MISSIONARIES

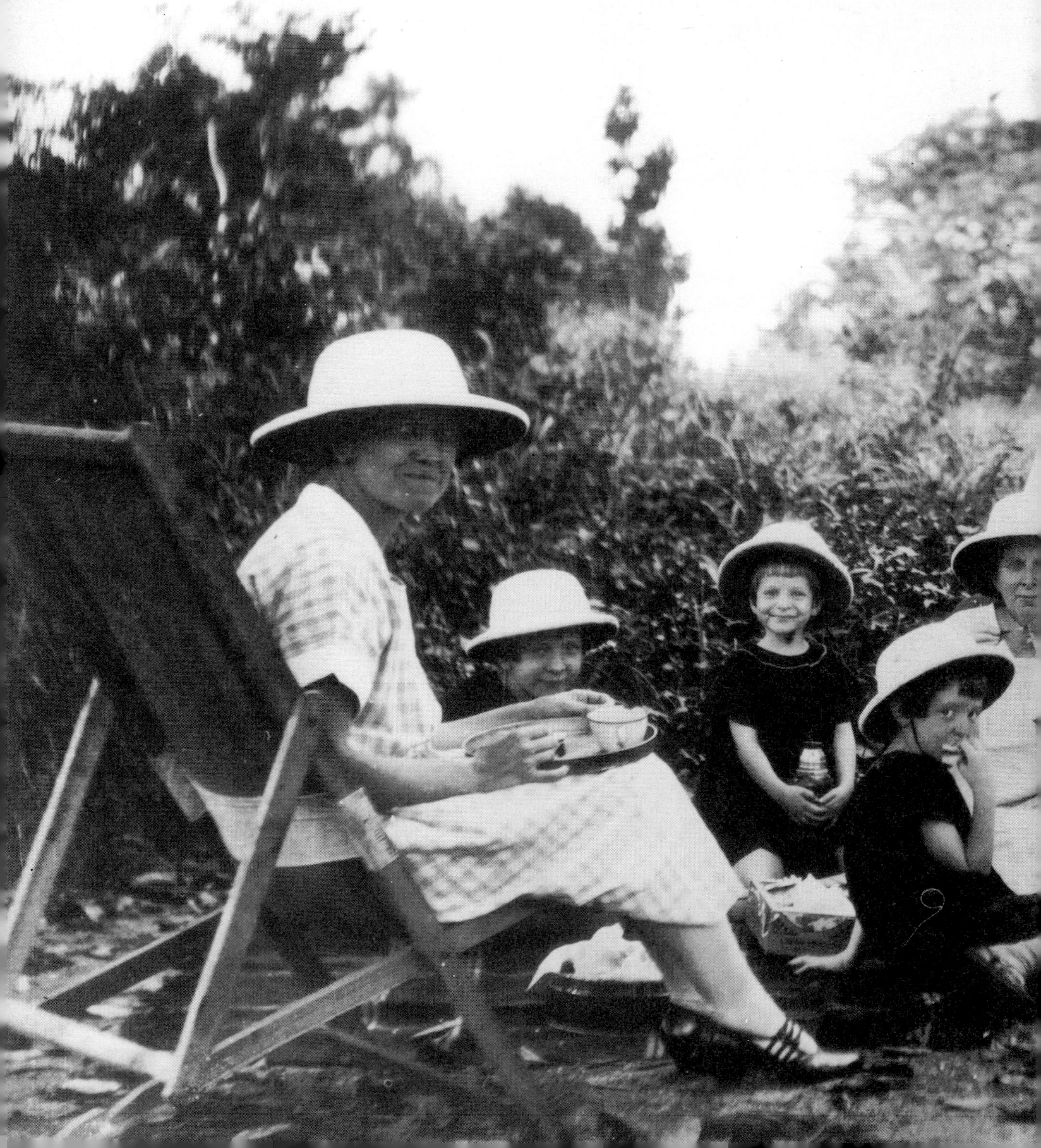

MISSIONARIES

Julian Pettifer and
Richard Bradley

Published by BBC Books,
a division of BBC Enterprises Limited,
Woodlands, 80 Wood Lane, London W12 0TT
First published 1990

ISBN 0 563 20702 7

Set in 11/13 pt Sabon by Butler & Tanner Ltd, Frome
Printed and bound in Great Britain by Butler & Tanner Ltd, Frome
Colour separations by Technik Litho Plates Ltd, Berkhamsted
Jacket printed by Belmont Press Ltd, Northampton

Contents

Preface   7

Acknowledgements   9

Map: The Spread of Christianity   10–11

1   The Great Commission   12

2   The Gospel of Tomahawks and Tobacco   31

3   A Bit of a Riot   53

4   Africa or Death   72

5   Plundering Hell to Populate Heaven   100

6   The Oppressors and the Oppressed   132

7   A Liberating God?   144

8   The Blood of the Martyrs is the Seed of the Church?   165

9   'And some fell on stony ground'   176

10 The Greatest Challenge   188

11 Into Darkest England   215

12 Coming Full Circle   241

Chart: Largest American Protestant Mission Agencies   266

Select Bibliography   267

Index   268

Picture Credits

The cover photograph was taken by Richard Bradley.

Preface

Much of the material for this book was gathered during the making of the BBC television series *Missionaries*. The aim of those six programmes was to take a long, close look at a largely forgotten band of men and women. Only sensational stories of missionaries disgraced, expelled, kidnapped or murdered ever attract the attention of the secular press and the general public. We were astonished to discover that when we mentioned to friends or acquaintances our plans to film with missionaries, the news was commonly greeted with incredulity or even hilarity. It seemed inconceivable to them that there could still be missionaries out there trying to convert 'the heathen'. There were also, predictably, a lot of well-worn jokes about cooking pots and the missionary position.

Flippant responses apart, people reacted very strongly to the notion of the series. Even among those who know very little about them, missionaries are a highly emotive subject. Those with a positive view of mission enthused about our project and reeled off the names of their particular missionary heroes and heroines whose lives they assumed we should be covering: Mother Teresa, St Paul, Albert Schweitzer, David Livingstone, William Carey, Lottie Moon, St Francis Xavier and so on. There was a widespread assumption that we were attempting a television *history* of Christian Mission, which we were not. Those with a less positive view, and there have been many, enjoined us to be sure to stress all the harm that missionaries have done. 'Why can't missionaries leave people alone?', 'What arrogance to assume they have a corner on the truth', 'They were perfectly happy until the missionaries came along and messed them up with feelings of guilt and sin', have been typical responses.

We have been urged to expose missionaries as cultural imperialists, iconoclasts, paternalists and even as agents of the CIA. Doubtless there are missionaries who have been all of those things and certainly missionaries have failed in many of their endeavours; but then, they have set themselves an awesome task. In the words of Stephen Neill: 'Christian missionary work is the most difficult thing in the world. It is surprising that it should have been attended by such a measure of success. And it is not at all surprising that an immense number of mistakes should have been made.' We have been able to witness first-hand some of these mistakes and some of the undertakings regarded by missionaries as their success stories on the present-day mission field. We have tried to address some fundamental questions such as: Why mission? Who are the missionaries? By what right do they take their religious beliefs to other cultures? Where and how are they working? How are they supported and what are their aims? What is the impact of the work done in Jesus' name?

Above all, we have been able to persuade a great many missionaries to talk about themselves and about their work. We asked them why they went, what they did and what they think they have achieved. What emerges from these encounters is a complex picture. At one extreme is a pair of American Bible Belt fundamentalists performing the whole of the Old Testament, book by book, in a remote jungle clearing to a bemused crowd of Papua New Guinean tribesmen, and at the other is an English Catholic Father teaching table manners to the children of the Ugandan middle class in a boarding school on the banks of the Nile. In between is a whole world of endeavour, in which we discovered some of the most impressive and least admirable examples of human behaviour. Missionaries as a group are frequently at odds with each other, but one thing unites them all. Each and every denomination has tried to interpret God's will, and to do what they believe He wishes of them.

A book like this can only scratch the surface of 2000 years of missionary and theological history: there are libraries full of missionary biographies, and erudite tomes on the most abstruse points of missiological debate. In short, this is not a book for the expert; it is hoped that it will interest the general public, those who are Church members and those who are not, and those who share a concern for the issues of religion and culture in a changing world.

Inevitably this is a highly selective work. The selection has been determined by the places we were able to visit and the people we were able to talk to within the constraints of a six-part television series. It will be noticed that we make no mention at all of the Church of Latter Day Saints (Mormons) or the Jehovah's Witnesses. Although they are both extremely active in mission, we are advised they do not fall within Christian orthodoxy.

Acknowledgements

The research on which this book is based was done largely for the BBC television series of the same name. We therefore wish to acknowledge the generous assistance of the BBC production team, and in particular Alan Bookbinder, Sue Bourne, Charmian Compton, Vivienne Griffiths, Virginia Nicholson, Kerry Platman and Tim Slessor. For a year and a half we were able to benefit from their insight, argument and enthusiasm. Our heartfelt thanks to Bryony Kinnear for wrestling with the manuscript and to Deborah Waller for her moral support at all times.

We have received advice from many quarters, notably from Peter Clarke, Colin Morris and Chris Sugden in the United Kingdom, and from Father Simon Smith, Paul Hiebert and Ralph Winter in the United States. Despite their best efforts, we shall undoubtedly have come to grief in the theological and political minefield that is Christian Mission. They bear no responsibility for what lies between these covers. The selection of material and the emphasis are entirely our own.

A special word of thanks is due to David Barrett, editor of the *World Christian Encyclopaedia*. At the Southern Baptist Foreign Missions Board where he now works as a consultant, it is said that one hears Barrett quoted more frequently than the Gospel! We are grateful for permission to use the factual and statistical material that flows so abundantly from his office computers. His work has provided a new insight to the history of mission.

Finally, we must thank the scores of missionaries world-wide who helped us and patiently put up with the tiresome demands of filming. In the remoter mission fields, they even provided us with bed and board and did so with unfailing generosity and kindness.

Julian Pettifer and Richard Bradley

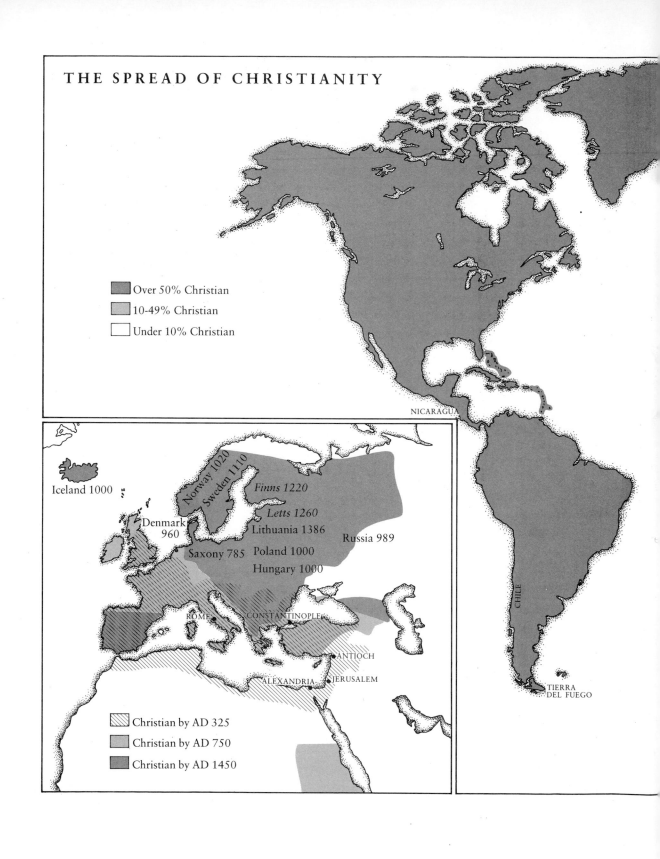

THE SPREAD OF CHRISTIANITY

Over 50% Christian

10-49% Christian

Under 10% Christian

NICARAGUA

Iceland 1000

Norway 1020

Sweden 1110

Finns 1220

Letts 1260

Lithuania 1386

Russia 989

Denmark 960

Saxony 785

Poland 1000

Hungary 1000

ROME

CONSTANTINOPLE

ANTIOCH

ALEXANDRIA

JERUSALEM

CHILE

TIERRA DEL FUEGO

Christian by AD 325

Christian by AD 750

Christian by AD 1450

1 The Great Commission

Mother Teresa, whose
Missionaries of Charity
are renowned for their
compassionate ministry
among the poor and
destitute. They now also
work in New York, in
Scandinavia, and Britain.

Dr Albert Schweitzer,
at Lambarene, his jungle
hospital in Gabon, a few
years before his death.
Schweitzer was an
accomplished musician,
writer, philosopher and
doctor – a remarkable
missionary.

God is working his purpose out as year succeeds to year.
God is working his purpose out and the time is drawing near.
Nearer and nearer draws the time, the time that shall surely be,
When the earth shall be filled with the glory of God, as the waters
  cover the sea.

A. C. Ainger

When that resounding mission hymn was written in 1894, it asserted with serene Victorian confidence that the 'Great Commission' entrusted by Jesus to his followers ('Go ye therefore and teach all nations . . .', Matthew 28:19) would rapidly be fulfilled and his disciples would indeed be found in all the nations 'even unto the ends of the earth'. Many people are surprised, and even shocked, to hear that missionaries are still to be found today. They had believed that the decline of Western imperialism and the independence of the nations of Asia, Africa and the Pacific Islands brought to an end the missionary era. In fact, there are many more missionaries now than there were during the heyday of imperialism; indeed, more than there ever have been in the whole history of Christendom. According to David Barrett, the editor of the *World Christian Encyclopaedia*, there are now 262 000 missionaries and, at the present rate of increase, there could be 400 000 by the turn of the century. Their numbers embrace the widest imaginable spectrum of activity: from Mother Teresa and her Home for the Dying in Calcutta, to Jimmy Swaggart and his 142-million-dollars-a-year evangelical TV empire.

All these new missionaries believe that they are obeying Christ's injunction to 'teach all nations'; but the manner of their teaching shows extraordinary diversity. In Zimbabwe, for instance, Father John Dove is spending his retirement years caring for elderly lepers, dreadfully mutilated 'burnt-out cases'. In cities throughout the world master illusionist Andre Kole thrills his audiences with a magical show that packs an evangelical punch which, he says, has brought thousands to their knees for Jesus. Dr Rick Goodgame, graduate of America's finest medical schools, tends AIDS patients in a dilapidated Ugandan hospital. In Tokyo, Father Neyrand stands behind the bar in the city's red-light district, mixing cocktails. In one of the remotest regions

Another face of modern mission. American television evangelist Jimmy Swaggart confesses to sinning in front of his wife, the congregation of his World Faith Centre and millions of television viewers, 21 February 1988.

BGP02:AM-SWAGGART:BATON ROUGE,LA.,FEB. 21 — Reverend Jimmy Swaggart, one of the nation's best known television evangelists, tearfully confesses he sinned against God and his family, Feb. 21 at his World Faith Center here. Swaggart stepped down from the pulpit amid allegations of adultery. REUTER/UPI sv/photo taken by videotape supplied by Jimmy Swaggart Ministry to WBRZ-TV 1988

of Papua New Guinea, Bob Kennell and his colleagues, their heads enveloped in dishcloths, act out Bible stories in a language spoken by no other white men.

These men and women who feel driven to leave their native lands and preach an alien faith to people who often do not wish to hear it are a curious and contradictory bunch. It is particularly confusing that they are unable to speak with one voice. For centuries they have quarrelled bitterly over the exact nature of the Good News they are trying to tell, and over the right to tell it. In carrying their differences into the mission field, missionaries introduce new tensions that divide families, villages, tribes and even nations. Conflict between Catholics and Protestants has frequently been the cause of church-burning and murder. Although at present Catholic missionaries outnumber Protestant, it looks as if that balance will soon change as the fastest-growing organisations are Protestant, particularly evangelicals, Pentecostals and fundamentalists of all kinds. The figures are impressive. In 1900 there were approximately 15 000 Protestant missionaries worldwide, nearly all from Europe and North America. Today there are 80 000, including 20 000 from the younger Churches of the Third World.

This is bad news for those who have a deep distrust of missionaries and for followers of religions other than Christianity who hear their beliefs condemned by some missionaries as idolatry, superstition and the works of Satan. But whether we admire missionaries or deplore them, their accomplishments have undoubtedly had a profound influence on the course of history. Christianity is the only religion that can be described as universal. Until the nineteenth century it was largely a Western belief but it is predicted that by the year 2000 Asia, Africa and Latin America will have substantially more Christians than the rest of the world put together; and although there are many countries, notably in the Muslim world, that are totally closed to missions, it is still claimed that every country in the world has a Christian witness of one kind or another. This has been the achievement of Christian missionaries. They have transformed an obscure, persecuted Jewish sect into a world religion with believers in every nation.

There are a growing number of missionary faiths. Many of the most active and aggressive are Eastern and North American sects: Jehovah's Witnesses, Mormons, Soka Gakkai, the Unification Church. But of the world's great religions only three, Buddhism, Islam and Christianity, are essentially missionary. Of these, Christianity has been most successful at spreading its message around the world. Dr Herbert Kane, a missionary academic, has no doubt as to why: 'The Bible is a missionary book. The gospel is a missionary message. The church is a missionary institution. And when the church ceases to be missionary-minded, it has denied its faith.' An exhortation to tell others the Good News is part of biblical commandment. In one form or another the Great Commission appears in each of the four Gospels. In Mark 16:15 the Apostles were commanded to 'Go forth to every part of the world, and proclaim the Good News to the whole of creation.' But this is only part of the missionary story.

From its earliest beginnings, Christianity was a missionary religion because it had to be. After Paul's dramatic conversion on the road to Damascus, he began to preach his new-found faith in the city's synagogues. Here was Paul, a Pharisee, telling Jews that the Messiah had come. The authorities were outraged, and branded him a heretic.

Paul was forced to flee, lowered in a basket from the city walls. These inauspicious beginnings set the pattern that was to follow. Rejected by the Jews, the only possible direction for expansion was into the Gentile world, and that meant into the Roman Empire.

Paul is the only Apostolic missionary of whose work and travel much is known: he is the missionary prototype. Christ commanded his disciples to go into *all* the world. Paul cherished a dream of taking his faith to the farthest limits of the then known world, to Spain. It is not known whether he got there before his death in Rome in AD 63, but there is no doubt about the general success of the early missionaries. Pockets of believers were to be found in Damascus, Antioch, Alexandria and even Rome, within a few decades of the crucifixion.

Yet Christianity was still the faith of the underclass, the marginalised and the persecuted. Within a year of Paul's death, the great fire, during which Emperor Nero is reputed to have played the violin, swept through Rome. To deflect accusations that the emperor himself had started the fire, Tacitus records how Nero turned on the most convenient scapegoat: 'Nero fastened the guilt on a class hated for their abominations, called Christians by the populace. Mockery of every sort was added to their deaths. Covered with the skins of beasts, they were torn by dogs and perished; or nailed to crosses; or were doomed to the flames. Nero threw open his garden for the spectacle.'

Christianity was not destined to be held in contempt by Rome for ever. Constantine's sudden conversion, following a vision as he marched into battle, changed that. In the process it profoundly altered the course of mission history. Christianity was no longer a minor heresy, but an imperial religion: its missionaries no longer persecuted agitators, but ambassadors of Rome. By AD 380 this transformation was complete. Emperor Theodosius turned belief in Christ into a matter of imperial command, threatening retribution for those who failed to comply: 'We command that those persons who follow this rule shall embrace the name of Catholic Christians. The rest, however, whom We adjudge demented and insane, shall sustain the infamy of heretical dogmas . . . they shall be smitten first by divine vengeance and secondly by the retribution of Our own initiative.'

Five centuries after the Crucifixion, missionaries could reflect on a period of extraordinary success. The vast area that had been the Roman Empire had become at least nominally Christian. The gospel had even spread beyond the fringes of Roman rule. In Ethiopia, two young men, Aidesius and Frumentius, were enslaved after being shipwrecked on the Red Sea, and found themselves at the Ethiopian court. They overcame the opposition of King Axum, and established a church that exists to this day. The Christian message was taken west into Armenia

A friar preaches to Muslims, Barcelona, c.1500. Relations between the two great missionary faiths were not always conducted so cordially.

by a missionary known as Gregory the Enlightener. And there was Patrick who journeyed north to Ireland. By the time of his death in AD 461, Ireland was largely Christian. It was, however, a uniquely Celtic Christianity, based on monastic communities and demanding extraordinary penitential discipline from its monks. These monks were infamous for the austerity of their lives: some would recite the entire Psalter while immersed in icy water; others, it was said, would stand immobile in prayer for so long that birds built nests in their hair.

In all by AD 500 Christianity seemed poised on the brink of unlimited progress. It had shown the strength to outlive the collapse of the Roman Empire, and the versatility to appeal to people of all cultures. However, what followed has been called 'The Thousand Years of Uncertainty'; a period of minor victories and major set-backs for the missionaries. The great age of Islam was about to dawn.

The rise of this new faith presented Christian missionaries with their greatest challenge yet. Barred from progress to the south by this mighty religion, missionaries turned north, slowly winning adherents among the wild tribes of Northern Europe. Among the most effective of their time were Willibrord, missionary to the Frisians, and Boniface, Apostle of Germany. In AD 596 Augustine was despatched on a special mission to England by Pope Gregory the Great. Gregory had what today would be called a 'burden' for England. Reputedly he cried on seeing English slave boys at market: '*Angli sunt, angeli fiant*' – 'They are Angles, let them become angels'. In Canterbury Augustine set about the task of converting them. Thirty-three years earlier, Columba had crossed the narrow stretch of water between northern Ireland and Scotland to begin the evangelisation of Britain from the north. He planted his cross on the island of Iona and commenced work among the heathen Picts. These, however, were isolated, meagre advances after the rampaging successes of the Roman years.

In 1500 Christian Mission rediscovered its impetus, with the emergence of the Spanish and Portuguese empires. The age of geographical discovery took explorers and Roman Catholic missionaries into new worlds. The Protestant sects, however, played no part in this dramatic extension of mission activity. The Reformation of Europe had failed to release the spiritual forces of Protestantism into mission. Between 1500 and 1700 the Catholics gained more converts in the Orient and the New World than they were losing to Protestantism in Europe. When the Protestants finally did join the missionary enterprise they had nothing to compare with the missionary orders of Catholicism, and certainly no equivalent to the rigid intellectual and military discipline of the Jesuits. Their largest mission was a sect called the Moravians. The missionaries were not scholars but artisans, men of unbounded, unquestioning zeal, and little education. They were often married with family responsibilities and domestic commitments. None the less, this unpromising group were in the vanguard of the most remarkable period of mission history.

First off the starting block was Count Nicolas Zinzendorf from Dresden. In 1732 he initiated the first Moravian mission to the Virgin Islands. Subsequent evangelical voyages took him to Greenland, South Africa, Jamaica and the North American Indians. It was to the Indians of the East that the first major British mission was launched in 1793. The mission was the brainchild of William Carey. A village cobbler, turned Baptist scholar and linguist, Carey has been called 'the father

Above, *'Would you care to say grace?' The missionary – especially the missionary in a cooking pot – has long been the butt of secular jokes.*

William Carey – known as 'the father of modern missions'.

of modern missions'. With his wife and children as reluctant companions, he set out for India in June 1793. Over the next thirty years, from their base in Serampore, he and his colleagues completed six translations of the Bible, and twenty-three complete New Testaments. Carey himself learnt Bengali, Sanskrit and Marathi. His theological view was uncomplicated and unexceptional for men of his time: the religions embraced by the Indians were delusions of the Devil.

Carey's departure for India engendered considerable excitement. On both sides of the Atlantic a flood of mission societies were formed. On 6 February 1812, the first five American missionaries, including Adoniram Judson, were ordained in Salem. Four months later they arrived in India. The missionaries of the English-speaking world were loose on the world.

These were men driven by a burning, blind commitment. Count Zinzendorf, the greatest of eighteenth-century missionaries, said, 'I have one passion. It is He and He alone'. Melville Cox, who died after just four months in Liberia, is supposed to have uttered the last words, 'Let a thousand fall before Africa be given up'. On arriving in India, Henry Martyn said, 'Now let me burn out for God'. Of Hudson Taylor, founder of the China Inland Mission, it was said that never once in fifty years did the sun rise in China without finding him on his knees. In their energetic devotion to bring the gospel to the 'heathen', they did more than pray. They wrote down hundreds of languages which had never been written before and introduced Western styles of education, medicine, bureaucracy and humanitarian thought.

Once again the missionaries were fellow travellers with the imperialists. One mission academic has called this association 'one of the unfortunate accidents of history'. But if the association has become an embarrassment in recent years for many Christians, for the spread of Christianity it has been anything but unfortunate. The nineteenth-century missionaries, like their predecessors, had few qualms about using the arteries of empire to further their own spiritual ambitions.

Our modern perception of missionaries is rooted in the nineteenth century, at a time when missionaries were firmly in the forefront of public consciousness. If the ordinary person is aware of missionaries at all, his stereotyped mental image is likely to be adorned with pith helmet, baggy shorts, cannibal cooking pots and gawping savages; and in the case of the missionary wife, with a long frock and frumpish hair-do, delivering a magic lantern lecture, chalking the words of a hymn on a blackboard, or pouring afternoon tea at a missionary picnic in a jungle clearing. Satirists have found this pervasive image irresistible, for example Noel Coward's song 'Uncle Harry', from his musical *Pacific*:

Our families have traditions, we've heard them a thousand times
Our ancestors were unequivocally right.
They frequently went on missions, to very peculiar climes,
to lead the wretched heathen to the light.
Though some of them were beaten up in the course of
                                        these rampages,
And Great Aunt Maud was eaten up whilst singing 'Rock of Ages',
On one of these expeditions an uncle we'd thought a bore,
turned out to be more spirited than ever he had before . . .

Poor Uncle Harry having become a missionary,
found the natives' morals rather crude.
He and Aunt Mary swiftly imposed an arbitrary
ban upon them shopping in the nude.
They all considered this silly and decided to rebel,
They burnt his boots and several suits,
which made a horrible smell.
The subtle implication was that Uncle could go to hell.

CURIOUS SAVAGES

written to his nephews and nieces, and accompanied by one of those droll sketches with which he often embellished his letters to familiar friends :—

"Fancy a set of hideous savages regarding your uncle as a strange, outlandish creature, frightful to behold! 'Are those your feet, white man?' 'No, gentlemen, they

THE BISHOP AND THE MUTINOUS BOATMAN
From a sketch by Bishop Hannington

are not. They are my sandals.' 'But, do they grow to your feet?' 'No, gentlemen, they do not; I will show you.' So I would unlace a boot. A roar of astonishment followed when they saw my blue sock, as they thought my

A page from a biography of missionary Jim Hannington. Exotic, amusing tales of encounters with 'savages' enthralled readers at home.

Missionaries have not enjoyed a very good press in recent years. They are frequently described as 'destructive', 'paternalistic', 'imperialist' and 'reactionary'. All this has left a bad taste even in the mouths of those who are not necessarily antagonistic to Christianity. One hundred years ago the Western perception of mission could hardly have been more different. Many missionaries enjoyed the kind of celebrity and adulation that today is showered upon astronauts and super-athletes. When Livingstone and Chalmers and McKay returned home and made their nation-wide tours, they filled the largest halls with ecstatic crowds and their activities were always headline news.

At the time, the mission societies wielded formidable power and wealth. The Church Missionary Society (CMS) was the largest of all, boasting a staff of 1300 missionaries, 375 native clergy and over 1000 native agents and teachers, and an income amounting to £400 000 a year (£20 million today). Its propaganda machine was equally impressive. In 1903, for example, the CMS issued nearly five and a half million publications, including ten quarterly and monthly magazines and numerous books on missionary matters. These publications were the source of the romantic picture painted of missionaries and their work. The titles and the vivid covers tell all: *The Romance of Missionary Heroism, Heroines of Missionary Adventure, Heroic Deeds on the Mission Field.* Hundreds of similar titles stress the danger, excitement and sacrifice of missionary life, the piety, bravery and nobility of the missionaries and the savagery, degradation and treachery of the heathens. Most of these books seem to have been written by hacks

God is an Englishman. The photo from Papua New Guinea was entitled 'Our boys at play, our church on the hill'. It was never just the Gospel that missionaries carried to the ends of the earth.

who knew their market. One example will stand for many – *Missionary Heroes, Stories of Heroism in the Mission Field*, an account of attempts to evangelise the Greenland Eskimos, who are described as 'dwarfs, ugly and repulsive looking to the last degree. Their minds matched their bodies and their habits were beyond belief for uncleanliness.' Attempts to convert them by translating the Bible fail, and even after nursing them through an outbreak of smallpox the missionaries are no nearer success. But, like all missionary tales, it has an uplifting ending. The missionaries achieve a miraculous breakthrough and 'before long the now joyful workers were counting converts by scores'.

A common theme in all this literature is the way in which missionaries bring not just the gospel of love and the promise of life eternal, but the benefits of Western industrial civilisation. The heathen are always characterised as primitive, superstitious, dishonest and, above all, dirty, while the missionary offers a promise not just of godliness but of cleanliness too. In the missionary periodical the *Quiver*, in an article entitled 'The Romance of the Missionary', Dr W. H. Fitchett does just this: 'In all the world there is no more thrilling romance than that of these pioneers of progress who have carried the gospel of the clean shirt side by side with that of salvation'. The supreme confidence

Europeans had in the superiority of their faith and of their civilisation
inevitably led them to believe that they had a divine right and duty not
just to convert the world to Christianity but to rule it too.

By its nature, missionary literature is hardly ever self-critical. Even
today, it is still as self-serving as a trade journal or a school magazine.
Quite unashamedly, its intention is to raise morale, money and manpower. In 1917 Ruth Rouse made a study of missionary vocation and
found that many who received 'the call' were first inspired by something

*Lady missionaries of the
United Society for the
Propagation of the Gospel
embark on an African
journey, 1900.*

they had read. No aspect of Christian mission is more puzzling than the call. Even in books written by missionaries for missionaries they agonise over questions like: 'What exactly is a missionary call?' 'How can I know that I have a call?' Some insist that God's will is made clearly evident in visions, dreams or voices. Others say that because all true Christians are by definition missionaries – in that they bear witness to Christ – no specific call is required. Judging from the uneven distribution of missionaries, the destination of the call appears to be determined by some of the same factors that influence anyone working abroad, it being easier and more pleasant to carry the gospel to simple rural communities or Pacific islands than to the slums of the big cities. Ruth Rouse examined 300 accounts of calls to the mission field. In nearly half, literature, and in particular biography, played an important or decisive part. All those highly coloured tales of missionary heroes and heroines did their job: the Bible was hardly, if ever, mentioned. Not even William Carey was prompted by the commandment of the New Testament, but rather by reading *The Last Voyages of Captain Cook*. In the case of women, Ruth Rouse was surprised to find that although missionary appeals to them were based largely on the social needs or sufferings of non-Christian women, these were rarely listed. It is clear that many women were drawn to mission because it offered one of the very few opportunities to escape from the rigid constraints of Victorian society. Even today there are three women in the mission field to every two men.

One factor Ruth Rouse does not mention in her analysis of the call is the desire for suffering and martyrdom. Yet judging from the prominence these subjects enjoyed in missionary literature, they must have played their part. The association of mission with suffering and death lies at its very foundation. In the words of David J. Bosch, 'the New Testament's highest and deepest point is reached in ... the son of man ... in his suffering and death he became the true missionary'. Bosch points out that the Greek word for witness is *martys*. This is the source of the word 'martyr', for in the early Church the Christian often had to seal his witness with his blood. According to David Barrett, the total number of martyrs since the crucifixion of Jesus is almost forty million. In certain tropical mission fields in the eighteenth, nineteenth and well into the twentieth centuries the mortality was appalling and the expectation of life was often as little as two years. The cemeteries are full of memorials showing that many did not outlast the year of their arrival. The greatest killer was malaria as there was no treatment of any kind until the arrival of quinine in the middle of the last century; and with no inherited immunity, with bodies weakened by poor diet, the disease often proved fatal. Father Henri Verjus was one of a group of French Catholic missionaries who went to New Guinea in 1885. He had prayed fervently for martyrdom before undertaking his mission. The party soon encountered hardship, lack of food and disease, but this suffering was not enough for Father Verjus. He inflicted other physical penances upon himself, believing the words of the Epistle to the Hebrews that 'Without the flowing of blood there is

A missionary prayer card devoted to Fred S. Arnot: such cards are still used to encourage those at home to pray for the missionaries' success.

no remission of sins'. In his exceptional appetite for penance, he went as far as lying on a cross of nails and engraving, in his flesh a bleeding Way of the Cross, which he kept open with salt and vinegar.

While there are still missionary martyrs today, their deaths are exceptional enough to make headlines even in the secular press. Today, when missionaries are unwelcome, they are rarely murdered, just excluded. A century ago, almost every country was open to missionaries of one tradition or another. Today, it is said that sixty-five countries are closed to all foreign missionaries, with three more closing their doors every year.

This trend has not inhibited missionary activities – on the contrary, the enthusiasm for mission continues unabated, particularly in North America. Until quite recently, America was itself regarded as a mission field, but now it is without question the predominant sending country. Ever since the Constantinian conversion, the ebb and flow of Christian mission has mirrored the rise and fall of the Western empires. Dr Keith Parks, President of the Southern Baptist Convention Mission, argues that this is evidence of God's hand at work: 'When people refuse to do what God has called them to do, he casts them on the junk heap of history and finds someone else to do his bidding. He's done it from the time he left Antioch and Jerusalem and Rome and Germany and England ... And God will move on unless you and I ... go out into a lost world.' For the time being God is backing America.

In the latest edition of the *American Mission Handbook*, which only lists Protestant ministries, there is information on 764 agencies supporting more than 70 000 overseas representatives: including the big and the bizarre, Habitat for Humanity Inc., Door of Hope Int. (USA) and Have Christ Will Travel. But this does not tell the whole story. America boasts a proliferation of Christian denominations. According to a recent count, there were 258 different denominational affiliations providing support for one or other of the recognised mission agencies. In addition, there are many independent Churches that also support one or more missionaries. These activities do not appear in the statistics.

The growth of American missions and the relative decline of the European is directly related to the rise and fall in the numbers of the faithful. In the 1790 census, only 5 per cent of US citizens professed any religious affiliations. Today, 95 per cent of Americans profess to believe in God and 40 per cent of adults attend church. By comparison, Europe is increasingly stigmatised as 'the Dark Continent'. In Britain, of 30 million baptised Anglicans, fewer than three-quarters of a million attend church on a typical Sunday; and throughout Western Europe attendance is rarely more than five or six per cent of membership. It comes as no great surprise, then, to find that while the number of European missionaries has stagnated over the past decades, the number of North American Protestant missionaries has risen by 82 per cent. This increase is due mainly to the determined efforts of large and wealthy evangelical missions. Some of these are recent foundations, others have their roots in the nineteenth century. The largest and one of the oldest is run by the Foreign Mission Board of the Southern Baptist Convention. With more than 4000 missionaries in 113 countries and an annual income of $180 million, the Southern Baptists have an operation that is comparable in scale and complexity to many multi-national business corporations. Dr Keith Parks, Foreign Mission Board president, believes that a major US contribution to overseas mission has been its success in adapting modern management techniques and communication technologies to the needs of evangelism.

The Southern Baptists have their headquarters in a modern office complex in Richmond, Virginia. A few miles away is the sumptuous Missionary Learning Centre where the 400 new missionaries each year spend the final seven weeks of their training. The recruits are almost always young, white, married couples with children. Typically, both partners will have received formal theological training and they will be embarking upon a lifetime career. Like other Americans working abroad, they will have a proper career structure, educational and health benefits, pension schemes and generous salaries. Few of them will have had much experience of cultures outside the United States or any close encounter with real poverty. At the Centre the families are housed in specially designed accommodation with shared kitchens and day rooms which is intended to prepare them for future curtailment of their privacy. A certain amount of 'ethnic' cooking is introduced into the diet and the children are taught something of the cultures they will be entering. Trips are made to worship in nearby churches where there are overseas congregations and there are lectures on how to present the gospel in its untrammelled essence.

In Matthew 24, Jesus declared that prior to his second coming to earth the gospel of the kingdom would be preached to the whole world. This gives a special urgency to evangelical missionary endeavour for, in the words of Billy Graham, it is 'the means to hasten the day when "every knee shall bow" before our great king'. As the year 2000 approaches, there is a strong whiff of millennialism in the air. Particularly in the USA, there are many Bible Christians who believe they are seeing sure signs that 'the end is nigh', thus adding an even greater urgency to the completion of the Great Commission. It is no coincidence that the Southern Baptists, like many other missions, have set the year 2000 as the target date for an ambitious expansion programme called 'Bold Mission Thrust'. Even the Catholics are touched by this heady millennial excitement: in 1987 the Pope announced a new initiative to win a billion new Christians by the end of the century 'as a present for Jesus on his 2000th birthday'.

The Baptist 'Bold Mission Thrust' has the precision of a multi-national's marketing strategy. Each mission area has a specific goal: in Kenya the aim is for one million baptisms by the year 2000. To reach that figure the Southern Baptists calculate they must plant 66 000 new churches. It means making headway among people hitherto antag-onistic to Christianity. Chief among their targets are the Muslims and the Masai. The missionaries and the Masai have been engaged in a battle of wills for over a century. Since the first missionaries, Krapf and Rebmann, ventured into the parched, thorny scrubland around Mount Kilimanjaro in 1847, the Masai have staunchly resisted the intrusion and defended their own beliefs. However, as the pressures have grown on the nomadic Masai life-style, there are signs that their resistance to Christianity is beginning to crumble.

In their pursuit of the Masai, the missionaries are applying the latest of techniques to the oldest of tasks: solar-powered cassette recorders that play hymns in the Masai language; the 'Jesus' film translated into Kiswahili; light aircraft that fly into the nomads' *bomas* (villages) with medicine and a missionary message. In one reported case, a pilot from the Missionary Aviation Fellowship flew a Masai elder over the summit of his sacred mountain, Oldonyo Lengai, where his god was believed to reside, to prove to him his god did not exist. As the time runs out for the Masai, the Baptist Mission in Kenya is celebrating, for as the Masai are forced into the new world, they become, in the words of Baptist director Jack Connelly, 'ripe for the Gospel'. And with each new Masai convert, the mission edges nearer its target for the year 2000.

In missionary jargon the Masai qualify as 'evangelised non-Christian people'. They are a small part of the world community of 21 billion people who have heard the gospel, but have not responded by accepting Christ. This figure includes most, if not all, Catholics and many Protestants who in fundamentalist terms are not true Christians and are therefore open to missionary attentions. Most missionary excitement, however, is reserved for another group: those who have never had a first chance to hear the Good News. The United States Centre for World Mission, Pasadena, has identified 16 750 such unreached groups, or 'Hidden Peoples'. To reach these people by the year 2000 is the evangelicals' dream.

The modern missionary makes every possible use of up-to-date communication tools. This is not new. Nineteenth-century missionaries were quick to harness the technological advances of their day to their task. Lantern slides and gramophones were widely used in the mission field and the bicycle became a most popular method of missionary transport. Today's missionary resources include not only fleets of vehicles and aeroplanes, but also radio and television stations with regular audiences of 1.1 billion, 22 000 books a year, four billion tracts, 42 million computers and 200 million computer specialists. There is also a huge output of gospel music, records, tapes, videos and films. The 'Jesus' film is an extraordinary project that, like so much of modern American missionary activity, emanates from California. More than 20 per cent of the 764 mission agencies are based there; and Southern California has the greatest concentration of Protestant mission organisations in the world. Among the largest is Campus Crusade for Christ which has its headquarters on a magnificent 2700-acre estate at Lake Arrowhead that was once a luxury resort hotel. In this unlikely setting, where Hollywood stars once gathered, young Christians come together to plan their mission strategies.

Campus Crusade for Christ began some forty years ago as a mission to evangelise college students throughout North America; but its founder, Dr Bill Bright, was determined to extend Crusade ministry overseas and he was convinced that the cinema was a powerful tool for doing it. He hit upon the idea of the 'Jesus' film. He approached several top producers, including Cecil B. DeMille, but none of the major studios would get involved in a ten-million-dollar movie based solely on St Luke's Gospel. Finally, the cost of the film was underwritten by American tycoon Bunker Hunt and his wife Caroline. It is Dr Bright's prayer that the film will be seen by five billion people in 271 languages and 1000 dialects by the year 2000. Over a hundred language versions of the film have already been completed. The organisers are convinced that Dr Bright's targets will be met.

In many ways Campus Crusade is the very epitome of the modern American mission: large, rich, optimistic and evangelical. It has grown rapidly and has more than 16 000 full-time and associate staff members in 151 nations and an income of around $80 million a year. Unlike the Southern Baptists who support their missionaries by 'corporate' fundraising activities (mainly a Christmas appeal), Campus Crusade expects all its missionaries to raise the money for their overseas duties themselves. This is what is called a 'faith mission': the money is raised by faith and prayer. Each would-be missionary family is required to canvass their relatives, friends and total strangers for funds. The sums are considerable: $3000 a month for a Campus Crusade family of four, and $20 000 for relocation expenses to the mission field. The missionaries do not seem to find this either worrying or embarrassing.

Ultimately of course they believe God is providing. 'Just as God has called us', explained one missionary, 'he has also chosen a number of people around the US who will become part of our support team. He knows their names – we don't. We'd like it if he'd just send us a list of their names but he hasn't chosen to do that right now. So we have the privilege of travelling around and asking.' If they fail to reach the target, they will not be permitted to go: but then they would accept failure as God's way of telling them it was not to be.

The American fundamentalist and evangelical missions have captured the high ground in what they see as a world-wide struggle against Satan. Anyone who is not for them is against them; and in the case of extreme fundamentalists, the adversary includes some other missionaries, notably Catholic. Catholic mission is vigorous and well financed but as vocations have declined in Europe and North America, the Church has had to cope with an ageing workforce on the mission field. At present, numbers are being maintained by recruiting more lay missionaries and by the increasing number of vocations from the Third World. Since the Second Vatican Council fundamental changes have taken place in the Catholic view of mission in the hope of improving the situation.

The liberal Protestant denominations – Anglicans, Methodists, Lutherans, Presbyterians, and others that provided the powerhouse for eighteenth- and nineteenth-century missionary expansion – are now a waning force in the mission field, outnumbered and, some would say, outflanked by fundamentalists and evangelicals. For liberal Protestants this withdrawal from straightforward evangelism has been quite deliberate. Instead of sending regiments of Western missionaries into the Third World, their emphasis today is upon supporting and training indigenous Christian workers, helping to solve basic social and economic problems, and fighting for social justice. In some mission fields this posture has exposed them to quite savage predation by the more aggressive evangelicals. Many of these liberals for their part believe the fundamentalists have usurped mission for their own ends.

Two thousand years after the events at Calvary, there is as much fuel in the missionary machine as ever. But for evangelical Christians a full tank is essential, for there is still far to go. By 1960, 34 per cent of the world's population was calculated to be Christian. By 1986 it had fallen to 30 per cent, and the percentage is dropping slowly every year. In India, for example, there are now twice as many non-Christians as there were when William Carey arrived in 1793. Yet, if Christianity is fighting to hold its position, the generals of the modern missionary army retain a fierce conviction that world evangelisation is achievable. In San Antonio, Texas, in the summer of 1988, Dr Keith Parks assured

7000 Southern Baptists that they were on the eve of the greatest Christian harvest ever seen: 'God has given us everything we need. We know how to do it; we have the money to do it; we have the people to do it; we have the technology to do it.' The only additional ingredient required is missionary zeal. North America has plenty of this; and if Europe can no longer provide it in sufficient quantities, the younger churches – from Africa, Central America, Korea and the Philippines – are eager to step in. By 1985 the Full Gospel Central Church of Seoul, Korea, was supporting 143 missionaries overseas. In the story of mission today, the headlong expansion of North American and Third World evangelical activity is the dominant theme. The scale of the ambition of these new missionaries is undiminished. 'If we as a people were willing to be used of God,' said Dr Parks with Pauline fervour, 'I am convinced . . . God would change the destiny of history.'

But with the year 2000 approaching, and millennial fever growing, there is a sense too that time is running out. A renewed urgency has been kindled in the missionary world. If the missionaries fail to respond, argues Dr Parks, 'The multitudes of the generation will die and go to Hell. I don't know what it means . . . but I don't want to stand before God with the blood of those unwarned multitudes that I was supposed to warn, dripping from my hands.'

The non-Christian world has been alerted. Better equipped, better financed, and as zealous as ever, Christian missionaries are relentlessly pursuing their Great Commission. 'Is the task of world evangelisation completed?', Dr Herbert Kane asks. 'From all four corners of the earth comes a resounding *No!* Far from being completed, we have hardly reached the halfway point. To quit now would jeopardise the entire enterprise.'

2 The Gospel of Tomahawks and Tobacco

*The Queen looks upon you as her children,
and will not allow anyone to harm you.*
Commodore J. E. Erskine, RN, Port Moresby, 6 November 1884

Missionary history as perceived by missionaries is invariably very different from secular versions of the same events. Nowhere is the gulf wider and more contradictory than in the history of missionary penetration of the Pacific Islands. Seen from the missionary standpoint, it was an extraordinary success story; but through the eyes of observers like R. L. Stevenson and Herman Melville it prompted the catastrophic destruction of ancient cultures and the end of primeval innocence. In 1796, thirty years after Captain Cook's landing, the first missionaries arrived in Tahiti. Not only Cook but all the other early visitors to the island had remarked on the beauty and friendliness of its people, the richness of its culture and the gentle charm of its life-style. The little party of men from the London Missionary Society might have been landing on a different planet. In his book *Out of the Darkness*, Andrew D. Stewart, a Director of the Society, describes the Tahitians as vile cannibals who indulged in all manner of vices; Pomare, their king, was 'a conceited, drunken and treacherous savage'. Stewart tells how the missionaries tried for nine years to make a single convert, being forced to flee to another island when war broke out among the tribes. In 1812 the Directors of the Society met in London to consider whether they should withdraw from the work in the South Seas as all had so far been in vain. At the end of the meeting, a few men stayed on to pray for the South Seas Mission and for the conversion of Pomare. Miraculously, they claimed, on the other side of the world, their prayers were instantly answered. Pomare sought out the missionaries in their island refuge and astonished them by seeking Christian baptism for himself and for his subjects.

According to Stewart, Pomare not only abandoned idolatry but pulled down the heathen temples of his people – the Marae – and in their place erected what he called the Royal Mission Chapel capable of accommodating over 6000 people. Here he promulgated a new code of Christian laws condemning murder, theft, rebellion and breaking the Sabbath. Then he presided over the destruction of all traditional ceremonial and religious objects. Concluding his account, Stewart writes that Pomare became 'a leader in good works, and an example to his people'.

The truth is that Pomare was an unreformed character who died of alcoholism and who was regarded with distaste even by his missionary allies. In the Pacific, the discrepancy between missionary and secular accounts was so great that it must raise doubts not just about missionary methods but about their honesty and integrity too. One of the problems the London Missionary Society faced was the quality of its manpower. The missionaries were certainly courageous, committed and God-fearing, but few of them were ordained ministers of religion or men of much education. They were mainly lower-middle-class artisans who wanted to teach their skills to the South Sea Islanders. They believed that once the savages had acquired the arts of Christian civilisation, they would desert their pagan ways and joyfully receive the gospel. Sadly, they saw no virtue in any aspect of traditional Pacific Island life or culture. Imbued with the Puritan work ethic, the missionaries regarded the traditional easygoing island life-style as inherently sinful. They therefore did their best to create the sort of market economy that required the lower-middle-class Protestant virtues of parsimony and toil.

In Hawaii Mark Twain witnessed the missionaries trying to instil the same ethic into the islanders, spoiling their quiet and peaceful life-style with exhortations to work, telling them 'what rapture it is to work all day for 50 cents to buy food for the next day as compared with fishing for a pastime and lolling through the eternal summer'. Robert Louis Stevenson too was shocked by the way missionaries abused their power in the islands. In his *South Seas Journals* he castigated the ease with which the missionary could obtain and use authority, where 'the temptation is always towards too much'. He believed that the Protestant missionaries had made life more or less unlivable for their converts.

Although the missionaries did their best to impress on their supporters at home how degraded and evil the islanders were, their own conduct often revealed their own fallibility. Some went native and struck up partnerships with island women. Others went into business and became wealthy by exploiting native labour; but perhaps most disconcerting was the ruthless way they won power over the island chiefs and used their influence to convert entire communities. The London Missionary Society made no headway at all in Tahiti until they entered into an unlikely alliance with Pomare. He delivered his subjects to the church door, while in return the missionaries met his requests for alcohol and firearms.

Caravaggio's painting of the dramatic conversion of Paul, the prototype missionary, on the road to Damascus (Santa Maria del Popolo, Rome).

'To the uttermost part of the world.' Crosses planted at Scott's Memorial, McMurdo Sound, Antarctica (left), and at Bela, Papua New Guinea (above).

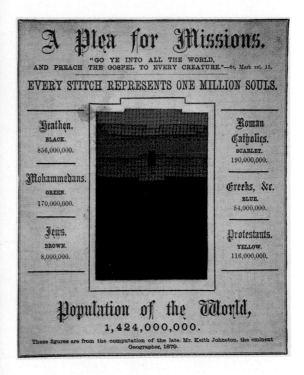

A Plea for Missions.

"GO YE INTO ALL THE WORLD,
AND PREACH THE GOSPEL TO EVERY CREATURE."—St. Mark xvi. 15.

EVERY STITCH REPRESENTS ONE MILLION SOULS.

Heathen.
BLACK.
856,000,000.

Roman Catholics.
SCARLET.
190,000,000.

Mohammedans.
GREEN.
170,000,000.

Greeks, &c.
BLUE.
84,000,000.

Jews.
BROWN.
8,000,000.

Protestants.
YELLOW.
116,000,000.

Population of the World,
1,424,000,000.

These figures are from the computation of the late Mr. Keith Johnston, the eminent
Geographer, 1879.

*Left: Cheap, popular
missionary biographies of
the Victorian period
imbued missionary life with
considerable romance.
Highly coloured tales of
heroic endeavour spurred
countless would-be
adventurers into the
mission field.*

*Above: A typical appeal for
recruits to take up the
Great Commission.*

A CURT DISMISSAL BY THE EMPEROR OF BURMA.

After reading Judson's petition that all Christians might be exempt from molestation, the Emperor disdainfully threw it to the ground.

Left: Missionary Mr Judson suffers unequivocal rejection in his attempt to defend the Christian population from 'molestation'.

Right: Postcards with a missionary message, one more way to rally support for those bringing light to heathen darkness.

Series Four.   A. B. Shaw & Co. Ltd., London.

THE WHITE MA TEACHING.

Series Seven.   THE ALL BRITISH PICTURE CO., LTD

The burning of the idols.

Series Four.   A. B. Shaw & Co. Ltd., London.

THE WHITE MA IN THE JUNGLE.

"I WONDER WHO HE IS!"

IN DARKEST ENGLAND, AND THE WAY OUT.

BY GENERAL BOOTH.

KEY TO THE CHART.

The Chart is intended to give a birdseye-view of the Scheme described in this book, and the results expected from its realization.

The figures on the pillars represent the appalling extent of the misery and ruin existing in Great Britain, as given in Government and other returns.

In the raging Sea, surrounding the Salvation Lighthouse, are to be seen the victims of vice and poverty who are sinking to ruin, but whom the Officers appointed to carry out the Scheme are struggling to save.

On the left, a procession of the rescued may be seen on their way to the various Refuges, Workshops, and

selves worthy of further assistance, are on their way to the Farm Colony, which, with its Villages, Co-operative Farms, Mills, and Factories, is to be created, far away from the neighbourhood of the public-house.

From the Farm Colony are to be seen Steamers hurrying across the seas, crowded with Emigrants of all sorts, proceeding either to the existing Colonies of the British and other Empires, or to the Colony-over-Sea, yet to be established; whilst the sturdy baker on the left and the laundress on the right suggest, on the one hand, plenty of work, and on the other, abundance of food.

The more the Chart is examined the more will be seen of the great blessings the Scheme is intended to convey, and the horrible destruction hourly going on amongst at least Three Millions of our fellow-creatures.

Cannibals quarrelling over lunch. According to the Revd W.G. Lawes 'Cannibalism in all its hideousness flourishes [in New Guinea]. The sanctity of human life is unknown and every man is a thief and a liar.'

Frontispiece from 'Into Darkest England', 1893, by William Booth, illustrating his grand social scheme to save the benighted city dweller from a sea of starvation, despair and sin, by transporting him to mission colonies at home and abroad.

Back in England, the London Missionary Society was releasing more terrifying accounts of the brutality of the islanders. It was cannibalism, more than anything else, that seemed to stir the conscience and stimulate the flow of contributions to missionary funds. Rarely were these allegations backed up by any scientific evidence but this failed to disconcert the supporters. The South American Missionary Society spiced their literature with terrible stories of cannibalism among the Indians of Tierra del Fuego. All of this was totally fictitious. The most superficial research quickly established that the Fuegians were disgusted by the idea of eating their fellows and that the stories were based on misunderstanding or had been deliberately embroidered for effect. Some missionaries heartily disliked the heroic and romanticised style of missionary literature and deliberately played down the hardship of their lives. They were frequently pestered to put anecdotes of adventure into their reports, but some refused. James Chalmers of New Guinea deplored the common practice in many missionary books of exaggerating and falsifying the truth.

Morbid interest in cannibalism reached its peak when the Wesleyan missionaries landed in Fiji in the 1830s. They had achieved remarkable success in Tonga, where they had converted the King, who before his baptism had been a famous warrior. It was with Tongan encouragement and support that the Wesleyans set out to take Christianity to Fiji where the practice of cannibalism was well established. While it is known that in many parts of the world at different times portions of human flesh have been eaten ritually in the belief that some of the virtues of the person consumed will be transferred to the consumer, the Fijians apparently ate human flesh simply because they enjoyed it. For once, it may have been true that the missionaries were regarded more as a possible source of bodily sustenance than of spiritual solace! In 1869 one of the Wesleyan missionaries, the Reverend Thomas Baker, was killed and eaten. In these circumstances, tales of Fijian cannibalism told by missionaries took on epic proportions. The old King Tanoa appears to have been particularly voracious: once a near kinsman had offended him and though the culprit begged his pardon most humbly, Tanoa responded by cutting off the arm of the poor wretch at the elbow and drinking the warm blood as it flowed. Next, he cooked the arm and ate it in the presence of his victim, and finally had him cut to pieces limb by limb.

Despite the unpromising circumstances in Fiji the missionaries achieved an outstanding victory by converting the young King Cacoban. He was even persuaded to seek the protection of the British Crown and, in 1874, he formally ceded the Fiji Islands to Queen Victoria. Nowhere had the alliance of missionary and imperial ambitions been so effectively demonstrated. However, it seems that Cacoban did have one reservation. Before accepting the gospel, he had been heard to comment anxiously: 'Wonderful is the new religion, is it not? But will it prevent our having men to eat?' The King had good cause to be worried. Not only was cannibalism outlawed but within one generation most other aspects of traditional culture had vanished. Fiji's gods, legends and oral histories had been replaced with Bible stories and Christian hymns. Thirteen hundred churches had been built and were filled with devout worshippers. The King even handed over his magnificent war club and ceremonial drinking bowl to the British Envoy as a sign of acceptance of the principles and forms of civilised society.

By the middle of the nineteenth century the whole of the South Pacific had been similarly 'civilised'. Once the missionaries had learned the strategy of converting the chiefs and the use of native evangelists, there was nothing to stop their progress. Above all, there were no physical obstacles like mountain ranges or forests, until they reached the island of New Guinea. This great island covers an area more than six times the size of England and its most notable features are the huge central mountain ranges which stretch over 1500 miles throughout its length, rising steeply to high peaks. By the time the missionaries reached New Guinea, they were buoyed up by their rapid progress in the more accessible Pacific Islands; they were also becoming better staffed and better equipped. No longer were the missionary societies sending off uneducated and unprepared men and women. The new missionaries

Breakfast on the beach. Notice the litter in which Mrs Dauncey was carried by uniformed bearers. Missionaries were a part of the colonial ruling class and despite undoubted hardships they had a status they would rarely have enjoyed at home.

often had superior education and high ideals and were able to take a somewhat broader view of their mission and of the native peoples. John Coleridge Patteson, educated at Eton and Oxford, a distinguished athlete and scholar, was one example of this new breed of missionary who spent his life spreading the gospel in Melanesia.

Another was James Chalmers, or 'Tamate', an agent of the London Missionary Society. By the time Chalmers arrived in New Guinea he had already spent ten years in Raratonga, where he had gained both experience and a certain reputation. Chalmers had friends and admirers in unusual quarters: Robert Louis Stevenson normally castigated missionaries for their part in what he called 'the extinction of the islanders' yet his regard for Chalmers was said to have verged on hero-worship. Another unlikely admirer was Bully Hayes, a notorious nineteenth-century buccaneer, who welcomed Chalmers and his young wife on board his brig for the 2000-mile journey to New Guinea. Chalmers had trained eight young Raratongan evangelists to assist him and they proved to be both zealous and courageous. He also had the benefit of a long report on conditions in New Guinea written by his colleague, the Reverend R. G. Lawes, who had already spent four years in discouraging work around Port Moresby. The report suggested that Chalmers would find himself in a country that offered every kind of obstacle to missionary work. It was a challenge that he relished. Like Livingstone, Chalmers was as much an explorer as an evangelist and nothing excited him more than the prospect of examining an isolated

*Ever yours
Tamate*

In his day, Chalmers was a missionary hero who enjoyed a measure of celebrity equal to Dr Livingstone. His murder by cannibals provoked a punitive expedition against the tribe held responsible.

country relatively unknown in the West. There had been earlier trading activity along the coast and, in 1849, an attempt to establish a Catholic Mission on Woodlark Island but any exploration of the interior had been abandoned because of the difficulty of the terrain.

Almost the first thing Chalmers did was to take a long walk inland until he was about eleven hundred feet above sea level. He soon discovered the nature of the task before him. The population was divided into hundreds of tribes and clans, each living at enmity with its neighbours. Tribal warfare was rife over the ownership of land, pigs or women. From the missionary point of view, one of the greatest obstacles was the multiplicity of languages. Around 700 languages were spoken, almost half of the world's known languages, most of them mutually unintelligible between neighbouring communities. Most languages were spoken by groups of several hundred people, or even fewer. There was no 'trade language' – like Swahili in East Africa – in which a Gospel translation would be widely understood. This led to the development of pidgin English which for many years remained the only means of communication. To add to his difficulties, Chalmers discovered that many of the languages were extremely complex. They presented the missionary translators with a challenge that has still not been wholly surmounted today.

There were also daunting cultural obstacles. Apart from the coastal regions New Guinea was still in the Stone Age. The people had no weapons, utensils or implements of iron or any other metal and they had yet to develop the use of money or the wheel. All the tribes practised polygamy, women changing hands for an agreed number of pigs. Their means of existence was slash-and-burn agriculture, the women doing much of the cultivation while the men hunted game, made war and performed endless rituals to propitiate any number of unpredictable gods and spirits. Above all, the spirits of the ancestors were constantly in attendance, ready to help and to guide the living, but also quick to take offence. The missionaries considered the natives to be devoid of any spiritual life whereas, in fact, they were intensely religious. The physical world and the world of the spirits were so closely woven together in their everyday lives that they made little distinction between them. Any injury, whether caused by magic or more down-to-earth forces, always led the injured party to seek redress by way of 'pay-back'. It was this elaborate and unrelenting system of vendetta that caused the greatest trouble to the missionaries. They discovered that in most of the tribal languages there was no word for forgiveness. Indeed the very concept was regarded either as foolish or cowardly. If a man did not seek revenge then one of his kinsmen would be obliged to act for him. Action often led to reaction and before long the parties found themselves involved in a chain of retribution that sometimes lasted for generations, although the original cause of the dispute had been quite forgotten.

It was into these warlike communities that Chalmers and his evangelists attempted to bring the Christian gospel. One of Chalmers's many qualities was the ability to see good in all people and in all places. He often remarked that conditions in the native villages were infinitely better than the abject squalor of the Glasgow slums in which he had worked in his youth. Even Lawes conceded that the New Guineans were industrious and the women more respected than in other parts of the world.

Although the missionaries were able to make contact with the tribes, the only basis for a continuing relationship was cargo. 'Cargo' was the term used to describe everything that came in on the supply ships, goods that the missionaries possessed and the people wanted. The inescapable fact that many converts are 'rice Christians', that their interest is not in the gospel but in material benefits, be they axes, education or tobacco, is something that missionaries have faced almost everywhere and at all times. Rarely has the trade-off been more blatant and created more tensions than in New Guinea. Among the missionaries, the argument focused on the use of tobacco, whether they were right to use it as a form of currency and as an inducement for the tribesmen to come to church. At Mission Headquarters in London, the Directors had grave doubts. Out in the field, Chalmers and Lawes had to live with the harsh realities. As Chalmers put it: 'Today's Gospel with the natives is one of tomahawks and tobacco; we are received by them because of these. By that door we enter to preach the Gospel of Love . . .' In practice, each evangelist used about 120 pounds of tobacco

Tobacco – the way to the heart of the Papua New Guineans. The perennial dilemma for missionaries was, and still is, 'What price the Gospel?'

a year. It was the currency that built the mission houses and churches, made their gardens and fences and purchased their wood and water, their fruit, vegetables and fish. Despite some misgivings Lawes and Chalmers saw no real harm in it or any possibility of substituting anything else. And they pointed out to their masters in London the indisputable fact that, without tobacco, the expenses of the mission would be greatly increased, 'The shortest way to a New Guinean's heart is through his tobacco pipe'. The use of tobacco was not the only cause of friction between London and Port Moresby. In many respects, Chalmers was a man ahead of his time. He argued that the missionary should live in the closest touch with the people he was attempting to uplift, not interfering too much in native customs.

It was largely due to the persuasion of Chalmers and Lawes that the British government extended its rule over part of New Guinea by establishing a Protectorate in 1884. This was largely in response to the German annexation of the north-eastern part of the island. Holland, the third colonial power, laid claim to the rest of the territory now called Irian Jaya. At a ceremony proclaiming the British Protectorate, Commodore J. E. Erskine's speech to the assembled chiefs was translated by Chalmers. It contained a line that today in Papua New Guinea

Learning English with the Apostles' Creed.

The Sacred Heart Mission at Ononge has changed little since it was established seventy years ago. Despite its new airstrip, it remains an isolated little missionary fiefdom under the benevolent rule of Catholic priests and nuns.

is regarded with particular amusement: 'Always keep on your minds that the Queen guards and watches over you, looks upon you as her children, and will not allow anyone to harm you . . .' It was paternalism of a kind that may even have stuck in Chalmers's throat.

In 1885 he wrote a paper on the future of New Guinea for the guidance of the new British administration in which he expressed views far removed from conventional missionary or Imperial thinking. He urged a policy of non-intervention, with the people being taught how to govern themselves. Even more controversially, and in opposition to his fellow missionaries, he recommended that the natives should not be forced to wear European clothes for the sake of decency: 'To swathe their limbs in European clothing spoils them, deteriorates them, and,

I fear, hurries them to a premature death ... Retain native customs as much as possible – only those which are very objectionable should be forbidden – and leave it to the influence of education to raise them to a purer and more civilised custom.' Unfortunately, very little notice was taken of his advice. Above all, his urgent insistence that education should *not* be left to the missionaries was wholly ignored. Indeed, throughout much of the colonial period, the only schools were those run by the missionaries. Nor was much notice taken of Chalmers's passionately held view that New Guinea must be governed in the best interests of its native people rather than for the benefit of white immigrants.

Although the colonial administration refused to follow Chalmers's advice, they admired him greatly, and when he returned home on furlough in 1886, he found he had become a national celebrity. He became a highly popular and sought-after speaker. As well as addressing Church groups, he delivered papers at the Colonial Institute and the Geographical Society; but the climax of his speaking tour was the meeting of the London Missionary Society at Exeter Hall. In his address Chalmers recalled Livingstone's promise to make an open path for commerce and Christianity. 'Gospel and commerce, but remember this, it must be the Gospel first ... Civilisation! The rampart can only be stormed by those who carry the Cross.'

Unlike most other missionary speakers, Chalmers deliberately played down the dangers of his chosen mission field, yet his diaries and those of his wife tell a different story. Chalmers was twice married and both his wives fell victim to tropical disease. Judging fom her journals, his second wife was a woman of considerable courage and resource, and she needed to be. Often, when her husband was on his travels, she was alone for weeks or months at a time. This could be a depressing experience, coping with sickness, mosquitoes and, above all, loneliness.

Chalmers was a courageous man with a love of adventure, and it was this, rather than the fever to which he had often fallen victim, which brought about his end. Early in April 1901 he accompanied a newly arrived young English missionary called Tomkins and a party of ten mission boys on a journey to Goaribari Island. As soon as they entered the village, surrounded by an excited mob, they were attacked from behind with stone clubs and knocked senseless. This was the signal for a general massacre. Chalmers was then stabbed and his head cut off with a knife. Tomkins suffered the same fate. According to one eyewitness, their bodies were cut up and eaten. The heads were retained as trophies and, when they were eventually retrieved by a search party, they were found stored in long houses that contained in excess of 10 000 human skulls.

Chalmers's gruesome death sent shock waves around the world. The story was told and retold and frequently embellished. One of the more bizarre accounts tells how the savages of Goaribari attempted to cook and eat Tamate's sand-shoes, believing them to be part of his body. Among many fulsome obituaries, one which appeared in the *Empire Review* provides a revealing insight into what the missionary role in the British Empire was perceived to be: '. . . the pioneer work done by James Chalmers in opening up communications with the natives, and thus rendering Europeans' exploitation possible, was emphatically Imperial in character. As an explorer and pioneer, his name should stand high in the annals of our Imperial history.'

Just as the Empire-builders found it perfectly proper to make use of the missionaries, so the missionaries tried to use their influence with the colonial government. The London Missionary Society urged the British authorities to exclude rival missions from the Protectorate, particularly Catholics, and in this they were partially successful. But in 1908, when Sir Hubert Murray became Lieutenant-Governor, the policy quickly changed. Murray came from an old Irish Catholic family and throughout his long term of office the Protestants angrily claimed that he favoured Catholic missions above all others. Be that as it may, the Catholic Fathers certainly flourished, as did all the other missions. Following the First World War, New Guinea experienced an extraordinary 'mission rush'. By that time the old British and German colonial administrations had been replaced by an Australian one, governing under a League of Nations Mandate. One of the terms of the Mandate provided for freedom of religious expression. Missionaries of every denomination – English Congregationalists, Australian Methodists, German and American Lutherans and French Catholics – hastened to stake their claims.

Very often, as with the French Sacred Heart Fathers, the missionaries were the first Europeans to make contact with the tribes even before the arrival of government patrol officers. After making the first contacts came the task of building and supplying the mission stations. While mission activities were confined to the coastal regions, this was a task for a fleet of boats, but when the Sacred Heart Fathers determined to push inland, they were faced with the problem of the terrain. The only solution was to build roads or pack-horse trails; their most ambitious route went from the coast directly inland to the mission station at Ononge. When it was completed, caravans of horses and donkeys took one week to go down to the coast and another week to return to the mission. The construction work was supervised by young men, most of them straight from the seminary, who laboured like navvies, with only unskilled native help. At great cost, a network of roads was

The kind of visible 'success' story the missionaries sought: natives clustered around the ruins of a spirit house they had been persuaded to destroy. Nearby is their newly constructed church.

constructed which permitted the establishment and maintenance of mission stations deep in the Highlands. Even today a few people still remember the days when a hundred horses and mules struggled up those tracks to the mission station at Ononge.

The journey was particularly difficult and the caravans were frequently delayed crossing flooded streams, landslides and massive potholes. Sometimes horses sank into mud up to their necks and sometimes they slid into ravines, losing their loads. Life in the New Guinea mission field was exceptionally rigorous and to meet its challenge there were among the missionaries some exceptionally tough and resourceful men and women. Even travellers who were not well disposed towards missionaries could not help admiring their fortitude.

Captain Frank Hurley, the Australian explorer, made several expeditions to New Guinea in the 1920s, and in his book *Pearls and Savages* he tells of a journey he made with Father Bach of the Sacred Heart Mission. Even before starting out, Hurley had been profoundly impressed by the qualities of his hosts, 'these Godly men', all well educated and many with distinguished war records. During the walk to Ononge, they stopped at a small mission station where they were entertained by a group of young natives singing oratorios in Latin.

Hurley was struck by the building and engineering skills of Father Fastre, the head of the mission, which he compared with the poor structures put up by the Anglican missions.

Hurley went to New Guinea to observe, to photograph and to film tribes that had never before been seen by European man. What he also witnessed was the beginning of the destruction of those cultures. With the arrival of the gospel, the tribes were encouraged, sometimes browbeaten, into destroying all the outward symbols of their old beliefs. Sometimes artefacts were confiscated by the missionaries and either destroyed or shipped out of the country. It was not just the missionaries who were guilty of this pillage. Hurley's own conduct was so outrageous that he was eventually reprimanded by the government and forced to forfeit some of his loot.

In New Guinea, as elsewhere in the Pacific, the missionaries have been a potent part of the impact of so-called civilisation; but only a part. In 1922, two prospectors, William 'Sharkeye' Park and Jack Nettleton, struck gold on the Bulolo River. The New Guinea gold rush was on, and the country entered a new phase of its development. The missionaries for the time being were forced to play a less prominent role. The gold rush provided the impetus for opening up the remote and inaccessible parts of the island, and led to a rapid expansion in air transport. The missionaries were not slow to exploit the new

The metal birds from the sky. The Missionary Aviation Fellowship, Tribal Air and Divine Word Airways: just three of the mission airlines that have supported missionaries in Papua New Guinea since the 1920s.

opportunities created by the mining, in particular they seized on the possibilities of aviation. The first to take to the skies were the Neuendetteslau Lutherans, followed a little later by other German pioneers, the Catholic Society of the Divine Word. Both missions obtained their own aeroplanes and set about constructing landing fields at their principal stations, often of barely sufficient standard for safe operations. It was an expensive decision but both the Roman Catholics and the Lutherans realised that if they were to have permanent stations in the Central Highlands, their greatest single problem was to keep them supplied. Although costly, the use of air transport was the only practical choice. It was not until the completion of the Highlands highway in the 1960s that any of the missions in the hinterland were able to dispense with their aircraft, and many are wholly dependent on aircraft to this day.

The introduction of the aeroplane brought with it another development which transformed life on remote mission stations: the installation of radio receivers. This communications revolution had a profound impact on the isolated worlds of the New Guinea tribes. It was the coming of the aeroplane itself rather than the missionaries it carried that turned their society upside down. Previously they were subsistence farmers: they grew enough to eat and that was the end of their labours. Suddenly, all over the Highlands, cargo made its appearance on board missionary aircraft. Even though they may not have wished to, missionaries found themselves running trade stores and participating in the beginnings of a cash economy. Suddenly, people were doing things for money rather than in a co-operative spirit. It was a change that affected their lives more deeply than religion. Sooner or later the people of the Highlands would have been compelled to abandon their isolation and join the rest of the world. But the missionary in his aeroplane ensured a great deal happened in a very short time. And there were more surprises to come.

3 A Bit of a Riot

*I believe in Goroka now, there are forty-six different churches within
a radius of a mile or two of the town. It has become a bit of a riot.*
                                                          Bishop David Hand

No country in the world has played host to a larger, more determined
missionary invasion than Papua New Guinea. The island's huge land
mass today supports a population estimated at 3 300 000. Yet a modest
calculation puts the total number of missionaries at 2300, or one
missionary for every 1430 Papua New Guineans. This undoubtedly
underestimates the true number of missionaries in the country, yet
even as it stands it gives Papua New Guinea the highest proportion of
missionaries anywhere in the world. In Indonesia the ratio of missionaries to native inhabitants is 1:120 000. In India it is 1:850 000. Even in
Kenya, a mecca for modern missionaries, the ratio is 1:11 000. For the
evangelical community the concentration of missionaries is the island's
blessing. For their critics, it has become Papua New Guinea's curse.

The full impact of such a large, diverse missionary community in
Papua New Guinea is hard to describe. They come from over forty
different Western Church denominations, each with its own headquarters and mission stations. Each needs housing for its staff and their
families; some run their own schools for their children, a few their own
airlines – Divine Word Airways, Tribal Air; one has even developed its
own 'mission city'. For the evangelical Churches, Papua New Guinea
is a perfect mission field, offering a welcoming open door. For the
older, well-established Churches the latest invasion of fundamentalist
missions threatens to pull their power base apart and splinter their
congregations. For most Papua New Guineans, the appearance of so
many rival Western Churches is bewildering and divisive. For the
anthropologists who flock to the island and for nationalist politicians,
the open-door policy is becoming a cultural disaster. Fifty years after
the first great mission rush, the mountains and jungles of Papua New
Guinea have become the backdrop for an extraordinary, latter-day
scramble for souls.

There are still a few missionaries in Papua New Guinea today who
were there in the 1930s and who were part of that great confrontation
that can never occur again: a million tribal people in collision with

Western culture. The Reverend Paul Freyburg, an American Lutheran, is one; he has no remorse and no misgivings about the impact of the missionaries: 'I rejoice in the memories of what I have done and seen done and pray that it will continue. I don't believe that our mission destroyed much of any value.' Now in his eighties, Paul Freyburg and his wife live in the hills overlooking the coastal town of Madang. In the past fifty years, he only left Papua New Guinea when he was forced to. Following the Japanese invasion of the island in 1942, most of the missionaries were evacuated; of those who stayed, over 200 died, many executed by the Japanese. Freyburg made a daring escape, trekking with a small party of Europeans through the mountains to a point where they could be shipped out to Australia.

As the war drew to an end, Freyburg and many other missionaries who had been forcibly evacuated returned to their interrupted task of evangelism. With them came many new missionaries representing scores of different societies and denominations. An open-door policy had been guaranteed by the League of Nations Mandate before the war. This was confirmed by the UN Trusteeship Agreement under which Australia governed in the post-war period. But the gentleman's agreement that had existed between rival missions was fast being eroded. The self-imposed comity of missions, in which the major groups – Catholic, Lutheran, Anglican, LMS and Wesleyan – recognised each other's rights to work in specific areas, could not survive the horde of new arrivals demanding a share of the action. Rivalry and so-called 'sheep-stealing' became an everyday fact of mission life.

The government tried to exert some control by dividing the country into pacified and non-pacified regions. No missions could be established in the non-pacified areas until they were officially opened up by an announcement in the government Gazette. When rumours got around that restrictions were about to be lifted, it was not unusual to find several 'mission scouting parties' camped out on the boundaries: the objective was to occupy the heavily populated areas that had the best communications before the opposition could get there. Right through the 1950s and 1960s and into the 1970s, missionaries were still entering areas whose inhabitants had had little or no contact with the outside world. Freyburg emphasises how dependent he was upon the work of local evangelists. Like James Chalmers and the other nineteenth-century missionaries, he helped to train his native pastors and then left the bulk of the work to them. They would enter a new area, bargain with the locals for land and then plant crops so that they could be self-supporting; the next task was to learn the language. To the tribes, these black evangelists, who might even come from the next valley, were almost as alien as the European missionaries. According

An effigy of the white 'messiah' and the plane in which he will bring his cargo. Throughout the Pacific Islands, cargo cults have frustrated missionary endeavours.

to Freyburg, evangelists were urged not to be in too much of a hurry to baptise new converts, but simply to live a Christian life, so that by example, the people would grow in their grasp of the gospel. The reality was very different from the theory. Once again it was the possessions, the cargo, which the missionaries had in abundance that mainly impressed the tribal people. Inevitably they assumed that since the Christian God blessed his followers with cargo, then they too would be rewarded for following the 'Gutnuis Bilong Jisas Kraist' (New Guinean pidgin for the gospel). This assumption has been the basis of the many 'cargo cults' that have bedevilled missionary work in Melanesia.

In their attempt to please the missionaries and secure cargo the people often collaborated in the destruction of their own religious or magical objects; thus it was that irreplaceable works of art were lost, together with the native festivals and craft skills. Like most converts, the black evangelists were often more zealous in these matters than the missionaries from overseas. Freyburg describes the 'renunciation festivals' at which he as the 'masta' was called in by his pastors to conduct an elaborate ceremonial destruction of 'the things of darkness' connected with magic and sorcery and the old religion. He would address the people from a high pulpit decorated with flowers, telling them the story of Abraham whom God had promised to protect when he went into a strange country; in the same way, God would take care of them when they gave up the things that were familiar to them. First the important men of the tribe would climb up into the pulpit bearing the magical objects; they would denounce them, describing their evil powers in words taught them by the missionaries, and throw them into a pit in front of the pulpit. In Freyburg's words, 'They would take those things and cry "Satan, I don't want your lies any more, take them back" and throw them down into the pit and spit on them'.

Then the women came, but their 'things of darkness' were what Freyburg described as 'vegetable items, roots, leaves, seeds and fruits which are supposed to have magical qualities'. When it was suggested that the women may have been throwing away valuable herbal remedies and that a priceless heritage of folk medicine might have been lost in the process, he was not impressed and dismissed it as superstition and magic. The missionaries were allowed to take their pick of the artefacts before the pit was covered in. Freyburg had a particular interest in collecting a type of fetish carved from black palm wood. He believes that the 'things of darkness' are better off in a museum than with the people, but it is not clear what happened to his collection.

It is not difficult to understand why anthropologists and ethnologists have become so frustrated by what they see as the missionaries' role in the needless destruction of cultures. Papua New Guineans too are becoming increasingly resentful as they learn what they have lost. Many of the works of art condemned by the missionaries as sinful – if they were not destroyed – finished up gracing the walls of wealthy Westerners' homes and filling the shelves of museums in London, Munich and New York. Sometimes, as with Paul Freyburg, it was the missionaries themselves who were the collectors.

Missionaries today claim to be aware that trying to force the pace of cultural change can be dangerous. Every missionary now knows the possible consequence of trying to change overnight the traditional attitude towards polygamy. In *Taim Bilong Masta*, a book based on interviews recorded with Australian administrators of Papua New Guinea, some of the officials had chilling things to say about this area of missionary endeavour. They reported cases of men divorcing their wives because the missionaries had refused to baptise them, which caused hardship to both the women and the children. One man with three wives simply killed two of them: 'He could see nothing wrong. He could now be baptised and he could go to heaven.' It was the government's view that this kind of disaster was largely the work of the new missionaries who had no regard for the local cultures and no wish to understand them, people described by Sir John Gunther, one Australian administrator, as 'grossly fundamentalist' and 'uneducated'.

Although many of these fundamentalists are sponsored by small

Pentecostal and evangelical groups in the United States and Australia, the largest belong to rich and powerful organisations, notably the New Tribes Mission (NTM), founded in 1942. According to the *American Missions Handbook*, NTM has an annual income of $15 million, supporting 1500 full-time missionaries overseas, 213 of them in Papua New Guinea. Since the Mission runs its own airline, Tribal Air, it is well equipped to operate in the most inaccessible parts of the globe. That indeed is its stated objective: 'The lost tribes until the last tribe' is their slogan. Missionaries are recruited on the evidence of their 'consistent passion for souls ... and ... grasp of the fundamental doctrines of the word of God'. In secular circles the word 'fundamentalist' has an increasingly pejorative ring; but for the NTM missionary it is the only label that guarantees Christian orthodoxy. If you are not a fundamentalist, you are not a Christian; and if you are not a Christian you are on Satan's side.

By adhering strictly to the inerrancy of scripture, the fundamentalist groups have armed themselves with the most powerful motive for taking the gospel to unreached peoples. They believe that even those who have never heard the Good News or had the chance to respond to it will suffer eternal punishment. Their duty is therefore clear. Ten years ago, Bob Kennell and George Walker of NTM started to work among the Bisorio people, small scattered groups of semi-nomads who inhabit the dense forests and mountains of the Sepik River region. At that time, the Bisorio were one of very few tribes to have escaped the attentions of the missionaries, which made them a special target for NTM. It was a challenging task as no one outside the tribe spoke their language and very few Bisorio spoke pidgin. Bob Kennell had deep reservations when he first encountered the Bisorio, 'some of the wildest looking people' he had ever seen. But the tribe agreed to let the missionaries settle among them, and the work of evangelism began. New Tribes Mission invests heavily in equipment and support services for their missionaries in remote places. The families working among the Bisorio enjoy a comfortable life-style in large houses complete with modern conveniences: solar panels, generators, washing machines, microwaves, televisions and videos. Food is flown in regularly by Tribal Air and their children flown out to be educated at the New Tribes school at Mission Headquarters in Numonohi. Half the NTM workforce on the island is involved in supply and back-up services. Harriet Walker, a New Tribes missionary, sees nothing wrong in providing themselves with living conditions that are in such marked contrast to those of the Bisorio: modern conveniences free them to devote more time to the people and to the evangelical task in hand.

One hundred years have seen immeasurable changes in the way

Blowing the conch shell was once the signal for feasting and dancing. Now it calls villagers together for Bible class.

missionaries live in Papua New Guinea, but their dilemma remains the same. In Chalmers's day, it was a gospel of tomahawks and tobacco. Today, it is a gospel of transistors and training shoes. Bob Kennell and George Walker had no illusions at all about the welcome given them by the Bisorio. Although they were an isolated group, the Bisorio had seen and heard of the benefits brought by the missionaries – airstrips, education, medical care, status and all sorts of cargo – and they wanted their share. During the three years George and Bob spent learning the language, there were tensions of the kind experienced by all missionaries working in similar conditions. The Bisorio expected a rapid delivery of material benefits and if they failed to get what they wanted, they were inclined to steal. This led to inevitable clashes. Still, after eight years, progress in missionary terms has been remarkable. Bob and George and their wives are now fluent in the Bisorio language and a translation of the New Testament has been completed. Several of the nomadic groups have been encouraged to settle permanently near the mission.

This is a familiar sequence of events that in the past has produced tragic consequences. It is likely that the forest surrounding the mission will become over-exploited as a source of food and that the women will have to travel ever longer distances to make new gardens. To compensate for any material shortcomings and to encourage the Bisorio to remain, George and Bob have provided employment and free hand-outs of clothing, medical care and some food. Inevitably, the Bisorio have become dependent on the mission and have fallen very much under the influence of the missionaries. It is difficult to see how it could be otherwise when so much time is taken up with religious instruction. The story of how George and Bob brought the gospel to the Bisorio is now so much admired that in *The Story of the New Tribes Mission*, the official history of the NTM, several pages are given over to it. Eager as they were to tell the Bisorio that Jesus died for them, they felt obliged to put the Good News in context. They therefore set out to tell the story of the Bible starting at Genesis 1:1 and progressing chronologically to the crucifixion and the resurrection. In order to engage the attention of the natives, they dramatised the Bible stories and acted them out as a costume drama, even using dishcloths in place of biblical head gear. The experiment began with just a small number of people in the village but soon grew as others got to hear of what was happening: '... they'd get caught up in the stories they were hearing and just stay on for months on end without ever going back to their families. The numbers grew and grew and they really became hungry for the message.' In the end, performances were taking place twice a day, five days a week. By the time the missionaries came to tell the story of Christ's passion, the Bisorio people were in a highly emotional state. The portrayal of Christ's crucifixion and death both horrified and confused them but when it came to the resurrection and the ascension George and Bob reminded them that by believing in Jesus Christ their sins would be forgiven and they would receive eternal life. 'Suddenly the first Bisorio spoke up. "I see it. I believe Jesus died for me, and had he not done so, I would have gone to Hell" ... Only a few did not speak up nor seem to understand.'

In other parts of the world, notably in Latin America, NTM has been bitterly attacked for enticing tribes away from their self-sufficient life-style and for forcing them into settlements simply to indoctrinate them with their Christian teachings. Although the Bisorio have not altogether abandoned their traditional way of life, they are at least part way down that same road. When it is put to the missionaries that they are misusing their influence and wilfully destroying a culture, they argue that the will to change comes from the Bisorio themselves. There is no doubt that the tribes people will look covetously at the modern homes of the missionaries and compare them with their own. The missionaries argue that in any case the Bisorio were bound to join the mainstream of life; that in time they were certain to encounter traders, planters, prospectors or government officers who are also agents of change. The government is apparently happy to see that missionaries are settling and 'civilising' its few remaining subjects that

Stopping at nothing: New Tribes missionaries exploit all the latest communications technology. Even in the remotest villages they carry public address systems, tape recorders and videos.

up to now have remained outside its administrative grasp.

The missionaries also claim – and this is the crux of their argument – that they are freeing the tribal peoples from the tyranny of fear. Bob Kennell believes that Satan was using fear of spirits to keep the Bisorio people in bondage. But what of the fear of Hell? Kennell does believe that the fear of Hell is an indispensable part of the message he has been commissioned to bring. Among New Tribes missionaries there is no danger that sin will be overlooked or the workings of Satan ignored. In the words of Mission Chairman Macon G. Hare: 'All Christians have a common enemy known as Satan, our adversary, supreme evil spirit, Apollyon, destroyer, god of this world, prince of darkness, accuser of the brethren, a liar, a deceiver.' They believe that Satan has blinded many Christians to the true will of God. To New Tribes supporters, 'many Christians' means all Christians who do not share their fundamentalist views. Although NTM is careful not to name names, it is no secret that, as good Calvinists, they equate the Papacy with Antichrist, which means in turn that Catholic missionaries must be regarded as agents of Satan. In the past, Roman Catholics have retaliated by branding their fundamentalist opponents Antichrist. All this name-calling does not lead to good relations between the scores of missions operating in Papua New Guinea. It has also caused great confusion among the people. In attacking the Catholics, some extreme fundamentalists have sunk to the level of distributing the most scurrilous literature: illustrated comics which portray the Pope as an ally of Hitler and Stalin and in which Catholic priests engage in bestial and degraded practises. In one illustration, monks are seen crossing by a secret passage from their monastery to a nearby convent to engage in sexual orgies. To complete the outrage, an underground cemetery is shown where their murdered offspring are buried. Understandably, no organisation will acknowledge responsibility for distributing this material which is manufactured by Chick Publications, America. For some young Papua New Guineans, however, these comics are among the first 'Christian' publications they have seen.

Bishop David Hand, whose ministry in Papua New Guinea began as an Anglican missionary more than forty years ago, believes that the proliferation of missions and the rivalry between them has been damaging to the Christian cause. In the Highland town of Goroka where he started his work, within a mile radius there are now more than forty different missions where there used to be two or three. Several of these newcomers are not averse to preaching against other missions or to poaching from them. Indeed, so saturated have the Highlands become with missionaries that this is the only way many can build up congregations. The culprits are not the traditional mainline

Churches, but the groups whom Bishop Hand describes as 'sects who believe they are the only ones in the world who are right and all the rest of us are wrong', and who are so keen to win souls that they will do anything, even threaten people with Hell.

Bishop Hand, who would disagree with NTM over most things, wholeheartedly agrees with Bob and George on one matter; that it is naïve to think that the Papua New Guinean was once the 'Noble Savage' living in some blissful state of nature from which he has been rudely plucked by over-zealous missionaries. That, he believes, is romantic nonsense. Bishop Hand has become part of the Papua New Guinean establishment, but as a young missionary he was just as zealous in pursuit of idolatory and witchcraft as the latest arrivals, the 'crackpot pioneers', about whom he expresses such reservations. He was made a bishop at the remarkably young age of 32, and went on to do pioneering work in the Milne Bay and Highland regions of the island. He would go from village to village to engage in trials of spiritual strength with the 'witch-doctors', challenging the villagers to burn their ancestor idols and smash their sacred stones. His approach echoed the actions of missionaries since earliest times. Boniface (*c.* 680–754), probably the greatest missionary of the Dark Ages, travelled around Europe performing similar acts of spiritual bravado, his most audacious being the felling of the sacred oak at Geismar in Hesse. The oak was a pagan sanctuary to the god Thor and the Germans were convinced that any who infringed the sanctuary would be punished by the gods. Boniface reassured them no such thing would occur. He felled the tree, unscathed, and the local population were convinced that the powers of Boniface's God were superior to their own. With the wood Boniface built a chapel in honour of St Peter. More than a thousand years later the same technique was employed by David Hand in establishing the Anglican Church in Milne Bay province. In one celebrated incident Hand broke uninvited into a sacred site and planted a cross above the sacred rock. To the Papuans' astonishment Hand left the rock unharmed. A church, known simply as 'The Church on the Rock', stands today to mark the event.

The Seventh-Day Adventists are probably the most successful, and thus the most resented, of the newer missions. The first Adventist plane flew into the country in 1964; today the Church membership numbers over 120 000. Few deny that their growth has been spectacular, yet no mission has a more forthright, uncompromising stance on customary practice. The Seventh-Day Adventist Church prides itself on its difference. Some mainstream missions feel it stands so far apart that it is a sect rather than part of the mainstream Christian Church. The Adventist Church worships on a Saturday. Each Friday evening to Saturday evening is given over in Adventist homes to 'family time' and worship. This, they believe, is the true Sabbath from which the rest of the Churches have strayed. The Adventists do not drink alcohol or smoke; many do not touch tea or coffee; they do not eat pork and many are vegetarians; and they place a high priority on personal cleanliness. All Adventists give a tenth of their incomes to the Church, and since many are successful in business and professional life, the tithe makes the Church one of the richest in the world. It has a multi-million-dollar health food business, 'Sanitarium'. On the mission field, the Adventist operation is one of the best financed and most well organised of all.

For many their success remains a mystery as their disciplines conflict with the traditions and habits of the tribal people. In Papua New Guinea, heavy alcohol consumption and tobacco smoking are endemic, and the pig is at the very centre of cultural and economic life. It is the most valued of possessions: the currency of the rural clans; a vital element in the negotiation that surrounds any marriage settlement; the compensation paid to settle disagreements; and the 'pig kill' is the focus of all great celebrations, a chance for the Highlander to display his wealth and status. Yet the mission has not bent the rules for its would-be adherents. The Adventists are equally uncompromising over traditional dancing, and in many cases forbid their members to attend the great celebrations for which the island is famous, the sing-sings. Chester Stanley, who heads up the Adventist mission, is unrepentant about any of these restrictions and believes that the motivation to take the step to give up traditional practices comes from God.

The Adventists delight in their nickname 'the clean mission', and are proud of the reputation their members have as honest and reliable employees. Some newspaper advertisements explicitly state that only SDAs need apply for the jobs. Chester Stanley feels this constitutes the attraction of their mission. 'If an Adventist young person is committed, the sky's the limit in terms of opportunity.' Christian critics of Adventism argue that converts have a profoundly legalistic view of religion: 'If I do not smoke, drink, or eat pork, and worship on Sunday I will go to heaven.' Adventist missionaries argue that rules help an individual to build a healthier, happier life. You can tell an Adventist, the missionaries claim, by his smile and his handshake. Chester Stanley explains, 'people tell me that you can walk into a village and ... they can identify whether it is an Adventist village ... The people have a sense of cleanliness. There is a sense of joy on their faces. Clean teeth. No gooey eyes and that sort of thing. We don't spend half a dozen baptismal classes thumping people about the importance of washing their shirts ... it seems to be a spontaneous reaction to the total message that we share with the people.' The gospel of the clean white shirt is still alive and well in Papua New Guinea. Adventist converts are distinguished by their clean white shirts, and the young people by the smart, almost military uniforms. While liberal mainline Churches repent the errors of their former ways, the cultural heavy-handedness, their inability to separate Christianity from the Western life-style, the Adventist mission has no such doubts.

It is not just the robust defence of cultural imperialism that earns the Adventists enemies on the mission field. They have little time for ecumenism. Their theology is virulently anti-Catholic. Heavy importance is placed on the Book of Revelation, with its warning of the forthcoming Apocalypse, and its description, as they see it, of the Pope as Antichrist. In the hands of barely trained converts these messages are explosive. Father Norman Crutwell is a retired Anglican priest, who speaks bitterly of his last days as an active missionary, beset by the anti-High Church propaganda of the Adventists. On several occasions he found leaflets that had been circulated among his congregation warning that all who worshipped on Sunday were destined for Hell. Crutwell is sure that much of the Adventist success can be attributed to playing on people's fear, not of the ancestor spirits, but of the Devil. Others suggest that it is its exclusiveness which makes it so appealing. As capitalism encroaches into the remoter parts of the island, joining the Adventist Church offers a chance to be a member of a successful upwardly mobile club. The Adventists have cultivated their separateness and have studiously avoided being drawn into the comity agreements worked out by the old firm of missions. The Adventists are ambitious: they know that to grow they will increasingly be drawing members, not from the unevangelised, but from the other Churches. They have no wish to enter an agreement that prevents them from entering Catholic, Lutheran or Anglican areas and drawing off the disillusioned and disaffected. At present the Church is baptising 10 000 new believers each year. Stanley admits that many of these will already be members of other Churches. In defence of this 'sheep-stealing' he states his belief in the importance of the democratic freedom to join whichever Church one wants.

The Seventh-Day Adventist mission is just one of some fifty battling it out for the hearts and minds of the island people. Sal Lo Faso belongs to another of the missions, the Pioneers. He is working among the Ningram people, in an area inaccessible except on foot. From the nearest settlement it is the best part of a week's walk to the Ningrams' home. The Pioneers are carving a landing strip from the jungle, essentially to enable Sal and his wife and children to get into the area with ease. In due course planes bringing all sorts of 'cargo' will regularly fly into Ningram country, ending their isolation for good. If they are pressing on with their task at full tilt, it is because nobody knows when Christ will choose to return. Like Chester Stanley, Sal Lo Faso has no reservations about being the agent of what will be a dramatic and potentially traumatic development for the Ningram. He has come to bring change in the form of the salvation message: 'as Jesus Christ comes into a person's heart he changes them, he changes their belief'. And if that means that their traditions must also change, then so be it. The 'haus tamboran', the spirit house, the focal point of traditional village life, will be destroyed, as most have been already, and a church built in its place. Sing-sings and traditional dancing will be forbidden, and the young children will soon be wearing baseball caps and T-shirts with a Superman or Masters of the Universe logo emblazoned across the chest. Such developments may be regretted by the new missionaries, but it is not something over which they lose too much sleep. Christ has called them to these places to bring new life to the people, that they should be 'born again': and being born again means making a clean break with the past.

Not all missionaries share this view. It is in fact the most established missions, in particular the Catholics, that are now committed to the defence of what remains of indigenous culture. They call their new approach 'inculturation'. For the nationalists and anthropologists this is a belated but welcome development. It is a concept as old as mission itself. In 601 Pope Gregory the Great, who had initiated Augustine's mission to England in 596, wrote: 'The heathen temples of these people need not be destroyed, only the idols which are to be found in them ... If the temples are well built, it is a good idea to detach them from the service of the devil, and to adapt them for the worship of the God.'

It was the approach of an arch-pragmatist, anxious not to alienate the heathen peoples, building the Christian Church step by step by carefully grafting Christian belief on to pagan practice. A thousand years later the same approach was reiterated in a series of instructions sent out in 1659 by the Sacred Congregation for the Propagation of the Faith, or Propaganda: 'Do not regard it as your task, and do not bring any pressure to bear on the peoples, to change their manners, customs, and uses, unless they are evidently contrary to religion and sound morals. What could be more absurd than to transport France, Spain, Italy or some other European country to China?' It was a piece of what now seems prophetic advice. In the three centuries of determined missionary endeavour that followed there were a few who heeded the instructions, but they were rare. Many more completely ignored it. By the time of the second Vatican Council in 1962–5, there was a dawning awareness that indigenous culture was acutely vulnerable before a combination of commercial and missionary pressures, and that culture was not a replenishable resource. Many argued that with the destruction of their culture, communities had been deprived of their life-blood, and robbed of their self-respect. There was a recognition that missionaries, however unwittingly, had been party to that process. Vatican II attempted to re-define the objective of mission: to encourage ritual, worship, and theology to grow out of the living culture of the people. Local churches were to be encouraged to a certain autonomy, in contrast to the previous emphasis on the unity and universality of the Catholic Church. Latin as the medium of worship was abandoned, and missionary priests everywhere were urged to push full speed ahead with 'inculturation'.

Bishop Firmin Schmidt is one of those struggling to work out what 'inculturation' means in missionary practice. Schmidt, a German American from Kansas, is the Catholic Bishop of the Southern Highlands. Until 1955 the area was thought to be too dangerous and was closed to missionaries. Then seven young Capuchin Franciscans from Pennsylvania were given official permission to enter. Among their number was Father Berard who had been stationed on the island during the war. He returned not in military uniform but in the brown cassock of his Franciscan order. Four years later he was joined in the small Highland town of Mendi by his former seminary tutor, Firmin Schmidt. Schmidt loved his new role captaining his team of Franciscans in

The floor of this little Catholic church is fashioned from thousands of beer bottles set, neck downwards, in sand. Designed by one of the Capuchin Franciscan fathers.

their pioneering work. They hiked and rode over some of the most inaccessible territory in Papua New Guinea. Schmidt encouraged the priests to live in Christian simplicity as even their simple life-style would seem like enviable affluence to the local people. The Franciscans have tried harder than any other mission group to embrace those aspects of Papua New Guinean culture which are not explicitly anti-Christian. As Schmidt puts it, 'God is the author of culture, we have to have respect. Our work focuses on the essentials of Christianity not the accidentals.' He and his priests are continually on the look-out for more 'culturally appropriate' ways of expressing their faith.

On 31 May 1988, 2000 people from the Pangia district of the Southern Highlands gathered for a great pig-kill and sing-sing or ceremonial dance. Long trenches had been cut into the ground in which fires were to be laid and meat roasted. At a chosen time the slaughter began. The blood of a hundred pigs splattered the grass, creating a striking red pool in the grey morning drizzle. The fires were lit and soon the whole area was subsumed in a swirling fog of woodsmoke. A pig-kill and sing-sing of such size is held only rarely in present-day Papua New Guinea, perhaps once in seven years. Usually they are held in order to cement alliances between friendly villages, or to demonstrate a man's power and wealth to his enemies. On this occasion, the pig-kill was being held for a very different reason: to celebrate the opening of the

Catholic Church of St Felix. A procession wound its way to the doors of the church led by the men of the Catholic congregation of Pangia, resplendent in full battle array. They marched at the front to ward off the evil spirits. Behind them came the crucifix, followed by the Franciscan priests in their brown cassocks. The great procession welcomed its guest of honour, Bishop Schmidt. In a symbolic gesture, the Bishop was wearing on his head a magnificent mitre made by local craftsmen from bird of paradise feathers.

This most unusual of church dedications made a magnificent spectacle. But it horrified many evangelical Protestants, who regarded it as a most dangerous liaison between the sacred and the profane. Most are unhappy with such attempts to seek cultural continuity with the past and look instead for clear statements of a new Christian order. For them it typified the ambiguous Catholic approach to the 'devilish' world of traditional worship. For the Franciscans, on the other hand, it pointed to the possibilities for a synthesis of Christian belief with traditional forms of worship and celebration.

This is illustrated most dramatically at Easter time. On Good Friday 1988 the Catholic population of Mendi decided to put on a dramatic re-enactment of the crucifixion. It was not staged to please the expatriates, but to satisfy the people; no missionaries were involved and none came to watch. Menacing black clouds were gathering over the limestone crags of Mendi, as villagers from several valleys arrived for the drama. The villagers dressed as they would for the death of one of their own. White clay to signify mourning was plastered on their faces,

Left and right,
The power of the cross. Re-enacting the crucifixion, the villagers dress as they would for the death of one of their own, white clay plastered on their faces and bodies as a sign of mourning.

arms and legs. They wore strings of white beads, and garlands of bright yellow flowers hung from their necks. A line of mourners, old men and women, stood clutching rough-hewn cedar crosses.

When the crucifix was raised into place, a terrible keening began, as the mourners wept for their crucified saviour. The actor playing Jesus yelled aloud, and there was a sympathetic round of applause. Jesus stepped off his cross to acknowledge the applause and to reclaim his clothing. Within a few minutes the site was deserted and the villagers had headed back into the hills. The Capuchin missionaries would probably have reflected with satisfaction at the evidence that the power of the Easter story had been successfully communicated to another group of people.

On Easter Saturday the Franciscans left their community base in Mendi and headed into the hills to celebrate man with the most isolated of their parishioners. They drove through rough, mountainous country and up into more fertile land, planted with banana palms and coffee trees. Father Matthew, one of the priests, headed for Tulum village, situated on a broad, grassy ridgetop. The Catholic church stood at the end of the village with a rough wooden cross at one side. A huge fire had been lit in front of the cross and the villagers had gathered around it. They began to tell stories, of Noah and of Abraham and Isaac, to the accompaniment of a strange chant, punctuated every few lines by loud 'Amens'. Sparks from the fire were leaping into the night sky. 'A house without a fire is a dead house', intoned Father Matthew, his arms outstretched and the reflection of the flames flickering on his white cassock. Father Matthew began to recount the Easter story in Tok Pigin, the lingua franca of the island.

The congregation left the fireside and processed behind Father Matthew into the little low-roofed church was decorated with ferns, leaves and branches. The air was thick with incense. The crowd huddled on the floor and listened while Father Matthew read the liturgy. Everyone joined in the prayers and a humming and murmuring filled the church. A young catechist walked among the congregation, with a palm leaf and bucket, spraying them with Holy water. Then five young girls, draped in wreaths of sunflowers, danced their way to the altar with the offering. An old man spat a stream of red betel juice on to the floor. Father Matthew announced that Easter had arrived.

Many of Father Matthew's fellow missionaries would have condemned the Easter celebrations at Tulum as little more than pagan practice dressed in Christian vestments. For them the Catholic inculturation goes too far, and the Christian message is submerged in an outpouring of heretical heathen worship. Father Matthew disagrees. He is searching for points of cultural contact and advocates caution before condemning traditional gods and beliefs. He believes that true conversion does not occur overnight, but takes time: 'We may have instant coffee and instant tea, but we don't have instant Christians.'

The Summer Institute of Linguistics (SIL) stand at the opposite end of the theological spectrum, yet they too claim to be working for the preservation of cultural diversity. Their main goal is to translate the Word of God into every known language in the world. Only then, they believe, will Jesus Christ return. To accomplish this purpose, SIL have a staff of almost one thousand in Papua New Guinea alone. The people here speak 696 languages. Its remarkable geography has ensured that it is one of the most linguistically complex societies in the world. An SIL missionary will often devote his or her entire working life to studying, learning and painstakingly translating the Bible into a chosen language. Though the aim is first and foremost to extend God's kingdom, they argue that their linguistic research does much to improve the self-confidence of the language groups among which they work.

In Papua New Guinea they have established the largest mission station in the world – Ukarumpa – which eats up a considerable proportion of SIL's $37 million annual budget. Known locally as 'little America', Ukarumpa is a town in its own right with accommodation for nearly 3000 expatriate inhabitants. Behind neat white fences stand spacious American-style bungalows, surrounded by neatly manicured lawns. Papua New Guinean employees water the gardens and wash the cars, which are driven around Ukarumpa's own mini-road network – Vietnam Street, Philippines Street. There is a guest house, a post office, a supermarket which stocks American food and the 'Teen Centre' where the teenage community meet for social events. Once a week the teenagers lay on a meal for the rest of the community, hamburgers, tacos and French fries, washed down with chocolate milkshakes and Coca Cola. There are tennis courts and horses for the young girls who enjoy riding. It is the epitome of American suburbia, in the heart of Papua New Guinea. There is a junior school and a high school, both open to the children of other mission agencies on the island. Missionaries are employed specifically to teach in the school, to act as house parents to the missionary children, to run the guest house, the post office and the supermarket. The mission employs printers for its publishing house, mechanics for its vehicle workshops, computer programmers and electricians.

Ukarumpa exists for the work of translating the Bible and a huge linguistic, anthropological and Christian library has been built up. An extensive computer system, armed with the latest and most sophisticated linguistic software available, is at the disposal of translators. For Gere Reesink, the Dutchman who is in charge of SIL in Papua

New Guinea, Ukarumpa is something of an embarrassment: while other missions are busily divesting themselves of their great institutions to establish small community projects, Ukarumpa keeps growing. But the task which SIL has set itself only gradually diminishes – by 1988, Gospel portions had been translated into 103 languages, New Testaments into 67, and the entire Bible had been completed in just five of the island's languages. It is painstaking work.

Dot James and Denise Potts have been working on the Siani translation of the Bible for a combined total of forty years. They have reached the Book of Revelation, at the end of the first draft of the Siani New Testament. Dot James, an American linguist, has been working with the Siani for the past twenty-five years. Denise Potts, who is British and a former primary school teacher, came out to join her fifteen years ago. Dot explained what convinced her to embark on such an extraordinary career: 'I thought what in the world would it be like if I had all my spiritual food in French or Latin or Greek? Here I sit at a banquet table ... They don't even have one verse in their own language that they can feed on.'

One of the ironies of Bible translation is that the people for whom one is working are mostly illiterate. They first need to be taught to read in their own language. For a long time, possibly forever, the only book that will be available in this language will be the Bible. Dot and Denise spend half of the year living in a simple thatched house among the Siani people. They have a lap-top computer powered by 12-volt solar panels, but it is the complex process of communicating biblical

Translating the Bible into the Siani language has been a lifetime's work for Dot James.

concepts that is most time-consuming. The potential for misunderstanding is infinite, as Dot explains: 'I was talking to one fellow about the phrase to turn the other cheek. We had translated it fairly literally into Siani. I asked him what he understood by that. He said, "Oh well, that's very straightforward. If someone hits you, and if you turn the other cheek and duck quickly, then you'll miss the next blow that comes in your direction."'

Forgiveness, sin, redemption, the Holy Spirit, they all constitute a translator's nightmare. After many hours' discussion of the word 'forgiveness' it was decided the nearest possible concept was 'not to demand "pay-back"', the traditional revenge payment. But the team explained to Denise that no Siani would ever do this. It was a point of honour to demand 'pay-back', and anyone who did not do so would be regarded as utterly foolish. One day, probably in several years' time, all such conceptual problems will be ironed out. The work will have been checked and rechecked by the Siani people, and by a team of SIL linguists. Then and only then will the 30 000 Siani people have a New Testament in their own language. The two women have no doubts about the usefulness of their task: if only one person is brought to Jesus then for them their lives will not have been in vain. In the meantime they feel that the Siani people have gained in self-confidence, by seeing they were so important that two strangers were prepared to spend their lives in studying their language.

Given the extraordinary concentration of missionary endeavour in Papua New Guinea over the last half century it is not surprising that 94 per cent of its population claim to be Christian. Statistically, Papua New Guinea is considerably more Christian than Australia, Britain or the United States. Yet new missions are still arriving, and the government continues to hold the door wide open. The missions offer a free, unofficial social services network, they bring in revenue and resources, they run several airlines and fly to areas that would be unprofitable for commercial companies, and they pay to build landing strips in inaccessible areas. The strict disciplinary code of the evangelical missions neatly counteracts many of the social problems, particularly alcoholism. As far as the missionaries are concerned, the fact that the overwhelming majority profess a Christian faith is no disincentive. When the last of the 'unreached peoples' has been reached, there will still be pastors and priests to train, schools to run, clinics to open. The missions will inevitably find a way to justify their presence to congregations back home. By enticing members from other Churches they will be able to claim a growing membership. The future alone will reveal the cultural cost and the political consequences of importing the theological bickering of Western Christianity into an already divided society.

4 Africa or Death

If heathenism, immorality, and sin had been left untouched in our own country, where once upon a time it had been rampant, the British flag would not be to the world what it is today, the emblem of Christian government.

A. B. Lloyd, missionary

In December 1856 David Livingstone returned to England at the end of his first great journey. In an age when missionaries were celebrities, Livingstone was a superstar. For his achievements he received the gold medal of the Royal Geographical Society, the freedom of several cities and an honorary doctorate from Oxford University. Even Queen Victoria granted him a private audience. When in November 1857 his book, *Missionary Travels and Researches in South Africa*, was published it sold 70 000 copies. But Livingstone had not returned simply to bathe in the glory, he longed to inspire others to follow him. In 1857 he told a large audience at the Senate House in Cambridge: 'I beg to direct your attention to Africa. I know that in a few years I shall be cut off in that country, which is now open; do not let it be shut again!' As he concluded, his audience let forth 'volley after volley of cheers'. He was expressing what they and thousands more pious Victorians fervently believed, that it was their uppermost duty to bestow upon Africa the benefits of Christian civilisation. This was 'the white man's burden', and it was the responsibility of everyone, most of all the missionary, to bear his share of the load. To the President of the Church Missionary Society, John Kennaway, it was a challenge worthy of a great Christian nation: 'Ruling, civilising, and Christianising the "silent peoples", of whom John Bull carries no less than 350 millions on his back. The duty is no light one, but it gives an outlet for the energies of our people, an object worthy of an Imperial race, of a Christian country, a call to put forth the highest qualities of the Anglo-Saxon character.'

Here was a supreme, unquestioning confidence. Nobody stopped to ask the African. They had no need to. They knew they were right. Africa was benighted, on her knees and desperate. According to the missionary A. B. Lloyd it was the missionaries who had been chosen by God to come to her rescue: 'The fiercest spirits that ever trod her

Top: South Seas missionary John Williams is clubbed to death on Erromanga Island, 1839, a classic instance of missionary martyrdom. Reports that he had been cooked and eaten as well caused an additional frisson of excitement at home.

Bottom: 'Baptism of the Maori Chief, Te Puni, Otaki Church' painted by C. D. Barrard. Missionaries to the South Seas focused their attentions on the island chiefs. Convert a chief, they calculated, and you convert the island.

Left: Sigute mission, Central Province, a typical mission station in the remote, rugged highlands of Papua New Guinea.

Top: Lamogai village, New Britain, a mission station for the zealous New Tribes Mission, whose motto is: 'Reaching new tribes until we've reached the last tribe'.

Bottom: A white man's graveyard in Alexishafen, Papua New Guinea. In this missionary cemetery are the graves of hundreds of early Catholic missionaries. Many did not outlive the first year of their arrival.

75

Left: Moving home by dugout. Unevangelised Fields missionaries Steven Eliott-Lockhart and his wife, Rhydwen, a former beauty consultant, transport their family and the essentials of modern living up-river to the Yoggi mission outpost.

Bottom: A mass baptism of the Seventh-day Adventist mission. The SDAs, known as 'the clean mission' for their puritanical code of social conduct, claim to baptise 10 000 new members a year in Papua New Guinea.

Top: Anglican pioneer missionary, Bishop David Hand, returns to the Siani Valley, an area he was first to evangelise.

*The raising of Lazarus,
re-enacted by a Highland
congregation in a Capuchin
Franciscan church.
The Franciscans are leading
the way in making the
Christian message
culturally relevant.*

An advertisement for light bulbs, 1890, capitalising on the Victorian missionary rallying cry for its own commercial ends.

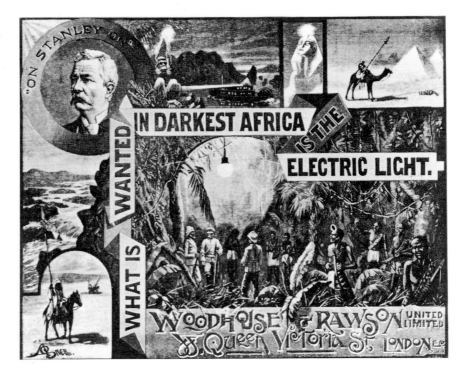

burning sands shall be brought into complete subjugation; not by the military fort and the roar of cannon and the rattle of musketry, for it will require a mightier power than this to bring peace to this troubled land. That which has made our Empire what it is to-day – "The Word of God"'.

Yet Livingstone's own experience had taught him that the Word of God alone was not enough to heal the 'open sore of the world'. When he told his Senate House audience, 'I go back to Africa to try to make an open path for commerce and Christianity', he was cheered to the rafters. In the mind of his audience these two aims, enterprise and evangelism, were wholly compatible. And history seems to have proved them right. Today the so-called Dark Continent is well on its way to becoming the most Christian continent. But if today the Church in Africa is claimed as a missionary success story, it was not always so. The romantic rhetoric masks a tale of compromise, failure and death.

Just north of Dar es Salaam, on the Tanzanian mainland, stand the crumbling buildings of Bagamoyo Mission Station. It is a melancholic place, a sad museum full of the mildewed relics of a more optimistic age. Like many of the once great nineteenth-century monuments to European Christianity, Bagamoyo is a testament both to the romantic illusion and the harsh reality that characterised the missionary occupation of the continent. Bagamoyo means 'lay down your heart'. It

A Highlander in full traditional dress for a 'sing-sing' to celebrate the opening of the St Felix Catholic church, Pangia. Several evangelical missions forbid their members from attending 'sing-sings', claiming they are pagan, devilish events.

was here that the slave caravans, often with more than a thousand slaves, stopped for the last time before crossing to the island of Zanzibar and the slave market. Those who survived the crossing were packed into caves before being sold. Those who were ill or dying were thrown overboard to avoid the duty payable on every slave brought into Zanzibar. In 1868 the Holy Ghost Fathers chose Bagamoyo as the site of the first mission station on the East African mainland. The first dwelling, a mud house, was soon replaced by bigger buildings with verandahs and arched colonnades, more in keeping with the grand pretensions and unbounded idealism with which the missionary priests set about their task. Their ambition was to build a Christian community of freed slaves. Ransoms were paid to the slave traders for the freedom of thousands of slaves. Most of those released were placed in 'Freedom Village' on the mission compound, but they soon discovered that their freedom was not absolute. The disciplinary code enforced by the missionaries was severe, with a rigorous timetable of work, Christian education and prayers. As the baptised ex-slaves grew up, they were married off in batches and resettled under the authority of a missionary priest in a Christian village somewhere inland. One visitor, Sir Bartle Frere, special emissary to the Sultan of Zanzibar, recommended the Bagamoyo system as a model, but for the Holy Ghost Fathers their involvement with former slaves dealt a fatal blow to their ambition to spread the faith along the East African coastline. The mission was too closely associated with slavery, and the Muslim population was anxious to distance themselves as far as possible from the slave population. They had no desire to become enmeshed with the new missionary guardians of the ex-captives.

On 24 February 1874 the body of David Livingstone was carried into Bagamoyo. For ten months, sixty Africans led by Chuma and Susi had transported the body from Chitambo's village near Lake Bangweolo to the coast. The body, preserved in salt and calico and dried in the sun, rested for the night in Bagamoyo and the next day was taken on to a ship specially sent from England for the journey home. Despite the euologies which filled the British newspapers, David Livingstone had in reality failed as a missionary. In the course of his missionary life he had made just one known convert, Sechele, and even he in time lapsed from his faith. What is more, not one of the Africans who bore his body to the coast was a Christian.

Livingstone was buried in Westminster Abbey with unparalleled pomp. Few of the people who flocked to the funeral would have been aware of the reality of his missionary achievement. For them Livingstone was the saviour of Africa, the man who single-handedly had cut a swathe of light through a dark, benighted continent. It was a myth that Livingstone had done as much as anyone to foster.

Mission work in Africa in the nineteenth century entered the realm of myth because the reality was too depressing to be told, a tale of intransigence and disinterest on the part of the local population, and of disease, discomfort and ignominious death for the missionaries. There were vested interests keen to ensure that a different picture was relayed to congregations and Sunday School classes at home. Brave men and women were lighting the lamps of Christianity all over Africa. Those who met with death did so heroically and as noble martyrs. Bishop Jim Hannington was one of the early casualties, murdered by the men of Mwanga, King of the Baganda, as he tried to enter Uganda from the west. His biography *Lion-Hearted* describes his death: 'As many a gallant soldier has fallen on the battlefield, while fighting for his country, so this fearless soldier of Christ fell while fighting the great battle of right against wrong ... It is a sweet and blessed thing to die for Christ.' No mission to Africa had a more disastrous start than the Society of African Missions: few missionaries had shorter careers than Monseigneur de Marion Brésillac, the eccentric and passionate Frenchman who founded the society. On 24 July 1858 de Brésillac with four priests and two brothers took an oath to work for

Missionary memsahib and her baby travel in luxury.

the mission for all their lives, pledging to accept suffering, privation and even death for the Lord. None of them can have known just how soon these pledges would be realised.

Africa was divided into spheres of influence for the various Catholic mission societies: Sierra Leone was dedicated to the Society of African Missions. On 14 May 1859 de Brésillac arrived in Freetown. It was an inauspicious beginning: just two people attended the first mass he celebrated. The town was in the grip of yellow fever and the Europeans were dying in droves. In such a situation it was impossible to retain any optimism. De Brésillac was assailed by a sense of failure, and a growing certainty that his missionary party would soon die. They tried to make plans for the future. But the disease had already begun to strike. Within two weeks three of their number were dead. De Brésillac wrote back to France, despairing of the failure of his mission before it had even properly begun, 'Blessed be God's holy name! His ways are impenetrable. Let us adore them and submit ourselves to them'. He was well aware of what the implications might be back home: 'This is going to frighten vocations off pretty badly, isn't it?'

Both de Brésillac and his last colleague, Father Reymond, had contracted the fever and were becoming weaker. As the disease took its course, de Brésillac realised he was dying. He was insistent that he needed the Last Sacraments. So Father Reymond struggled from his bed, got into his cassock and stole, and was led to de Brésillac. One dying man ministered the last rites to another. The next day de Brésillac was buried, but there was no Catholic priest able to assist at the funeral. Neither could the Protestant bishop conduct the service. He too was dead. When Father Reymond died a few days later there was no one left to minister the Last Sacrament for him. Within a few weeks, all the members of de Brésillac's first mission were dead. In the history of the Society they were regarded as martyrs, brave men who had planted the seeds of the faith on the continent. But in truth their practical achievement amounted to nothing. De Brésillac and his men were not killed in action, they died before ever reaching the front.

During the next twenty years one priest in every four died each year. Missionaries had no special resistance to the diseases they encountered, no divine protection. Yet despite the risks they continued to return – death was part of the process, part of God's great, undeclared plan for Africa. Their faith was total and unconditional: 'Africa or death', the motto coined by one missionary pioneer, Daniel Comboni, said it all. It was not for them to question why. Christianity would triumph and flourish all over Africa in God's time.

If the West African coast was notorious, it was not unique. All over Africa, missionary initiatives ground to a halt almost before they had

A missionary carved in wood by a Yoruba sculptor, Nigeria, 1930.

started, dogged by disease, African hostility or an excess of naïve idealism. One of the most inglorious fiascos involved David Livingstone himself. The speech he made in 1857 provided the impetus for the formation of the Anglican Universities Mission to Central Africa. By 1860 it was ready to send out its first mission, to be led by a young bishop, Charles Frederick McKenzie. McKenzie's plan for Africa was ambitious but unrealistic. The mission aimed to penetrate central Africa along the Zambezi River, relying on Livingstone to provide them with transport. Once inland, they would establish a station in the fertile highlands of what is now Malawi, and use it as a base from which to combat slavery and to spread their Christian beliefs.

They arrived at the mouth of the Zambezi on 7 February 1862. For three difficult months they followed Livingstone on an unplanned detour as he explored the waterways around Lake Malawi. When they finally left the rivers and set out on foot they came upon a slave caravan which, in a burst of unrestrained fervour, they attacked. The Arab slavers fled, and the missionaries found themselves with eighty-four extra fellow travellers. From then on the party was doomed. Cut off from the coast, in hostile territory rife with fever, the mission steadily disintegrated. Six months after they had established a station at Magomero, Bishop McKenzie and one of his priests caught a fever and died. The remainder of the party moved down river to be nearer the junction of the Shire and Zambezi rivers. Two more of them died. Most of the freed slaves meanwhile had been abandoned. Bishop William Tozer was called out to replace McKenzie. He was furious at the inept way the mission had been handled and accused Livingstone of 'the blindest enthusiasm'. He decided to withdraw the mission from the Zambezi to the island of Zanzibar. For Livingstone this was an act of cowardice and he retorted scornfully: 'What would Gregory the Great have said if Augustine had landed on the Channel Islands?' Yet in truth it represented the most sensible ending to a foolish episode. In Europe, idealistic young men and women were signing up in growing numbers for the mission field. In Africa, the missionaries were still struggling to find, let alone sustain, a toehold on the great continent that they wished to convert.

The going was no easier in southern Africa. It was to this region that the first European missionary had journeyed three centuries before Livingstone. With two other Jesuits, the Portuguese Gonzalo da Silveira landed in Sofala. Da Silveira successfully made his way inland to the court of the King Mwene Mutapa, in what is now Eastern Zimbabwe. At first the King showed a courteous interest, and accepted a statue of the Virgin Mary as a gift, but his tolerance did not last long and, on the advice of others at the court, he had da Silveira strangled to death.

Robert Moffat, Scottish gardener who became one of the great missionaries to Southern Africa: father-in-law of David Livingstone and friend of the Ndebele king, Mzilikazi.

In the years that followed there were limited attempts to resurrect the work that da Silveira had begun, but in 1667 the missionaries were withdrawn altogether. When Livingstone passed through the area he found a ruined chapel and a broken bell, all that remained of the early mission.

The Society of Jesus was suppressed in 1773, but in 1814 the Jesuits were officially restored as a missionary body and turned their eyes once more to southern Africa. From the Cape in South Africa, they pushed northward into the territory of the Zulu and Ndebele people but once more they failed to make any headway. By 1886 prospects looked so bleak that they were withdrawn to the Cape. Ten of their members had died and they had not made one single convert. The Jesuits were tenaciously pursuing the same area to which the London Missionary Society had already laid claim for the Protestant Church some years before. Robert Moffat had established the Kuruman Mission which became base camp for the Society's thrust to southern Africa. He had already persuaded the Ndebele king, Mzilikazi, to accept the presence of a few missionaries, including his son John and his wife Emily. The elder Moffat was convinced that the Ndebele people were in urgent need of a dose of Christianity: 'I am among a people who are living in Egyptian darkness, in beastly degradation, everything in their political economy diametrically opposed to the spirit of the Gospel of God.' Mzilikazi assigned the missionaries some land at Inyati, just north of present-day Bulawayo. From the start John Moffat and his wife were under considerable pressure. They had just lost a child and they faced a strained relationship with the Ndebele people. Within a short time John Moffat had to confront a major dilemma. The Ndebele wanted to get some work out of the missionary they had allowed to stay on their land. Most of all they needed someone to mend their guns. 'Are we justified, as missionaries,' Moffat wrote anxiously, 'in mending firearms and using ammunition for purposes of barter among a people like the Ndebele ... there is no means of gaining influence in South Africa so potent as gun-mending.' It was a severe jolt to his sense of missionary purity, but it was not an unusual situation. The powerlessness he felt was shared by most missionaries at that period. Currying favour with the local chief was virtually a full-time occupation. John Moffat and his small mission had been allowed to stay with the Ndebele on sufferance. There did not seem to be much that he could offer them in return – they showed no interest in his religion, but his skill with munitions was a different matter. By 1863 he had abandoned his finely wrought principles, 'I have taken to gun-mending ... my ideas of missionary work are very different from what they were; perhaps I have come down a peg'. The missionary who had come to save souls found himself greasing shotguns: such deals and compromises were the stuff of early mission work.

At home these Christian men and women might have been taught to believe the mighty power of the gospel to win over African hearts. At the court of a chief they soon realised that a length of calico or a round of ammunition could be far more eloquent. Yet it was not always the case that missionaries found themselves weak and indebted to the local ruler. There were others, like Bishop McKenzie, who attempted to begin Christian communities from scratch with a group of freed slaves, who found themselves with a different set of problems, resulting from too much power. Their plight was neatly summed up by a Plymouth Brethren missionary, Daniel Crawford, 'Many a little Protestant Pope in the lonely bush is forced by his self-imposed isolation to be prophet, priest, and king rolled into one – really a very big duck he, in his own private pond'. At either extreme, the consequence was the same. The missionaries found themselves in situations they were ill equipped to deal with, doing everything but preaching.

In the case of the Ndebele, the London Missionary Society was able to retain the friendship of Mzilikazi. He allowed them to begin a school and ordered his people to attend classes. On the first day a great many obeyed the King's command, but the numbers dwindled rapidly and within three weeks the school had disappeared. John Moffat was forced to conclude that after almost three decades with the Ndebele the mission had made almost no impact. Indeed, rather than having been a positive influence, Moffat sensed things had grown worse: 'It is awful to see how they have degenerated in the thirty years I have known them.'

For these pioneers there was little comfort, still less what they would have called progress. It was at best a tale of heroic failure and, missionaries being human, it was often less than heroic. Yet for those far from the field, at home in Britain, this was the golden age of mission. The lantern-slide shows presented their Christian hero standing beneath a tree with chest thrust out and Bible in hand, preaching to a crowd of enthralled and radiant African faces. Some, who were not missionaries but who themselves had travelled to Africa, resented the fraud being perpetrated on eager, generous congregations. Captain Napier Hewett was one such. He wrote in 1862, 'Little do the subscribers to foreign missions dream of the purposes to which their money is devoted; little do they comprehend the character of the men to whom the distribution is intrusted ... and little do they conceive the false colouring bestowed upon the reports of missionary labours!'

Despite, or perhaps because of, the colouring applied to accounts of these early missionary endeavours, the numbers volunteering for missionary service mushroomed. As the experiences of men like Moffat and Livingstone were published in scholarly tomes and rehashed as popular editions, they immediately became best-sellers. The thousands of people who were inspired to follow them had many motives, but one common goal: to lift the African continent out of degradation and bestow upon it all the benefits of civilisation. It was a sentiment which Livingstone himself expressed. 'We come among the Africans as members of a superior race and servants of a Government that desires to elevate the more degraded portions of the human family.' Livingstone was to develop a more perceptive view of the African personality through a lifetime of working among the people, but at the time, few argued with his diagnosis. The only real debate was about how far, with God's grace, the African could be raised, and whether, if ever, he could attain the position of the ultimate and perfect expression of the human race, the European. The general view was that the African had the potential, perhaps not actually to achieve the level of Western civilisation, but at least to mature to a stage at which he could accept and truly appreciate the greatest of gifts, the Christian gospel. It was the European missionary who had been chosen to lead him down that path from childhood to maturity.

In order to bolster the missionaries' confidence and morale for this task, and perhaps to impress those at home, it was felt necessary to emphasise how very degraded and depraved the African was. The American Methodists at Old Umtali Mission in Eastern Zimbabwe published *A True Picture Story of the Tragedy and Triumph of Human Africa* in which the heathen African is contrasted with the Christian in a series of captions:

Heathen man: the tragedy, heathen, ignorant, helpless.
Christian man: the triumph, intelligent, Christian, force for
    righteousness and social and economic good.
Heathen motherhood: Savage childhood has but one teacher,
    the mother. Savage motherhood makes the future generation savage.
Christian motherhood: The Christian mother is the maker of
    future generations of Christians. Without her the task seems
    almost hopeless.
Heathen family: The heathen family, a savage with many wives,
    dozens of children, the school of savagism.
Christian family: The Christian family is the foundation of a
    new born race.

Today it seems outrageous but then such racist and cultural arrogance was shared among missionaries, traders and colonialists alike. The letters of the Umtali missionaries show just how they regarded the people among whom they had come to work: 'Heathen and naked as new born babies, and as ignorant as beetles'. To such missionaries, all that was African was devilish, their music, their dancing, their nudity, even their names. Part of the process of turning Africans into good Christians was to give them a Christian name, meaning a European name. Many were named after the missionary who baptised them. Sometimes the names given were not names at all, but simple English nouns, such as Kitchen, Tobacco, Sixpence or Bottle. E. H. Greeley, another Umtali missionary, revealed his aspirations for the African people in a letter to the United States in 1916: 'Heathen mothers do not know much, but many boys and girls go to our schools now and are begging to read God's word and write and to take care of their bodies and be clean and dress like the people of America.'

The African's clothing, or rather lack of it, concerned the missionaries to an obsessive degree. To them nudity symbolised the African condition: naked breasts were synonymous with shamelessness and depravity. The battle to clothe Africa was highly symbolic. The Victorian woman in her tightly laced, cumbersome clothes was respectable, the image of Christian decorum; the African woman in her loincloth and beads, breasts bared, was the quintessential pagan. First the African had to be persuaded that nudity was sinful, or at least shameful. If this did not work, then there was always the hope that the aspiring African man or woman might wish to don Western clothing as a status symbol. One observer archly described the consequences: 'At every mission-school you see the boys looking like so many monkeys in dreadfully fitting coats ... and the girls attired in

All part of a rounded Christian education: the Boys' Brigade of the Church Missionary Society, Ugogo mission, 1910.

print frocks with waists up under their arms, and tawdry hats adorned with common ribbons perched on the top of their wool. Vanity is thus encouraged to such an extent that many of the natives squeeze their feet, which are themselves as hard as leather, into boots, although it is perfect torture to them to move.'

Over a century later the voluminous robes of the Baganda women in Uganda, or the remarkable outfits of the Herero women of Namibia, modelled on the garments worn by early German missionaries, still testify to the lasting effectiveness of this particular aspect of the civilising mission.

The missionaries' prudery attracted considerable ridicule from some people outside missionary circles. The seasoned traveller, A.B. Ellis, poured scorn on such narrow-mindedness: 'He lays down the dogmatic rule that the loose drapery of the natives is immoral and indecent. He seems to have an idea that Providence specially designed trousers to go hand-in-hand with the Gospel, and to be introduced into every country, whether suited to it or not, for the ultimate benefit of tailors.' For Ellis, clothing was but one example of the absurd shortsightedness of early missionary activity. The missionary arrives, he writes, 'horrified at finding these people contented and happy ... He tries to awake them to a sense of sin, and the horrible future of baked meats which awaits them'. Then, Ellis sharply observes, the missionaries send home a report of conversions: 'It is received by the Exeter Hall army with joy, and speeches are made about the glorious work of spreading Christianity; whereas ... the natives have been transformed from good heathens, with many excellent qualities, into accomplished liars, hypocrites and scandal-mongers ... Thus the glorious work of civilisation goes on.' Yet such attacks on their integrity of purpose failed to deflect the missionary movement that was sweeping through Europe, and the belief of the missionaries held firm. At the same time they were force to question why their message was not being taken up more readily. It seemed obvious to them that the benighted African had everything to gain by becoming Christian. To most Africans the opposite was true. It is perhaps more pertinent to ask why the missionary ever expected to be successful, since for the African in the precolonial period there seemed no point in becoming Christian.

Conversion exacted a high price in those early years. The experience of the Gusii people in the Kisii area of western Kenya was typical. Two missions were particularly active in the area: the Catholic Mill Hill Mission Society, and the American Seventh-Day Adventist Mission. The approach of each was very different, but both spent twenty years in the wilderness, looked on with suspicion by the people, with few adherents and fewer still true converts. Permission to enter the area was first given to the Catholic priests in 1911. It was one of the last areas in East Africa to be occupied by missionaries. Their task was to teach the Catholic religion and they decided to build up a class by asking each local chief to donate a son to the mission. A few fathers did agree, either because they had many sons, or so as not to displease the white man. Few of the sons, however, had any intention of going to stay with the missionaries. They planned to join their age-mates in the *egeserate* or cattle villages, where they looked after cattle, played bravery games, drank beer and smoked marijuana. The missionaries grew increasingly frustrated as the boys kept running away from the mission, despite the use of force to make them return. In the end, the mission school was little more than a holding operation.

After four years in the area the Roman Catholics had baptised just thirteen converts. The Seventh-Day Adventists had none at all. Even the few converts the Catholics claimed seemed precariously close to giving it all up. Father Stam, the priest at the Mill Hill mission, records his frustration: 'It is said Atanasi has married a girl, paid five cows for her and walks naked and painted; that Pio has paid three cows for his girl and married her; that Adriano lives with a woman ... Very consoling.' It was all becoming too much for the old priest. His letters record a growing desperation: 'I have been spending a lot of money ... with results amounting to nil, simply on account of those older idiots who fear their depraved practices are going to be tampered with'. He interpreted the reluctance of the Gusii people to join the mission as pig-headed obstinacy. In this he was not unusual. Most missionaries attributed the African's reluctance to convert to his stupidity. Few could see that from an African perspective there was little to gain and a great deal to lose. To enter the mission compound the Gusii man or woman had in effect to abandon their family commitments and social obligations, their way of dress and their social life. All this for a set of religious beliefs that at first seemed irrelevant to them. The Seventh-Day Adventists, for instance, took a categorical stand against drinking beer. Yet in Gusii society beer-drinking was an inseparable part of most rituals and social events. Beer was the currency with which one man paid for co-operative work done on his behalf by his friends. Throwing a beer party was the accepted way of redistributing wealth, extending patronage and displaying social status. The Catholics required that their mission boys remain celibate and unmarried. Yet a wealthy man in Gusii society was judged by how many wives he had, and poverty was despised. The Seventh-Day Adventists required married women to cut off their wedding anklets. To the missionaries the ring was a symbol of witchcraft. To the Gusii woman it was a sign of her fidelity and her lifetime commitment to her husband.

Polygamy was the main institution to which both missions were resolutely opposed. They encouraged a polygamous man to give up all but his eldest wife. Yet as polygamy was an essential part of the social fabric this meant asking him to relinquish a whole set of acquired family commitments, and to abandon his other wives to poverty and shame.

What of the young mission boy who found himself against his wishes learning catechism at the Mill Hill mission? He would have been renamed by the priests, Francis, Abel, Jacob, Abraham, or Lazarus perhaps. He would be forbidden to put ochre on his hair like other boys of his age. He would be given a white shirt to wear and white rice to eat. Far from being a role model to others, he was a social outcast. It was little wonder that the missionaries were treated with suspicion. They were not just asking the Africans to embrace the religion of Europe but its life-style as well. They were not simply advocating Christian conversion, they were selling a cultural revolution.

Livingstone recognised that Christianity posed a threat at every level to tribal society. His father-in-law, Robert Moffat, not only realised this but feared for the consequences of a mass conversion to Christianity; this, he felt, would only result in confusion and break-down of the tribal system, for which the only remedy would be annexation by a colonial power. The Gusii saying, 'iyanagokwa etairanetie getondo' – 'nothing dies without a cause' – could be a motto for the early story of African mission. The missionaries believed the Gusii to be sunk

His Master's voice. The missionaries were quick to harness the technology of their day to the task of evangelism.

The Chishawasha mission band – the pride of Southern Rhodesia. Jesuit fathers imported musical instruments to form this massed brass band at Chishawasha, just outside present-day Zimbabwe.

in stupidity. In fact they were making a reasonable and pragmatic calculation. They knew their own beliefs and their practices to be perfectly adequate and the missionaries had demonstrated no reason to abandon them. Until they could see such a reason for joining the mission, they would stay away.

But the tide was about to turn. As the colonial powers concluded their scramble for African territory, the missionaries sensed that their wilderness years might be coming to an end. What appeared to be the supernatural ramblings of a fiercely determined group of white eccentrics was on the way to becoming the professed religion of most of sub-Saharan Africa. At the mission schools, the baptism, confirmation and catechism classes were growing. For the missionaries, God's unseen hand was showing itself for the first time. The first shoots were sprouting from the gospel seed they had planted and patiently tended. If the missionaries felt the allotted time on God's timetable for Africa had arrived, there were good practical reasons why they were having more success. Livingstone's speech of 1857 in which he vowed to return to Africa 'to try to open a path for commerce and Christianity'

contained the key. When he spoke of commerce combined with Christianity he was thinking of the slave trade, which he believed would only be destroyed by the growth of legitimate commerce. Christian conversion without commerce was not enough. Others agreed with Livingstone that the natives must be taught the discipline of industry and work as the only sure way to redeem them. Thrift, diligence, discipline and a sense of duty were not just Victorian values but Christian values too. Like all good children of the Industrial Revolution, the missionaries needed no convincing of the redeeming power of labour and the gospel of hard work. In the mission schools and industrial colleges all over Africa, it was these values they endeavoured to inculcate. Commerce and Christianity went hand in hand: a holy alliance.

In a copy of a missionary magazine, *African Advance*, of June 1916, one author pondered what effect the evangelisation of Africa would have on commerce. It involved some ingenious calculation. In an article entitled 'Gospel of the Whole Man' he wrote: '200,000,000 Souls – 200,000,000 Bodies, Life and its power wasted, and worse. The wants of more than 90% of these cannot be described in terms of a single commodity in the Christian world. So far as the world's commerce goes, they are neither producers nor consumers ... Gospelizing this whole population within a year would mean an increase of at least $1,000,000,000 in the commerce of the world.

'The Gospel heals, feeds and clothes soul and body. The demand for Bibles, books, pens, ink, paper, slates etc. springs up in a night. Flour, meat, rice, sugar, tea, cookies, fish, milk and vegetables are considered necessary diet. Medicines, implements, dishes, cutlery, beads, wire, candles, kerosene, matches, lamps, soap etc. are purchased in large quantities. Trousers, coats, shirts, hats, boots, collars, skirts, blouses, blankets, umbrellas, underwear, cloth and scores of other things swell the evangelised African's legitimate wants.

'To supply these wants he sells his labor and becomes at once a real economic factor.'

If this is not quite how Livingstone himself would have put it, it accurately predicted how the alliance between commerce and Christianity would work. And as the traders were joined by the colonial administrators, the missionaries were drawn into a close triangular relationship with their white colleagues. If each had rather different goals, there was a great deal of common ground. By and large they shared the same derogatory view of the African, while placing Western civilisation at the pinnacle of man's achievement. Imperial government *was* Christian government and there were few who doubted that colonialism was a force for good. A.B. Lloyd had no doubt that the Imperial army and Christ's footsoldiers marched to the same drum: 'Thank God! Britain's sons have planted the Union Jack in her very centre, not to suck her life-blood for the sake of her wealth, but to bring to her the priceless treasures of Peace, Prosperity, and Religion.'

A Jesuit father playing hymns to the faithful few, some of the earliest converts in Southern Rhodesia.

Missionary and colonialist had the potential to be mutually most beneficial. Sir Harry Johnston, an administrator of extreme imperialist views, although himself an atheist, was none the less quick to appreciate

how useful the missionary might be to Her Majesty's Empire: 'They strengthen our hold over the country, they spread the use of the English language, they induct the natives into the best kind of civilization, and in fact each mission station is an essay in colonization.'

For their part the missionaries did not shrink where necessary from availing themselves of the protection offered by the colonial forces. Twice the Jesuits in southern Africa had been defeated in their attempts to establish a mission in what is now Zimbabwe. In 1889 the tattered remnants of the Jesuit Mission regrouped in Pretoria where the Pioneer Column was assembling. The British South Africa Company was after gold and the tools of its trade were guns, but the Jesuits sensed an opportunity. In return for the patronage and protection of Cecil Rhodes, they offered themselves as chaplains to the expedition. Rhodes, who had appropriated vast areas of land for his British South Africa Company, donated some 50 000 acres to the Society of Jesus. By September 1891 the claim had been staked and the Chishawasha mission was built. It still stands, a monument to the collaboration between the missionaries and Cecil Rhodes, the quintessential imperialist. He further assisted the mission by encouraging the Africans to send their children to school. In return the missionaries agreed to collect the hut tax from the Africans on their property. The tax had been designed to force the Africans to work to earn the money to pay it, in order to supply much needed labour for the white mines. In collecting the hated taxes, the missionaries did the dirty work of the Company.

With full colonial support the mission went from strength to strength. It became a model farm and a showcase for Western farming techniques. Tobacco was planted and within a short time the mission even had the resources to cure, grade and treat it. Chishawasha also had an extraordinary massed brass band, which only added to its celebrity. Puffed with pride, one priest remarked, 'What an advertisement Chishawasha has proved to the Chartered Company, *the* show place of Rhodesia.'

A brief interruption to mission life, when the Shona people rose against Company rule and attacked the mission in 1896, did little to check the new confidence of the Jesuits. They set about creating a string of Christian villages, in which converts would live together away from danger and temptation, and where Christian would marry Christian. By 1907 the mission boasted of 150 Christian couples living in Christian villages. In one of these lived the mother and father of Robert Gabriel Mugabe. As was true of many who would later lead their countries to independence, the mission featured large in his childhood.

The relationship between the Company and the mission would not always be so cordial. But the partnership had served its purpose, the Company had sheltered the mission until it could stand on its own feet. The missionaries repaid the debt by collecting taxes, and introducing Africans into the ways of work.

No single story better expresses the common interest of missionary and colonialist to the detriment of the African, than that of Charles Helm, missionary of the London Missionary Society. Helm lived at Hope Fountain on the land of the Mashona king, Lobengula. Helm had done his job well and was a trusted and respected friend of the King. In September 1888 Charles Rudd representing the British South Africa Company arrived at the King's court to negotiate for mineral rights and land. Lobengula trusted Helm, and allowed him to act as adviser and interpreter. On Helm's advice, the King accepted Rudd's proposal. But in effect Lobengula was tricked and the proposal authorised the occupation of Mashonaland by the BSA Company. When Lobengula discovered the betrayal he put Helm on trial. Sentence was passed that Helm should no longer be a missionary, but only a trader. It was the end of Helm as a missionary. He retreated to live in a house in Kimberley, given to him free of charge by Cecil Rhodes. Why Helm betrayed Lobengula, indeed whether he intended to at all, is still debated. But whether a conspiracy to defraud or an unfortunate accident, it plainly exposed a deeper alliance of interest, in which the

All in a day's work. The early missionary was expected to be a jack of all trades. Here, the Revd David Carnegie extracts a tooth at Hope Fountain Mission, Southern Rhodesia, 1901.

Johnston Kenyatta, a mission boy at the Church of Scotland Mission, Kikuyuland, who became Jomo Kenyatta, first President of Kenya. Most aspiring nationalist leaders passed through the mission gates: the roll-call of former mission school pupils includes Robert Mugabe, President of Zimbabwe, Joshua Nkomo, Bishop Abel Muzorewa, Revd Canaan Banana, former President of Zimbabwe, Milton Obote, former President of Uganda, Kwame Nkrumah, first President of Ghana, Emperor Bokassa, Hastings Banda, President of Malawi, Kenneth Kaunda, President of Zambia, Samora Machel, former President of Mozambique, Oliver Tambo, Nelson Mandela

missionary was much nearer the colonialist than the African.

Few missionaries were able or willing to develop such a convenient and close working relationship with the colonial authorities as Charles Helm or the men at Chishawasha, but none could escape the ambiguity of their position. All over the continent the foundations of empire were being laid, the hut taxes and the poll taxes, the district courts and the local administration. The day-to-day world of the African villager was changing at a frightening rate. For the first time men were having to leave home in large numbers to find work, to the mines or to war. They returned changed men. They abandoned native dress and customs and many showed a desire to learn to read and write. To be a reader might lead to a job as a clerk in government service. The missions held the only key to literacy. Going to school meant accepting, at least on the surface, the denomination of the missionaries who ran it. Every new school pupil was a potential convert. If the young African wanted to read to secure a job, the Protestant missionary wanted him to read in order to have access to God's word. The missionaries' first priority was to train up an army of evangelists and catechists. These Africans, the first to receive a basic education, would then take the Christian message out into the villages. With their knowledge of the local language, and their understanding of traditional beliefs and customs, they were to prove far more effective at spreading the Christian message than the missionaries had been.

The missions almost had a monopoly of education. It is small wonder that most of those who emerged to lead their countries through colonialism to independence spent their formative years in the mission school compound: Jomo Kenyatta, Kenneth Kaunda, Joshua Nkomo, even Emperor Bokassa, among others. For the ambitious youngster there was no choice. At the mission the boys were exposed to new ideas, and met others from different tribes. But they also underwent a rigorous and comprehensive indoctrination in the ways of the West. They were taught industrial skills, from welding to knitting. With these went lessons in discipline and callisthenics, in the best public school tradition. Boys and girls were taught to march, to drill, to do press-ups, to play cricket and to run the sack-race. No British mission school was complete without its boys' brigade, its scout troop or its brownie pack. Native dancing was outlawed as heathen, but in its place they were encouraged to learn British traditional dances, whose pagan origins were quietly ignored.

Many Europeans were sceptical about the first products of mission schools as they felt that the natives had been 'spoiled' in some way. Yet in a real sense the association with the Christian missionaries had positive connotations for the first time. In the new world that was

Dancing to the missionaries' tune. A Jesuit priest taught these Rhodesian youngsters the morris dance. Their own dancing was forbidden as pagan, and morris dancing's roots in Moorish dancing and fertility rites were conveniently forgotten.

emerging, of money and taxes, mining and military conscription, the syringe and the bicycle, the book and the blackboard, the white shirt and the wellington boot, this was the way to get on. The bravery games in the cattle villages and the lessons learned around the village fires had little to say about this world. Old solutions no longer seemed to be working; old systems no longer guaranted a man status and respect; old beliefs ceased to be convincing. In growing numbers Africans turned to the missions. The missionaries had had many barren years of sacrifice and failure. Their harvest was just beginning.

5 Plundering Hell to Populate Heaven

'Africa shall be saved,' shouted Pastor Reinhard Bonnke, punching his fist into the air, 'If you still have got two knees, that you can bow before Jesus, if you still have got one ear, with which to hear the gospel of Jesus Christ, you can be saved today. You shall be saved today.' It was June 1988, and the 150 000 Kenyans jammed into Nairobi's Uhuru Park had come to hear the words of the electrifying white preacher, the 'Billy Graham of Africa', the man who vowed 'to plunder hell, to populate heaven'. With his Kiswahili interpreter echoing every word, Pastor Bonnke called upon the Holy Spirit to enter the hearts of unbelievers and to cast out wickedness and witchcraft. The babble of thousands of voices speaking in tongues swept through the crowd and several people had hysterical fits. To deafening cheers, witchcraft fetishes, a rusty can and a broken drum, were brought on to the stage by a repentant medicine man and smashed with a hammer. God had triumphed over Satan.

Attention then turned to the sick and the infirm. They displayed a full spectrum of illness – blindness, polio, mental handicap and cancer. Many of them were unable to walk. 'Sickness', Bonnke cried, 'is the

'Sickness is the work of the Devil.' German evangelist Reinhard Bonnke, with his Kiswahili interpreter, brandishes a pair of crutches: for him the proof of another healing miracle.

work of the Devil. In the name of Jesus I come against every power of disease.' A woman and a young child wearing callipers forced their way through the crowd. Her mother undid the straps, the child took a few awkward steps and fell over. Pastor Bonnke helped her to her feet, placed his hands on her head, and prayed that Christ would continue the healing work that had begun. A man came to the stage to reveal he had just been cured of epilepsy. As more and more people came forward to proclaim they had been cured, Bonnke gave thanks for the miracles which had taken place. By the end of the evening, crutches, callipers and walking sticks, discarded by their owners, littered the stage. The Christ for all Nations crusade had come to town.

Almost a century and a half after David Livingstone first set foot on the African mainland, Africa is rapidly emerging as the most Christian continent on earth. Nothing better illustrates this than the unorthodox missionary ministry of the West German pastor, Reinhard Bonnke. In 1979, while a Pentecostal missionary in Botswana, Bonnke claimed to have had a series of night visions of 'Africa washed in the blood of Jesus'. He interpreted his dream as a command to spread the word into all of Africa. Within five years Bonnke had raised enough money from private donations, principally in Germany and South Africa, to fulfil his dreams. He commissioned the building of an enormous marquee, big enough to seat 35 000 people, standing seven stories high, and held in place by twelve masts and eighteen tons of steel cable. On 18 February 1984, on the edge of Soweto, a crowd of 50 000 witnessed the dedication of the Big Tent. He then set out on a series of crusades across Africa. The vehicles in which he travelled were purchased half-price in West Germany: they had originally been ordered by Colonel Qadhafi of Libya, but he had been unable to pay for them. The irony was not lost on Bonnke: 'The trucks designed to carry rockets and bombs will now be transporting the dynamite of the Holy Spirit'. Cecil Rhodes had once envisaged a great colonial corridor bisecting Africa from Cape Town to Cairo: with a typical flourish, Reinhard Bonnke's great convoy left Johannesburg with the slogan 'From Cape Town to Cairo for Jesus'.

Bonnke's brash showmanship makes him an unlikely inheritor of Livingstone's missionary mantle, yet he sees himself firmly within a great missionary tradition. Bonnke claims the lineage of Livingstone, but were the good doctor alive today would he recognise the German pastor's missionary technique? Bearers carried Dr Livingstone on the last leg of the final journey from Ujiji to Chitambo's village where he died. Pastor Bonnke has a fleet of nineteen six-wheel-drive trucks to carry him and his equipment across the continent. Bonnke preaches in the world's largest tent, as if he were the ringmaster of the greatest show on earth: 'I want to win souls for Christ. I want new blood to enter the Kingdom of God. The crushing burden of my heart is to get the unconverted converted.' His preaching has a raw power, his message is simple. And on the face of it, it works. He meets none of the hostility or bemused indifference faced by his predecessors. His mission team count their converts not in fives and tens, but in tens of thousands. In Cameroun, Ghana, Nigeria, Bonnke regularly draws crowds of 100 000. In a crusade dubbed 'The Malawi Miracle', President Banda invited Pastor Bonnke to address the Malawian Parliament. In Zimbabwe in 1985 the crusade claimed the President's wife, Sally Mugabe, as one of 31 000 converts. In Kenya three years later, President Moi visited Bonnke's crusade and was so impressed that he ordered its immediate live transmission on national television.

Bonnke avoids expressing political opinion, but the politics of Africa have inevitably shaped his ministry. His first headquarters was in a whites-only suburb of Johannesburg and many of his key staff were white South Africans. Bonnke soon realised that to stand any chance of taking his crusade into Black Africa and fulfilling his pan-African vision, he would need to sever his South African ties. He asked South African staff to secure a different nationality or to resign from the crusade. In a pragmatic rather than an ideological move, his mission relocated to Frankfurt. Yet the mission team remain keenly aware of the wider political agenda of Africa: 'The forces of Islam and the insidious agents of Marxism are also at work on the African continent. The stakes are high in Africa.... For those with true spiritual perception Africa is simply a giant chessboard with the nations as pawns and the players, the devil and the Church ... God has raised up a man in Reinhard Bonnke who has the boldness to proclaim that "Africa shall be saved". Not by feeding programmes. Not by communism – but simply by the Blood of Jesus Christ.'

Once the gates of a country open to Bonnke's convoy, every effort is made to ensure they stay open. The message of individual redemption which he spreads is politically neutral and unthreatening. If the government embraces the crusade, then Bonnke will support the status quo and will offer prayers of blessing for the President. The principle has not changed. A century earlier the missionary was dependent on the goodwill of the chief to allow him to set foot in a village. Even in the age of the public address system and the articulated truck, the missionary must be an astute politician.

No one knows how deep the impact of mass evangelism in Africa is. In the short term, Bonnke has brought both unity and disunity. A great rainbow coalition of African Churches is formed in each host country to prepare for the crusade and to deal with the huge numbers of new Christians. In Nairobi in 1988, in an unprecedented display of ecumenism, a Catholic archbishop shared the stage with Protestant evangelicals, to support Bonnke's Pentecostal message. But if some Christians welcome this unorthodox missionary, others criticise his flamboyant showmanship, the huge costs and his murky South African connections. His simplistic emphasis on a personal relationship with Christ, and his call for a return to Bible-based morality, has been attacked for failing to address the complex and profound social problems which beset the daily lives of those who come to hear him. The individualistic thrust of his Pentecostal message is seen as inappropriate to African society which is based on the community instead of the individual.

Despite the criticisms, Bonnke has clearly connected with the religious needs of many Africans. His faith has a fiery, emotional urgency, that makes it unrecognisable from the dour, pious Christianity brought by many Victorian missionaries: 'What I'm preaching is the eternal word of God. It's not an option, it's an ultimatum.' Like the traditional medicine man, Reinhard Bonnke offers a concrete explanation for illness and suffering: all disease emanates from Satan, and the cure lies in Jesus Christ who heals both physical and spiritual ills. Christ for All Nations insist that many medically acknowledged miracles have occurred on the crusades. Critics argue that Bonnke has raised many people's expectations of healing and left them cruelly unfulfilled. 'In that case,' retorts Bonnke, 'we should pull all the hospitals down, because not everyone gets healed in a hospital.' He has shown indisputably that many Africans feel more at home with the charismatic, healing-centred Christianity he espouses, than with the intellectualised theology of many historic missionary Churches.

The aim of Christ for All Nations is the conversion of a continent. Their belief in Christ's transforming power is absolute. Conversion alone is sufficient and all else follows from this. Yet historically, conversion has been only one of the missionaries' ambitions for Africa. Livingstone was in no doubt that in itself conversion was not enough to heal what he saw as the great open sore of the world: 'If we call the actual amount of conversions the direct result of Missions, and the wide diffusion of better principles the indirect, I have no hesitation in asserting that the latter are of indirectly more importance than the former.'

Father Damian Grimes, a Mill Hill missionary and school headmaster, has given his life to 'the wide diffusion of better principles'. He stands at opposite poles from Pastor Bonnke, in both theology and missionary practice. He arrived in Uganda in 1959, a Yorkshireman from Wakefield, a graduate in Medieval History from Glasgow University. Little did he know as he set foot in prosperous, beautiful Uganda that over the next decades the country would be torn apart by bloody dictatorship and tragic civil strife. A tide of nationalism was sweeping the continent. It was the eve of British Prime Minister Macmillan's famous recognition of this fact: 'The wind of change is blowing through the continent.' By the end of the following year, Nigeria and the Congo were both independent, and sixty-nine people had been killed in Sharpeville, South Africa. The missionaries watched closely. Where would the winds of change blow them? Before long the sights of the new African governments fell upon education. By 1970 many countries had gained the confidence to nationalise their schools. In the Kenya Education Act of 1968, and a variety of similar legislation across Africa, the independent nations brought the formal era of the mission school to an end. It symbolised a profound defeat for the conservative missionaries, like the elderly Walter Carey, once Anglican Bishop of Bloemfontein, who had seen education as the key to a process which would take two hundred years. 'I want these Africans to be educated: but it must be education by christian teachers, in christian principles, and in a christian atmosphere. Otherwise you will create more clever savages. I wouldn't touch that sort of education with a barge-pole.' Some mission societies reluctantly bowed out of education, others did so with some relief at the end of a heavy administrative and financial burden. But many, and the Catholics in particular, had no intention of abandoning education altogether. Compromises were struck which enabled many missionaries to retain a presence in the African classrooms.

You are how you eat. Father Grimes teaches Ugandan fifth-form pupils the finer points of a Christian education: a class in table manners.

Father Grimes was one of those who stayed on. His first posting had been at Namayango, a boys' school with a reputation for producing fine boxers. He set about learning the skills of the ring and within a few years emerged as a formidable boxing referee and coach, even training competitors in the Commonwealth Games. In 1967 he was offered the headmastership of Namasagali Secondary School in central Uganda. The school stands in a remote area on the banks of the Nile, and is housed in the buildings of a disused railway station. It made an unusual setting for the extraordinary school that was to evolve.

Many schools in Africa are still deeply imprinted with the heavy hand of missionary authorship. Remote and far from effective authority, many missionaries, like 'little Popes in the bush', had virtually a free hand to develop the institutions under their authority as they wished. So Namasagali developed out of Father Grimes's unusual and fertile imagination: part English public school, part finishing school and part progressive co-educational establishment. It is run by a cabinet of student ministers, policed by 'reeves' and a complex heirarchy of school courts, where Ugandan boys and girls are taught to bow and curtsey, to recite Shakespearean verse, to dance to Western pop music and to master the mystery of Western table manners.

By 1967 Uganda had been independent five years. The Kabaka, King of the Baganda people and the first President of Uganda, had been overthrown and driven into exile. The kingdoms of Uganda had been abolished in favour of a modern unitary state. Against this background Father Grimes developed his own particular school ethos that would best prepare his graduates to face the changing world outside, a synthesis of two cultures, traditional and Western. He was intent on creating a mini-society at the school and began with a school cabinet, complete with ministerial portfolios. The chosen students wore special robes and attended regular cabinet meetings. As a student himself, Father Grimes had specialised in medieval history. Out of this had developed a belief in the importance of law as a foundation for any society. A court system and the separation of powers were introduced, and instead of prefects, he created a band of law officers, known as 'reeves' after the shire reeve of feudal England. The system included judges who had a full range of appropriate punishments at their disposal. In a gesture against the male-dominated society outside, the most senior judge was the Lady Chief Justice. This was not simply an exercise for fun. Father Grimes felt he was training the citizens and leaders of tomorrow, in what he believed to be Christian principles.

On the cultural side, it was decreed that English only would be spoken. Language has always been a potent, explosive issue in Africa: in English-speaking colonial Africa, English was insisted on in most

*Father Grimes and his
school dance troupe in a
clearing at Namasagali
School, Uganda.*

mission schools, and in the French West African colonies the same
principle for French was applied even more rigorously. Students who
spoke their own language were punished, those who failed to master
the alien language failed altogether. To many Africans it was a constant
reminder of their subjugation and assumed cultural inferiority. Father
Grimes staunchly defends the exclusive use of English in his school,
firstly as a means of combatting tribalism to ensure school unity, and
secondly as a passport to the wider world where English is a valuable
currency.

International acceptance for his students is very important for Father
Grimes. Final-year students are given special tuition in Western table
manners, essential skills in the international communities of business
and diplomacy. Traditional Ugandan society placed heavy importance
on politeness. Father Grimes tries to keep this spirit alive in his own
inimitable way: young women are taught to curtsey, young men to
bow. Like the principal of some extraordinary tropical finishing school,
Father Grimes forbids girls to wear excessive make-up, or to have
cracked nail varnish because that is 'unacceptable in good social
circles'.

Creative dance was introduced into the timetable. It was this area of the school's activities that earned most criticism. Some conservative Ugandans were unhappy about the prospect of boys and girls in leotards dancing together, even if supervised by a well-respected missionary. In this was a certain irony. The first missionaries to Uganda had been horrified by the nudity they encountered. A style of dressing evolved, that is still worn today, based directly on the voluptuous, bustled dresses of the Victorian women missionaries. Father Grimes defends his action as part of his wider ambition to turn out healthy, well-balanced, high-achieving graduates.

He talks with pride of the Namasagali girl who found a job working on the perfume counter at Harrods in London, or the former student who won a place to the London School of Economics, and who wrote to him to thank him for teaching her about Metternich whom she was now studying. He is convinced that his work has been based on Christian principles in the service of God: 'I like to think this is a microcosm of a real Christian society ... I also say to the children at times whether they listen to me or not, that the approach is based very much on the perennial philosophy you know, if you go back to Aristotle and Plato: their approach is very similar to ours now.' He is one of a disappearing generation of missionary educators. His eccentric, highly individualistic regime has never been typical, yet in another way he subscribes to much of what Africans have come to expect from missionary education. Namasagali has become one of the most sought-after schools in Uganda. Father Grimes offers what missionary education has always offered, a means of upward mobility, a route to enhanced social status founded on the bedrock of 'Christian civilisation'.

While Father Grimes has spent his missionary years grooming the élite of Africa, Father Dove has spent the last years of his life in the patient service of those whom society has cast out. Near the small market town of Mutoko in Eastern Zimbabwe is Mutemwa Leprosy Settlement, a sprawling collection of seventy little brick huts amid the huge granite boulders that litter the scrubby plains of Eastern Zimbabwe. In its attitude to leprosy, pre-colonial Africa was much like medieval Europe. It was a fearful disease, a threat to the entire tribe. Someone discovered to have leprosy would be driven from the village, sent out into the bush, and left to fend for themselves or die. In the eyes of many European philanthropists, leprosy was a potent symbol of the suffering of benighted Africa. It provided a challenging context in which to express the universality of Christ's love; a challenge to which many missionaries responded. African attitudes to the disease gradually changed, but not quickly enough for many of the leprosy patients at Mutemwa. Father Dove continued to assist and support the elderly patients who were left behind, in the hope that his presence gives them a sense of worth. Moreover, their suffering, he believes, makes them valued in God's eyes: 'I, as a missionary, am always very moved by their death and think how rich they are, even though there's no coffin, no flowers, no candles ... I feel very moved by it, and feel at the same time how rich they are and I feel a little bit of sorrow for big business men and others who die with what? They can't take any of their worldly wealth with them, but these people can take with them their wounded bodies, in the likeness of Christ.' For John Dove, mission is a process of trying to be more like Christ and he almost admits to envy of the leprosy patients in their suffering. Each morning he says mass for them in the little round hut that is the settlement chapel. His missionary life has become one of quiet religious devotion and friendship to the Mutemwa patients.

Both Father Grimes and Father Dove are among the last survivors of a generation of Catholic priests who came to Africa, never intending to leave, and devoted their lives to the schools and hospitals. The missionary contribution in education and medicine has often been positively acknowledged but Africans have not always repaid the missionaries by joining their Churches. For some the alien imported faiths could never be turned into comfortable spiritual homes. They sought their religious life outside the mission compound, in the independent Churches. By 1989 there were 6700 of these, with over 30 million members.

Christianity as many Africans first experienced it was not a monopolistic, omnipresent religion. Rather it resembled a colourful, cut-throat, religious free market, with so many traders selling their own orthodoxies, wrapped in their own particular packaging. That made the choice more rather than less confusing for the customer. In some areas the largest Christian traders formed cartels and divided up the market. In other areas independent Churches proved a potent, popular recipe: a highly spiced mixture of missionary and traditional ingredients. In any sub-Saharan African city at a week-end, knots of worshippers gather together dressed in white or coloured robes, beating drums and singing, exuberantly worshipping God: the Jake Nation, swirling in circles until they collapse exhausted; the Apostles of Johannes Maranke, with their large beards and shaved heads, carrying shepherd's crooks; the Maria Legio, resplendent in their multi-coloured robes, carrying large wooden crosses with outsize rosary beads hanging at their belts. In some the Christian ingredient seems small, in others the missionary roots show clearly. One wonders whether David Livingstone, Dr Laws, or Robert Moffat would recognise any of it as part of their legacy to Africa.

The origins of independence are as diverse as its manifestations. For some, independence was a spiritual issue – the white-led mission Churches with their formal liturgy and alien ritual did not offer the right kind of religious experience. For others, it was a political issue, an issue of authority. In colonial days it was hard for an African to be a leader of anything but a Church. For still others, independence was not a reaction to missionary Christianity, but a response to being excluded from it. The early missionaries laid down rigid social requirements before allowing membership of their churches. A polygamist, or the wives of a polygamist, faced automatic disqualification from joining a mission church.

Among the independent Churches, the Zionist movement has swept through Southern Africa since it first emerged over fifty years ago. Zion, the ideal society first envisaged by the Jews, a heaven on earth so often referred to by the missionaries but so often passed over in their teaching, struck a deep resonance with many Africans; a heavenly city, a holy rock in a period of turbulent change, Jerusalem somehow realised in Africa. 'Zion Cities' sprang up all over Southern Africa. One was founded in 1917 in Basutoland by a Sotho Zionist, Eduard Lion, another in the Drakensberg mountains at Ekukhanyeni. Some followers decided to live in these 'cities', others came as pilgrims, for festivals of prayer and worship, and above all for healing. The missionary approach to healing was rooted in years of scientific medical school training. It taught that the pill and the syringe were the weapons with which to fight illness. For many Africans this was too narrow a notion. Instead they were drawn to the spiritual, prayerful approach offered by the independent Churches. In the troubled years of colonisation and the struggle for independence, the Zionists offered a safe and secure home. As always in times of social instability, the context was right for the emergence of 'prophets', men and women who claimed unique revelatory powers and the ability to interpret visions and dreams. There was no room in the inflexible mission Churches for these black prophets. In southern Africa, it was to the Zionist movement that many of them turned.

In the south-eastern corner of Zimbabwe, beneath the rocky hillside of Mount Moriah, stands Bishop Mutendi's Zion City. Samuel Mutendi had been a migrant worker in South Africa when he discovered the Zionist Church. He returned to Zimbabwe to found the Zion Christian Church, and in time emerged as one of Zimbabwe's great independent bishops and healers. He built up what was in essence a sizeable spiritual hospital, catering for both physical and psychological illness. Today it is his son who welcomes pilgrims from all over Zimbabwe for celebrations of healing which are held throughout the year. Each pilgrim and each vehicle is splashed with

J OB suffer'd many sorrows, but was
  patient to the end;
Knowing, in all his troubles, that the
  Lord was still his friend.

Above, *Old Testament
illustrations provided by
the missionaries were
copied to the last detail by
the African independent
Churches.*

Right, *Faith healing in
Zion City. Bishop Mutendi
prods two barren women
in the stomach with his
cane. His followers believe
this perfunctory ritual will
make them fertile.*

holy water on arrival, to cleanse them of evil spirits. The pilgrims are
welcomed with a fanfare of trumpets, before Bishop Mutendi the
younger emerges, resplendent in his black and gold cassock and mitre.
His many wives and scores of children stand inside his compound. The
pilgrims remain outside. They come forward one by one for treatment.
To the casual observer the healing part of the process may seem
perfunctory – a prod in the stomach for a barren woman – but his
supporters have no doubts about his power to heal all ailments.

Not far from Bishop Mutendi's Zion City, at Mount Moriah,
another Zionist Church, the Zion Apostolic Church, meet annually for
a week of feasting and worship. They have followed a commandment
in Deuteronomy and trek many miles deep into the bush for their
celebrations. They dress in brightly coloured robes copied precisely
from the lantern slides and Bible illustrations they were shown by the
missionaries. In a scene reminiscent of the Old Testament, they gather
on a river bank for a baptism. A bottle of milk is squirted over each

new convert in a final, symbolic act of purification. The ritual slaughter and feasting takes place in a clearing. Here the Zion Apostolics dance, chant and beat drums for hours on end. The music and movement is frenzied and intoxicating. At a given moment the priest and his helpers grab a woman who they believe has the Devil in her. The priest repeatedly pierces her with a hat pin to let out the demons. Jesus set the example of exorcism which they follow: the hat pin is their own contribution.

For the followers of the Apostolic Church, belief in the supernatural requires no leap of faith. The parable of Christ casting out demons into the swine makes literal sense. The Apostolics claim membership of the Christian Church. They point to biblical passages as validation for many aspects of their worship, and to the centrality of baptism as evidence that they are within the Christian tradition. To missionaries, and to mainstream Zimbabwean Christians, they are pagans in Christian robes, their beliefs a devilish distortion of the Christian message.

Another young African is baptised. Africa, south of the Sahara, is described as the most Christian continent on earth.

While it might be difficult to find traces of the missionary tradition in the Zionist Churches, they do share Protestant parentage. The story is the same throughout Africa. It was out of the Protestant missions, with their history of schism, that the independent Churches grew. In one spectacular instance in East Africa the opposite occurred: a secession from the Catholic Church. And here the notion of independence was taken to its extreme.

The members of the Maria Legio claim that their leader, Simeon Ondeto, is the Black Messiah, the second coming of Christ. Ondeto began religious life as a catechist for the Ulanda Catholic Mission. In 1963 he went to Kadem, near the border between Kenya and Tanzania, to join a lay organisation, the Legion of Mary, run by the Catholic Mission. The Legionaries travelled in small groups around the villages to pray for the sick. Ondeto exorcised spirits, in return for food. His preaching gained in authority and he began to have 'visions'. In one of his sermons he claimed he had died twice and seen heaven. Only Catholics were there. But so too were Jacob, David, and Abraham, enjoying polygamy in heaven as they had on earth, and telling Ondeto that polygamists should be baptised. In April 1963 a Luo woman, Gaudencia Aouko, came to visit him. She too claimed to have had visions. Jesus and Mary had appeared telling her to start a new religion and to call it 'Maria Legio'.

The partnership took off and they both began to baptise. The Catholic Mission had required religious instruction before baptism, and a baptismal fee for each candidate. The Legio embraced those who had been turned away by the mission, polygamists and their wives in particular: they were baptised immediately and for free. Ondeto announced a new headquarters on a mountain top called Got Kwer, otherwise known as Mount Calvary. Gaudencia launched an uncompromising attack on witchcraft, winning great popularity for her supernatural trials of strength. All the accoutrements of Catholic ritual were retained in some form, from vestments and outsize rosary beads to the sacraments and the speaking of Latin. There were added elements: trances, spirit possession, exorcism, speaking in tongues. The new spiritual leaders specialised in curing 'juogi', a spirit known to afflict barren, over-worked, old or adolescent women. Within a year of their first meeting Ondeto and Gaudencia had 60 000 followers.

The authorities became worried and in April 1964 Ondeto and thirty-eight others were arrested and charged for holding an illegal public meeting. The magistrate denounced them as lapsed Catholics and pagans, guilty of heresy. Gaudencia retorted that it was because the missionaries had failed to understand the heart of the African people that the Legio was so successful. 'We get the key to heaven

'The last mile.' Livingstone's last journey before his death at Chitambo's village, near Lake Bangweolo, 1873. As an explorer, Livingstone's achievements were remarkable: as a missionary he made just one known convert.

THE LAST MILE

German pastor, Reinhard
Bonnke, claims to be
'treading on the tears of
Livingstone'.

Above: *Crowds of over
100 000 congregated in
Nairobi in 1988 to hear the
evangelist's Pentecostal
message.*

Far right: *One of the huge
containers that transports
Bonnke and his entourage
from 'Cape Town to Cairo
for Jesus'.*

Right: *A member of the
Maria Legio breakaway
church, possessed by
demons.*

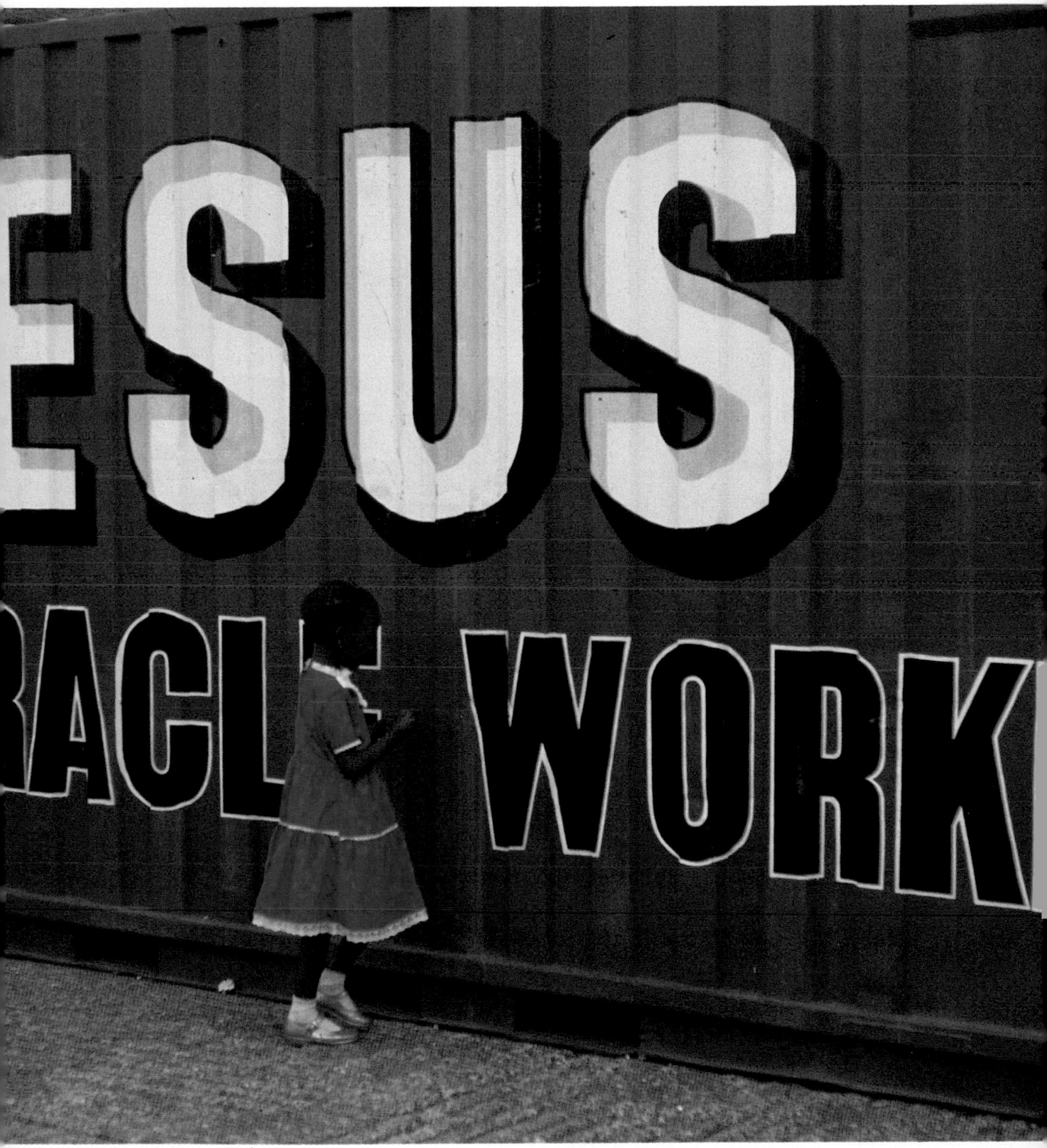
ESUS
RACL WORK

Above: Serima Catholic
Mission, Zimbabwe, is
renowned for its dramatic
Christian sculptures by
local artists.

Above right: Young
member of the Zion
Christian Church,
Zimbabwe.

Right: Self-appointed head
of the Zion Christian
Church, Bishop Mutendi.

Far right: Herero woman,
Namibia. The Herero still
wear costumes styled on
the dress of nineteenth-
century German
missionaries.

Left: Deep in the Zimbabwean bush, the Zion Apostolic Church carry out their baptism ceremony. The new convert joins more than 30 million others who have made the independent Churches their spiritual home.

Above: A Zion Apostolic Church member worshipping in her own way.

from Jesus and not from Rome.'

With the imprisonment of Ondeto, the newspapers triumphantly declared the movement had been 'virtually smashed'. On the contrary: by the end of 1964, 90 000 had joined the Legio. A constitution was drawn up, and a full ecclesiastical heirarchy established. Ondeto appointed himself Holy Father, or Pope, while Gaudencia was declared the Auxiliary Spiritual Leader of the Faith. Beneath them ranged a full complement of prelates, including six cardinals and seventy-five bishops. The women wore white dresses, in imitation of the angels in the Holy Pictures.

Polygamy, even among the bishops and cardinals, was allowed. But despite the conciliatory stance on marital relationships, membership of Maria Legio was not an easy option. Ironically, the movement took a much firmer stand on many social issues than the missionaries, such as smoking, drinking, dancing, the wearing of shoes in holy places and the use of European medicine. Furthermore, the Legio retained the use of Latin in worship, even as the Catholic Church throughout the world was turning to the vernacular.

Ten years after its birth the membership of the movement was calculated at 150 000. Twenty-five years on, the Maria Legio itself claims a quarter of a million members. In time they have developed into a strong, mutually supportive movement. One of their members owns a large bus company in Nyanza Province, which provides their transport; another is an MP in Kenya's national parliament. Ondeto's position within the movement is shrouded in some uncertainty, his supporters obviously believing his is no merely mortal presence. Though Ondeto repeatedly denies that he is Christ returned, each denial prompts a flurry of protest from his disciples.

Visiting the Black Messiah is an unsettling experience. At the gate of the village all visitors are forced to stop. No one is allowed to enter without the Messiah's permission, and for every decision he consults his internal angels. If your presence is felt to be benign you will be admitted: if not you are warned you will be turned to dust. The high perimeter fence encloses a complete village. There are stalls scattered around the compound selling religious bric-a-brac – small framed paintings of Christ and the Virgin Mary, tin crosses, strings of beads. But they also sell pictures of the Messiah Ondeto, and Mama Gaudencia. The compound is crowded with men and women in brightly coloured robes and headdresses, some carrying crosses, others swords, all wearing large rosary beads. A frightening cacophony of chanting, grunting and cursing emanates from the people who stand, lie, kneel in various attitudes of devotion or trance-like reverie. Some people are tied up, others encircled by noisy worshippers. The appearance of

Students of the Annie Walsh School, Sierra Leone. For missionaries in Africa, there was no better model for a 'civilised' Christian education than the English public school.

Baba Simeon Ondeto, 'the black Messiah', once a lowly catechist at a Catholic mission, now spiritual leader of the Maria Legio, western Kenya. Below, the rosary, a crucifix, and a portrait of the black Messiah, hang together around the neck of a Maria Legio follower.

Ondeto, resplendent in gold vestments, in a procession of holy officers is greeted with chants of 'Hosanna'; as he passes, his followers prostrate themselves on the ground. He punctuates his sermons with protestations that he is not the Messiah. Each such declaration provokes a volley of dissenting screams from the congregation. For a man who began his association with the Christian missions as a humble auxiliary catechist, it represents a great personal triumph. For his disciples, membership of the Maria Legio seems to be a fulfilling, intense, thoroughly African religious experience. It directly addresses the fears and worries of their daily life, it offers them care, support and prayer in times of crisis, and it accords them a status within their community which they could never have obtained in the missionary-dominated Church.

The Legio is dismissed by many as a movement of disgruntled Catholics and pagans, that has lapsed into a messianic personality cult. It may well have long since ceased to be Christian in any meaningful sense, certainly to Western eyes. But today independence comes in many varieties, spanning a whole spectrum of religious expression. In a historic gesture, Africa's greatest independent Church, the Kimbanguist Eglise of Zaire, has been admitted to the World Council of Churches. It is a sign that the West and its missionaries no longer have the exclusive right to define what is an authentic expression of Christianity.

Pressure from within and without is forcing the historic missions to come face to face with their own inflexibility: from the huge independent African Churches; from the Pentecostalism of men like Reinhard Bonnke; from the vociferous lobby of African bishops to the Anglican synod, anxious to reintroduce polygamy as a valid subject of Christian debate; and from the heart of Roman Catholicism, where Archbishop Mlingo has rattled the establishment with his charismatic healing prelacy. Despite the considerable defections, most Africans still remain loyal to what were the missionary Churches. However, even here there has been talk about the end of the missionary era. This peaked in the 1970s when those who had witnessed the successful birth of independent government felt the time was approaching when the Churches should also be allowed to break free of their colonial sponsors.

Some missionaries themselves felt the time had come, even as early as 1958, at an assembly of the International Missionary Council in Ghana. Ghana was just independent and a new era was beginning. Professor Freytag, a leading missionary theorist, appealed for a reduction in missionary numbers. Other missionary voices publicly reiterated his call for the gradual voluntary liquidation of missionaries to Africa. Missionaries who had become famous in the 1950s and 1960s handed over to black successors and left for home: men like Colin Morris, Methodist missionary in Zambia, scourge of white Copperbelt society, friend and advisor to Kenneth Kaunda; Bengt Sundkler, Swedish Lutheran, the Bishop of Bukoba, Tanzania; and Trevor Huddleston, the young radical of Sophiatown, South Africa. These missionary liberals, fired by their positive experience of African nationalism, sensed it was time to go.

It was in this climate, sensing that white missionaries might not be around for ever, that in 1963 an Italian Catholic, John Marangoni, founded the Apostles of Jesus, an all-African missionary congregation. The aim was simple: an African Catholic missionary force to evangelise Africa. It was partly an acknowledgement of the nationalistic times, and a realisation that Africans were more effective missionaries to their own people. But it was also partly preparation for the departure of the European missionaries. Up to this point the debate about when might be the right time to go had been conducted between missionaries. This changed in 1971 at the Mission Festival, Milwaukee. For the first time on an international platform, John Gatu, then the General Secretary of the Presbyterian Church of East Africa, called for a moratorium, a total halt in the flow of missionaries and money from the West. It provoked a storm of protest. Many missionaries were stung by the implication that they were no longer needed and that their presence might actually be impeding the true growth of the Church. John Gatu was denounced in one impassioned outburst as an 'ecclesiastical Idi Amin'. But Gatu was asking for the African Church to be given a chance to develop in its own way, free of the distortions of external finance and foreign personnel. Only then, he argued, would African Christians be able to stand as adults in the world Church. In 1974 the All African Conference of Churches, meeting in Lusaka, resolved the moratorium. The feeling was articulated, a fleeting storm of debate ensued, and the harsh reality of economic dependence prevailed. Much as Church leaders might aspire to complete autonomy, financial dependence on the Western missions was a fact of life for most African Churches and many of the leaders were loath to give up the personal privileges they enjoyed as a result of their links with the missions. Despite the rhetoric, the missionaries did not leave the mission field in droves. A few left when their allotted time ended, but more arrived to take their places. The moratorium movement died.

If the bottom line showed a fairly constant number of missionaries in Africa, it concealed a changing balance sheet. The numbers of missionaries from the theologically liberal Churches was dwindling. Home congregations were losing confidence and charities like Save the Children, Oxfam, World Vision and Tear Fund were competing successfully for their financial support. Mission societies were forced to reassess their position and their role. There were even attempts to drop the very word missionary, with its colonial, paternalistic connotations, in favour of 'partners in mission', 'missioners' and, in the Salvation Army, 'reinforcement officers'. But no change of name could disguise the economic reality: the West still held the purse strings.

No such self-doubt racked the American evangelical Churches. Fired

Father Hans Burgman, a Dutch priest, plays his flute on the doorstep of his home in the shanty area on the outskirts of Kisumu, Kenya.

with all the gung-ho enthusiasm of their British counterparts a century earlier, Bible-belt Baptists and Pentecostals arrived in Africa in unprecedented numbers. Ironically, it was to Kenya, the home of John Gatu who had called for the moratorium, that the largest contingent of new missionaries came. But Africa had changed. In Zaire by 1989 there were nearly 200 times as many evangelical Christians as in the Churches of its coloniser, Belgium. In Britain, around 11 per cent of the population attended church: in its former colony Kenya, 65 per cent claimed an active affiliation to a Church. In Malawi, 68 per cent of the population, four million adults, professed to be Christian. In Scotland, the home of Livingstone and Laws, 37 per cent of the population were Church members, and half as few again attended regularly. Even Mozambique, torn by war and a bitter colonial legacy, claimed ten times as many evangelicals as Portugal. Despite the irony, missionaries continued to leave for Africa, to promote a set of beliefs which their own countries had ceased to hold.

Few European countries have become more thoroughly secular than the Netherlands. Father Hans Burgman is a Dutch missionary priest in western Kenya: he has come to a country with many more Christians than the one he left. He is unapologetic about the continued presence of missionaries in Africa. He is in the process of a Christian experiment, the building of a gospel community in an African slum. For him the issue is not whether there should still be missionaries in Africa, but rather the depth of their commitment to missionary life, and their motivation for being there. In a small mud house in a shanty town on the margins of Kisumu, a city which sprawls on the shores of Lake Victoria, Father Hans Burgman celebrates mass. He has not chosen an easy missionary life. It could have been otherwise. He was once the Vicar General of the Mill Hill missionaries in North London. As a philosopher he might have pursued an academic career in Europe. As a missionary priest he might have come to the comparative comfort of a rural mission, or to the protected institutional environment of a school or hospital compound. Instead he chose to live in Pandapieri, a shanty town, where sanitation is poor and malaria is endemic. At night he sleeps in the humble homes of his parishioners: the former Vicar General beds down on a reed mat on a beaten mud floor. Outside the front door of his humble home runs a road, a road he likes to call the widest in the world. It separates the corrugated iron and mud houses of the shanty town from the smart European-style villas: a frontier between slum-living and respectability, the distance from Africa to Europe. Father Burgman is pleased to be living on the wrong side of the tracks. It is where he believes that today's missionaries should be.

The physical hardships are overridden for him by the spiritual rewards of life in such a community. Hans Burgman accepts that however hard he tries, he cannot change his Western spots. In a small room in his house he keeps those possessions that remind him he will always be a European: his papers, his books of philosophy and poetry, a flute, and a music stand. He accepts that he will always be a foreigner: 'Everybody likes a well-to-do foreigner. I remain well-to-do. I have a white skin, I have trousers, I have a pair of spectacles, so I am rich, but people prefer a friend who is rich to a friend who is poor. That's a great boon, it's a great asset.' Burgman is unapologetic about the role of past missionaries in Africa. For him, the coming of Christianity was an inevitable consequence of Africa's growing aspirations: '... they needed a kind of religion that could comment on aspirins and bicycles and wrist-watches and that is the Christian religion, because that is the religion that goes with the articles of modern life...'

The slums in which Father Burgman works are also a fact of modern life. How does Christianity begin to comment on that? At Pandapieri they are developing a series of community health projects, training women in the community in basic health care and holding regular clinics; there is skills training in carpentry and tailoring; an art centre; a project making roofing tiles. The emphasis is on the simple, small-scale answers to needs articulated by the community. Pandapieri becomes a temporary, and sometimes permanent, home for the children who live on the streets, involved in drugs and petty crime. Father Burgman is resisting the lure of huge capital grants from the aid charities which he feels will drastically change the nature of the projects and take them out of the hands of the community. He is anxious that the work should run on spiritual rather than financial fuel, by tapping the religious reserves of the people, rather than the financial reserves of Europe. It is an approach which requires complete commitment and considerable faith.

Hans Burgman believes that the challenge to modern missionaries is twofold: to live with the same radical, total commitment as the earliest missionaries did: and to step across the cultural divide. The modern missionary in Africa is likely to live in a suburban villa in a respectable part of town, with modern comforts and amenities, able to send his or her children to a first-class boarding school. The invitation to step across into the muddy stinking streets of a shanty town, with its mosquitoes, its open sewers and mounds of rotting rubbish, is not an attractive one. It is a challenge which he believes many members of his own and other missionary societies are too frightened to take up.

Mission, in Father Burgman's terms, is a complex, demanding spiritual adventure. But many of the new missionaries do not have the inclination for such an adventure. They respond to a cruder, more belligerent vision: Africa conquered for Christ. Africa is increasingly Christian, but there is still a belief among many of the newer Churches that the leaders cannot be left to run things on their own. So while there are growing numbers of African pastors and priests, the number of missionaries stays constant.

The completion of one missionary challenge gives rise to another. Modern missionaries have discovered perpetual motion, a never-ending cycle of tasks to be done, which justifies their presence in Africa in perpetuity. It has become rare these days to hear missionaries talk of working themselves out of a job. There are the independents to win back to Christian orthodoxy, the millions of nominal Christians, the Catholics and the High Church Anglicans to be 'born again', the battle to prevent the growth of secularism as Africans flood into the cities, each new generation of young Africans to evangelise. And over all this towers the greatest challenge: the battle with Islam.

The social missionary also faces many new challenges. Modern Africa is no longer blighted by slavery, but there are a host of problems that spring from poverty and under-development, social and ecological disaster. Here is a bottomless barrel of new missionary rallying cries: famine, drought, apartheid, civil war and, above all, AIDS. Few areas of Africa have a more tragic story to tell than the area of green and fertile farming land north of Kampala, known as the Luwero triangle. In the tragic war of retribution that bloodied the years of the Obote regime in Uganda, the area was systematically destroyed. As many as half a million may have died in the savage atrocities. Gradually those left alive returned to the ruins, to the mass graves of the dead, to the full horror of what had happened.

In this grim climate, Ian Clarke, a Christian doctor from Northern Ireland, came to visit Luwero. For some time he and his wife had been contemplating giving up their comfortable middle-class existence to become missionaries, but with three young children they had not considered Uganda. But his trip changed everything. He felt God was calling him to Uganda, and to Luwero in particular. Within a year, the family was installed in the village of Kiwoko, in one of the few houses left standing in the heart of the Luwero triangle. For the Clarkes, the change in life-style could not have been more dramatic. Ian Clarke opened a clinic on the steps of a bullet-riddled church. In a side room he sees the hundreds of patients who queue up for treatment each day. The floor of the church is his operating table, and in the doorway the local pastor, ironically named Livingstone, dispenses the drugs. Once the clinic was established, Ian Clarke began a series of open-air surgeries in the countryside. Under a tree he lines up the children for inoculations, while from a branch hangs a scale for weighing the babies. He examines the patients on a small piece of sacking on the ground. It is a scene Doctor Livingstone himself would recognise. Over a hundred years after the arrival of the first missionaries it is back to medical and missionary basics.

Health provision of this kind in an area devastated by war is a challenge to Clarke's skill and ingenuity as a doctor. It is AIDS, in the face of which his medical skills are of little use, which reveals Clarke the missionary. In the bush, where most people are now homeless and diversions are few, indulgence in alcohol and sexual promiscuity have become more prominent. Warnings about the danger of AIDS are not heeded: the people argue that if they have to change their life-style so dramatically they might as well be dead.

Clarke is attempting to overcome such fatalism with spiritual rather

A priest visits parishioners in Rakai district, south-west Uganda: the couple are both dying of AIDS. For missionaries AIDS is the latest and most testing challenge, but also a potent new rallying cry.

than medical argument. Government information about AIDS calls on Ugandans to practise 'Zero Grazing', an agricultural metaphor for restricted sexual activity, as the best protection against the disease. For Clarke the motivation has to be deeper than the lessons of health education: an acceptance of Jesus as Lord is the best, and only, safeguard.

The nature of AIDS and the way it is spread makes it a perfect vehicle for the missionary doctor's evangelistic message. Inevitably it has come both to dominate Clarke's work, and to define his missionary goals: 'There's a passage where Abraham interceded with God about Sodom and Gomorrha and said – if there be ten righteous men will you not destroy the city. And I feel that we are here as missionaries, and one of our functions is to proclaim the Gospel in order that God can raise up righteous men here in Uganda. I don't necessarily feel that the Gospel will stem the tide of AIDS ... but sufficient people can hear the Gospel ... and can be raised up as examples.'

AIDS, or 'Slim' as it is commonly known, has reached staggering proportions in Uganda. In 1988 about half of the adult medical patients at a hospital in Masaka were shown to be positive for the HIV virus. A survey of truck stops showed about 70 per cent of the prostitutes and 33 per cent of the truck drivers to be infected. In a Kampala hospital one in five babies was born HIV positive. In one survey 19 per cent of blood donors and the same number of pregnant women also tested positive for HIV antibodies. Dr Rick Goodgame, a Southern Baptist missionary working as a consultant gastroenterologist at Mulago Hospital, Kampala, reports that on any one day about 50 per cent of the admissions are AIDS patients. It is estimated that as many as half of the population may be infected with the virus by the year 2000, with probably a million deaths and possibly many more.

Dr Goodgame came into the midst of this crisis almost by accident. A graduate of John Hopkins University in America, he married the daughter of a missionary and took a post at Makerere University, once the finest university in Africa. The Mulago Hospital where he was to work was battered and demoralised after twenty years of civil war. Even as the hospital was adjusting to the first real spell of peace, the scale of the AIDS epidemic was becoming apparent. For a born-again Christian like Goodgame the parallels between this medical imperative and the urgency of the salvation message were irresistible: 'For both the central mood and emotion is that of urgency and the truth that can save ... The main objective is persuasion that leads to altered behaviour. The main adversaries are ignorance, unbelief and lies. The target population is the whole world ... The crises which the gospel addresses (sin, death and judgement) and the crises which the AIDS message addresses (HIV, suffering and death) are both so great that it has been almost impossible ever to preach the Gospel without giving the AIDS message, or to give the AIDS message without preaching the gospel.'

With the aid of $250 000 from the coffers of the Southern Baptist Convention he launched a most unusual national AIDS awareness campaign. The government had already attempted a 'Love Carefully' campaign. Several Catholic sisters were unhappy about the government's emphasis and launched their own poster campaign, 'Love Faithfully'. The Catholics were deeply reluctant to condone the use of condoms. Goodgame shared their concerns. His response was the 'Answers' project: 100 000 Bibles with sheets pasted into them giving both the medical and the Christian 'answers' to AIDS, were distributed throughout Uganda. Then leaflets were produced in several languages giving the same information. Goodgame's aim was to get a leaflet into every home in Uganda. Readers were advised to turn to selected scriptural passages, including a dire warning against adultery in Proverbs 5: 'The lips of another man's wife may be as sweet as honey and her lips may be as smooth as olive oil, but when it is all over, she leaves you nothing but bitterness and pain. She will take you down to the world of the dead; the road she walks is the road to death ... If you do ... you will lie groaning on your deathbed, your flesh and muscles being eaten away, and you will say, "Why would I never learn?"'

Seminars all over Uganda, led by missionaries and Ugandan Christian volunteers, gave out the same message in schools, businesses, army barracks. For Goodgame this is a way of salvaging something good from a terrible crisis, and at least a partial answer to the difficult question of God's involvement in AIDS. He denies the charge of distasteful opportunism: the accusation that missionaries are using the fear of AIDS to fill their churches. He insists that the church is where people should go when they are troubled or afraid. For Goodgame and other evangelicals, AIDS may be the stimulus of a revival; if AIDS patients can find peace after hearing the gospel then the same can happen throughout the whole country. Goodgame's prediction of revival may or may not come true. But one thing is clear: AIDS is set to dominate the future of mission to Africa. Not since the call to end slavery have Christian missions been presented with a rallying cry of such potency. The spread of AIDS may well spur a Christian revival and a return to biblical morality in sex and marriage. But if AIDS offers tomorrow's missionaries unique opportunities, it also involves unique dangers. Mission to Africa has never been without risk, but the personal dangers of AIDS work in Africa are considerable, and for the would-be missionary a severe test of faith.

AIDS is just one need among many that will draw Western Christians to Africa. The missionary era is clearly not over, and will not be until the politicians decide that it is; and economic reality suggests that few African countries either desire or dare to expel their missionaries. At the very least the missionary is a valuable source of income in post-colonial Africa. For countries crippled by debt repayments, natural disasters and insufficient aid, the mission organisations have become a vital, if ad hoc, source of aid for African social programmes. Like much aid, there are strings attached, but the price of the presence of a few missionaries is one most countries are prepared to pay.

Africa is in many ways a missionary success story. In the words of Reinhard Bonnke: 'Africa was once called the Dark Continent. Now it is the Christian lighthouse to the world.' In that sense a success, but also a failure. The early missionaries truly believed in the benevolent power of their faith to affect things for good, in particular to defeat slavery. One hundred and fifty years later Christianity has failed to prevent the poverty of under-development, or famine, or civil war, or apartheid or AIDS. Yet still the missionaries, like some great motley volunteer army, range back and forth across the continent tackling its social problems. For many of them Africa remains as it has always been, a 'benighted continent' dependent on the beneficence of the West. Africa may be Christian but it may also still be 'the Dark Continent'. In Father Burgman's words: 'The west has that irresistible urge to come to the aid of everybody, without realising themselves that they are also in need of help ... All they want to see is the picture of a child emaciated and with outstretched hands. I call it the principle of African misery ... The modern missionary is one who not only brings but who also comes and fetches the good things the continent has to offer, a two way bridge, or sometimes I call it a two-way umbilical cord.' Some missionaries are happy to come as guests, to give their experience and to learn. Others still arrive with conversion goals and baptism targets, and wild dreams of winning Africa for Christ. And the Africans continue as they have always done to worship in a way which expresses their aspirations. The religious faith of the African people has survived the transition from animism to Christianity: they have never completely lost the grasp on their own religious worship. Today the missionaries have at best a marginal role in African religious life. As African self-confidence grows the tables are turning. It is they who are beginning to shape the missionaries' religion. In the words of Joseph Kelly of the Church Missionary Society: 'We Christianised Africa. Now Christianity is being Africanised.'

6 The Oppressors and the Oppressed

A people had died out, but the Gospel had reached them in time.
Text of present-day missionary lecture

St Brendan says mass on the back of a sea monster. The belief that St Brendan was the first Christian missionary to reach the New World is colourfully expressed in this fifteenth-century engraving.

Nowhere is present-day missionary endeavour so grimly haunted by its past than in South America, and nowhere have the lessons of history been so carelessly ignored. By the end of the fifteenth century Spanish and Portuguese explorers had opened up the great new sea routes for conquest, colonisation and Christianity. To prevent wasteful competition for the plunder of the New World, Pope Alexander VI created two spheres of influence; he determined that the whole of the Americas,

Spanish priests through the eyes of a fifteenth-century Inca artist: above, cruelly punishing little children; below, giving charity.

with the exception of Brazil, should belong to Spain, while Portugal would take Brazil and whatever could be seized in Asia and Africa. It was decreed that along with territorial gains would go the duty to incorporate any native peoples into the Catholic Church.

Thus it was that the conquest of Central and South America very rapidly brought the Indians under the heavy hand of the Spanish monarchy and the Spanish Church. With the invading armies came priests and friars whose presence justified the subjugation of the people and the use of whatever coercion was judged necessary to bring them to the faith. Under the guise of evangelism came harsh exploitation and eventually the enslavement of the Indians. This was not the intention of the missionaries but it was the inevitable consequence of their wholly compromised position as part of the colonising power. Much of the cruelty and injustice stemmed from the system of *encomienda* by which settlers were permitted to demand labour from the Indians in return for protection and religious instruction. The brutality was such that between ten and fifteen million Indians were estimated to have died.

Faced with this genocide, a number of priests campaigned bravely on behalf of the Indians, well aware that in so doing they were courting the wrath of the conquistadors and even risking martyrdom. Bartholomeo de las Casas (1474–1566) is the best known of those who took up the Indian cause. He wholly rejected the idea of conversion by force and maintained that mission must be carried out with love, gentleness and kindness.

Yet even those priests who were sympathetic to the Indians adopted courses of action that had dismal consequences. The Indians were often drawn together into 'Christian villages' where, under the scrutiny of the Fathers, they were taught their catechism and were encouraged to forgo their 'savage' practices for Christian customs and virtues. Cut off from their own people and denied the self-sufficiency based on hunting, gathering and the cultivation of their gardens, there was only one way for them to go. Judging from the numbers baptised, the conversion rate was astonishing, with records of 8000, 10 000 and even 14 000 people being baptised in a single day. Bearing in mind that the priests' grasp of the language was often feeble, that there was no scripture in the vernacular and that the 'converts' were totally illiterate, it must have been evident even then that the 'conversions' were meaningless. What the missionaries brought to Central and South America at that time was not evangelism but mass baptism. The Church demonstrated its awareness of this fact by withholding the sacrament of communion from the Indians and by making little attempt to build up an indigenous priesthood. These failures have had a lasting negative effect on the Indian population, and upon the Church in Latin America. The missionary legacy is a muddle of traditional beliefs and superstition overlaid with Christian symbolism.

From the very beginning, missionaries in Latin America found themselves involved in a massive contradiction: on the one hand, they were playing a key role in the subjugation of people by conquerors whose only real interest was booty; on the other, the New Testament told them their true place was alongside the victims. How could they align themselves at the same time with the oppressors and the oppressed? This same question has been asked again and again throughout the history of mission in Latin America, and is still being asked today. Although the conquests were accomplished with astonishing speed, there were still huge areas where neither settlers nor missionaries managed to go. In Brazil, Portuguese settlement was largely confined to the coastal regions, and although the region that is now Chile and Argentina was occupied by the Spaniards, the southern tip of the continent was considered too inhospitable for colonisation. So it remained until 1826, when the British ship HMS *Beagle* arrived with a scientific party that was to undertake a four-year hydrographic survey of Cape Horn and the adjacent waters.

For the small group of native tribes known as Fuegians, the arrival of the *Beagle* was to have unforeseen and fatal consequences. The relationship between the Europeans and the Fuegian Indians was chronicled by Lucas Bridges, the son of one of the pioneer missionaries who worked among them. His book *Uttermost Part of the Earth*, about his father's life among the Fuegians, is a most unusual missionary biography and shows great compassion and understanding. Bridges was born in Tierra del Fuego and grew up speaking the Fuegian languages: he therefore does not always see things only from the conventional missionary point of view. The fatal sequence of events started on that first voyage of the *Beagle* when the Captain decided to take back to England four young Yaghan Indians who were unfortunate enough to fall into the hands of the crew. It was fashionable at that time to bring back exotic savages from journeys of exploration. The practice was usually justified by the intention of giving them a Christian education before returning them to raise up and enlighten their own people.

The first step in the civilising of the Fuegians was to give them Christian names; unaccountably, the three boys were named Boat Memory, York Minster and Jemmy Button, while the 9-year-old girl became Fuegia Basket. On arrival in England, Boat Memory promptly died of smallpox. The three survivors began their Christian instruction at the home of a Walthamstow clergyman. Gossip about Yaghan

Despite their fearsome appearance, the Fuegian Indians were not cannibals. The assertion that they were was made by Charles Darwin, among others, and was only corrected when Thomas Bridges learned their language and discovered their disgust at the idea of eating human flesh.

The Fuegians who went to Walthamstow. Despite their Christian education and their collars and ties, Fuegia Basket, Jemmy Button and York Minster quickly reverted to their old ways and were later spotted 'practically naked in their bark canoes, eating seal, birds and fish when not eating each other'.

savagery and degradation quickly made them considerable celebrities and rumours of their former cannibalistic habits ensured them a presentation at Court to King William IV and Queen Adelaide. After two years of 'good Christian living', during which the children learned how to dress modestly, eat with a knife and fork and say their prayers, they were embarked once more upon the *Beagle* for their homeward journey. Their fellow passengers included Charles Darwin and Richard Mathews, a young missionary sent by the Church Missionary Society.

It was hoped that Richard Mathews would continue to instruct the Fuegians during the voyage and then, with their help, establish the first mission station in Tierra del Fuego. In accordance with this plan, the Captain of the *Beagle*, Robert Fitzroy, put the little party ashore in a suitably sheltered spot and helped them to construct cabins for themselves and the considerable quantity of goods and provisions that had been donated by well-wishers. At first, all this activity attracted hundreds of Yaghans who watched from their canoes, but since the Indians showed no animosity and soon drifted away, Captain Fitzroy set sail. The first intimation that all might not be well came when a watchman on the ship noticed the usually naked Yaghans passing in their canoes wearing various items of European clothing. Captain Fitzroy at once turned back to the mission station and found Mathews in a state of collapse. Despite the combined efforts of York Minster, Jemmy Button and Fuegia Basket, the stores had been ransacked and almost everything stolen. It was decided that what little provisions remained should be divided among the three young 'Christians' who would then be left to their own devices. Mathews stepped gratefully on board, thanking God that he had not been killed and eaten.

Even today, when Tierra del Fuego is easily accessible by air, it can seem a remote and forbidding place. That most seasoned of contemporary travellers Gavin Young described it as 'surely one of the most terrible regions to be found on earth'. In Darwin's day, apart from the well-known physical rigours of the place, there was the fearsome reputation of its inhabitants that the *Beagle* episode had done nothing to modify. Indeed, Darwin was so struck by what he took to be the primitive savagery of the people that he was inclined to think they might even be a subhuman species – the missing link that he was seeking. It may well be that reports brought back by Darwin, Fitzroy and Mathews were so alarming they acted as a deterrent to further missionary ventures, at least for some years.

The next person to figure prominently was Captain Allen Gardiner, RN. In the book *Missionary Heroes* published in 1910, a chapter is devoted to 'Captain Allen Gardiner, Sailor and Saint', which tells how he promised his dying wife to devote himself to the work of God among the heathen. This is, in fact, romantic nonsense. Gardiner was still unmarried when, in his early thirties, he decided to exchange the navy for the mission field. Far from exhibiting the qualities of prudence, organisation and planning so admired in the armed services, it seems that he was beset by uncertainty about which mission field to enter. He is reported to have tried first Zululand and then New Guinea, in both cases unsuccessfully. He next made his way to South America, to preach Christianity to the Indians, but there encountered bitter hostility from the Roman Catholic priests. It seems that the Jesuits persuaded the Chilean authorities to refuse Gardiner's request to settle among the Indians, and it may have been this set-back that prompted him to look further south, to Tierra del Fuego.

Gardiner returned to England and founded the Patagonian Missionary Society (which was to become the South American Missionary Society), whose efforts would be devoted specially to the natives of Tierra del Fuego. There then followed a catalogue of incompetence and folly. Although the new Society was desperately short of money, its founder was impatient to save souls and immediately chartered an ancient schooner, whose owners regarded her as no longer fit to go to sea. Despite a drunken and troublesome crew, Gardiner reached his destination, only to realise the impossibility of making any headway without some help and more adequate equipment. He returned to England and over the next eight years mounted three more expeditions, all of which ended in more or less ignominious failure. In 1850 he made a fourth attempt. Compared with the other abortive expeditions, this one appears to have been better planned and provisioned. With Gardiner went a doctor, a catechist, a carpenter and three experienced seamen. The party was equipped with two sturdy metal boats and a six-months' supply of food, and this time it contrived to arrive during the relatively better weather of the summer months. However, not one member of the party spoke a word of any of the Indian languages. It seems they were trusting entirely in the possibility of making contact with Jemmy Button, York Minster or Fuegia Basket and using them as go-betweens and interpreters. What Gardiner may not have known was that when Jemmy Button was last sighted by the crew of the *Beagle*, only fifteen months after returning to his own people, he was practically naked, entirely filthy and utterly unrecognisable as the pomaded youth who had been presented at the Court of St James's.

What happened to Gardiner and his party in the months that followed their arrival was pieced together by Lucas Bridges from the accounts of those who found their bodies and who read their letters and diaries. What was recorded in these documents was a series of errors and misfortunes, the first and worst being the immediate discovery that most of their ammunition had been left behind and was already en route back to England. Without any means of killing game or defending themselves against native attack, it became vital that they contact Jemmy Button and somehow establish friendly relations with the Indians. This they failed to do. On the contrary, the Indians grew ever more threatening until the missionaries were obliged to take to their boats and seek some place to hide. Their chosen refuge, Spaniard Harbour, was where their bodies were eventually found. They had died, one by one, of exposure and starvation. In his diary Gardiner had written detailed suggestions of how the task he had set himself might be successfully concluded. The most obvious was that before any further effort was made to put missionaries among the Fuegians, a safe haven be established within striking distance of Tierra del Fuego, on the Falkland Islands. The missionaries should travel back and forth from this base camp until sufficiently friendly contact had been established to induce some of the Fuegians to cross to the Falklands. Only then could the missionaries win allies among the natives and gain a thorough knowledge of their language.

Back in England, the South American Missionary Society followed Gardiner's suggestions to the letter. A settlement was established on

The death of Captain Allen Gardiner: a typically melodramatic portrayal of what was a foolish and ill-planned episode.

Keppel Island in the Falklands and a schooner named the *Allen Gardiner* was fitted out and despatched to Tierra del Fuego to re-establish contact with Jemmy Button. Up to that point, the plan succeeded. Jemmy was located, unclothed and unkempt and unwilling to take the ship to the Falklands; nor was he able to persuade any of his companions to accompany the white man. In desperation, the Secretary of the Society, the Reverend George Despard, determined that he himself would take charge of another expedition; included in his party was his 13-year-old adopted son, Thomas Bridges. At last the missionaries began to see their efforts rewarded. Over a period of four years, the *Allen Gardiner* plied to and fro between the Falklands and Tierra del Fuego, and with every trip relations with the natives became more cordial. Several Yaghan families were persuaded to travel to the Falklands where Thomas Bridges was able to acquire from them a useful knowledge of their language. So friendly had the intercourse become that the missionaries judged the time was right to set up their mission station. A party of nine set sail for Wulaia, the chosen site for the mission. Neither the Reverend Despard nor Thomas Bridges was included in the party.

Six months later, when nothing had been heard of the ship, Mr Despard set out in search and found her anchored at Wulaia, stripped of every movable item, including every square inch of canvas and every nail. The only survivor was the ship's cook, Alfred Cole, who told how things had gone badly from the beginning, with the Yaghans incessantly begging and trying to steal from the ship. Chief among the trouble-makers had been Jemmy Button. Undeterred, they went ahead with the building of the mission and on Sunday, 6 November 1859 the missionaries and all the crew, except the cook, went ashore to give thanks to God for this historic church planting. No sooner had the first hymn begun than the singing was drowned in a chorus of shrieks and yells. The missionary, Garland Philips, and one of the sailors ran from the building and headed for the sea, only to be clubbed and stoned to death in the shallows. The rest of the party were murdered with their hymn books in their hands. For some reason, the Yaghans spared the life of the cook, although when they captured him they stole his clothes and pulled out all his facial hair including his eyebrows. Mr Despard took the tragedy badly, feeling responsible for those he had sent to their deaths; he also believed he had been betrayed by the natives whom he had treated with kindness. His faith shaken, he returned to England but, even in his despair, he refused to sanction a mission of reprisal against the Yaghans.

The small party that remained in the Falklands included Thomas Bridges who, after five years mixing with the Fuegians who had visited the Falklands, had now become fluent in one of their languages. For the first time there was a missionary who was able to communicate with the Indians and begin to understand something of their culture. This was the beginning of a rather more positive, if brief, chapter in the history of the Fuegian mission. Although Captain Gardiner and Mr Despard and the other pioneers were men of courage and piety, these qualities were not enough. Thomas Bridges possessed a measure of sound common sense and he began to compile a dictionary which helped him pass on his skill to the new missionary recruits coming over from England. One of the newcomers was John Lawrence, a nursery gardener who was to play a vital role in the new plan to evangelise the Fuegians. Groups of Indians were to be brought to the Falklands where they would be taught animal husbandry and how to grow crops; in this way they would become less dependent on uncertain supplies of fish and game. They would also, of course, be introduced to the gospel message and to the basic tenets of 'civilised' behaviour. These 'tamed' Indians would then return to their homes where they would serve as an example of the benefits that came from the Christian life. Among these benefits were the use of simple tools and utensils and the wearing of trousers – Lucas Bridges recalls that one of his earliest recollections of his father is seeing him busily engaged making tin drinking cups and stitching sailcloth trousers for the natives.

For once, it was not prudery alone that prompted the missionary to put clothes on the Indians; it was also to protect them from the elements. The Yaghan people, who inhabited the coastline, were particularly poorly clad, mostly in small pieces of otter or fox skin. In most other aspects, too, they represented the essence of primitive savagery from the missionary point of view. They lived in roughly constructed wigwams and did not use metals, instead hunting with bows and arrows and spears with bone or flint tips. Whale meat was an important part of their diet; carcasses were cut up and buried and quarrels over the ownership of these hidden caches was a frequent cause of bloodshed and family feuds. If the feuding was not over stolen meat, it was almost certainly over stolen women. The Fuegians were polygamous, with the unusual variation that there was often a very wide discrepancy in the ages of the partners. It was quite usual for a young man to have one wife of 16 and another of 60. From the woman's point of view, she was unlikely ever to have to face life alone as an elderly widow. One of the women who found comfort in this custom was Fuegia Basket. Forty years after she was presented at the Court of St James's, Thomas Bridges encountered in a remote part of Tierra del Fuego a wild-looking, toothless woman who, to his surprise, spoke a few words of English. It proved to be Fuegia Basket. From questioning

A Fuegian Indian trying a cigarette aboard a whaling ship, Moresby Sound, Tierra del Fuego, 1920.

her in her own tongue, Bridges concluded sadly that the painstaking efforts of the Vicar of Walthamstow to instruct the little girl in the Christian faith had been quite fruitless for she remembered not a word of it. At the time Bridges talked to her, she must have been well over 50 years old and yet she was accompanied by her new husband, a youth of 18.

Despite the set-backs of the early days, the missionaries began to establish a position of power and influence among the Fuegians. This they did by a well-judged application of stick and carrot. Over a period of four years, more than fifty Indians went to the Falklands for training. On their return home, those who had been co-operative were helped with gifts of tools and seed potatoes and livestock. The settlement soon divided into two: the traditional wigwams by the shoreline, and the neat houses of the 'Mission Indians' further inland. This was social engineering on a grand scale. Garments from England were regularly distributed among the natives, but they were generally second-rate and unsuitable for the life-style and the physique of the people.

During the 1870s and 1880s, while the missionaries were getting established, they were a law unto themselves. Although the Fuegian archipelago was nominally under Chilean and Argentinian sovereignty, neither country had bothered to extend its administration into such inhospitable and apparently valueless lands. Thomas Bridges and his fellow missionaries virtually ruled over the Indians: they felt they had a God-given right to do so. However, that period of well-intentioned paternalism was brought to an abrupt end by a number of developments. Both Argentina and Chile began to take an interest in their southernmost territories, stimulated in part by the knowledge that the missionaries had done what had been considered impossible: they had shown that crops could be grown and animals could be raised in those seemingly barren lands. Once that became known it was not long before white settlers began to push further south, given further impetus by talk of gold.

Thomas Bridges realised that an influx of white settlers was imminent and that their influence was bound to reach all the Fuegian tribes sooner or later. He argued as many have since that if civilisation did not come to the Indians by the way of the Bible, it would come via the bullet and the whisky bottle. The only way for the Indians to survive was for them to be able to compete with the intruders on more or less equal terms. Bridges wanted to obtain from the Argentinian government a grant of land sufficient to support the Indians in agriculture and stock-raising enterprises. When his plan was put to the South American Missionary Society in England, the committee turned it down on the grounds that an Anglican Mission should concern itself with saving souls and not with the trivial matter of earthly survival. Bridges resigned his position of Superintendent and determined to pursue his plan independently. But it was too late.

The Indians were overcome, not by the white man's gun or his alcohol, but one of his childish ailments: measles. The first serious epidemic was brought by the crews of the Argentine navy vessels that came to establish a government presence in 'Fireland'. When the Yaghans began to fall sick, their symptoms were so severe that the ship's surgeon was convinced they were suffering from typhoid-pneumonia. In a matter of days, the dying outnumbered the living. It took the practical common sense of the missionary wives to realise that typhoid was not responsible as all of their own children were becoming ill and then recovering, whereas the same symptoms were having a devastating effect among the Indians. This was the first of a succession of epidemics – measles, scrofula, influenza – against which the Indians had no inherited resistance. Only those of mixed blood survived. Very soon their numbers were so diminished that Thomas Bridges abandoned any idea of trying to found a permanent mission settlement and concentrated on looking after the interests of his own family. He received a grant of fifty thousand acres of land from the Argentine government and, in the end, went the way of many, settling down to life alongside the oppressors rather than the oppressed.

It was perhaps fortunate that Thomas Bridges did not live to witness the final humiliation and annihilation of the people to whom he had planned to bring the Good News. However, his son Lucas saw it all and, although he was now firmly identified with exploitation rather than with enlightenment, he retained a measure of sympathy for the Indian cause. In the 1890s the Argentine government sold off the vast traditional hunting grounds of the Ona tribe to immigrant sheepherders but at the same time made a small grant of land to the Roman Catholic Silesian Fathers who were invited to establish a mission for the benefit of the Indians. This was all that was done for them. Conflict was inevitable as the tribesmen attempted to protect their land. So determined were the ranchers to get rid of the troublesome savages that some of them offered a bounty of £1.00 a head for every Indian killed. The natives were tracked down like vermin and their only escape was into mission compounds, Indian reserves where they could be confined and disciplined. A reward of £5.00 was given for every Indian delivered to the safekeeping of the missionary enclaves.

The missionaries were in yet another impossible dilemma. However much they may have disapproved of the policy that deprived the Indians of their lands, they could hardly refuse to take them in. They therefore found themselves in league with men like Mr McInch. Not only did Mr McInch boast of having killed fourteen Indians on a single hunting trip, he claimed it as a humanitarian act: better for them to die of a bullet, he felt, than to languish at a mission station or to perish when the next imported disease swept the land.

Those Indians who managed to escape the murderous forays of the settlers either sought asylum with the missionaries or were physically confined at mission stations. There is a fine irony in the fact that Dawson Island, where General Pinochet confined members of the Allende government after the 1973 coup, started its prison history as a Silesian Mission where 700 Ona Indians were held captive at the turn of the century. Bridges describes the conditions he saw when he made a brief stop at Dawson Island. The Indians had been put to work by the Silesians on what were intended to be useful occupations; the women were weaving blankets and the men were occupied in a sawmill. They were all decently dressed, although the clothes were old and generally too small. Despite the obvious disapproval of the lay brothers, Bridges was able to converse with the Indians in their own language. He learned that although they were treated kindly, they were little more than captive slaves. There was no way for them to escape from the island and they were obliged to work for their food and lodging.

Most of the Indians died of disease, with those who were confined at the missions being specially vulnerable. Infections spread in a matter of days with catastrophic consequences. In providing the Indians with a refuge from the murderous settlers, the missionaries found themselves presiding over their final extinction. When the first missionary set foot in Tierra del Fuego in the 1820s, there were perhaps ten thousand Fuegian Indians living there. Today there are none. The missionaries cannot be blamed entirely for what happened to the Fuegian Indians, but the part they played in the tragedy is not an heroic one. It bears uncomfortable similarities with events that are unfolding up to the present day and, above all, it reveals a certain missionary attitude that is hard to understand and even harder to accept. Although Lucas Bridges grew up with the Fuegian Indians, although he spoke their tongue and admired their culture, he could still write: 'Allen Gardiner's plans were followed to a successful conclusion. Although I am well aware that, within less than a century, the Fuegians as a race have become almost extinct, I deliberately used the word "successful".'

Any lingering doubt about what exactly Bridges meant by 'successful' is dispelled by the text of a present-day audio-visual lecture on the history of the South American Missionary Society. It concludes with the observation, 'A people had died out, but the Gospel had reached them in time'.

7 A Liberating God?

The God we know in the Bible is a liberating God ... He is a God who liberates slaves, who causes empires to fall and raises up the oppressed.

Gustavo Gutierrez, 1971

In Eastern Europe, the Catholic Church is identified with anti-communism. But in Latin America it is now supporting revolutionary movements of the left.

In Tierra del Fuego today, there are no Indians but there are still representatives of the South American Missionary Society. Peter and Elizabeth Dooley and their young family are the latest English missionaries to follow the trail of Captain Allen Gardiner. They are based in Punta Arenas, said to be the most southerly city in the world. It is a modern community of 80 000 people which has seen its prosperity grow steadily since the recent discovery of oil and gas. Only in its cemetery, filled with memorials to settlers and crews of shipping disasters, is there a reminder that not long ago this was a lawless land of pioneers where Indians were shot down in cold blood. Despite its air of modernity, Punta Arenas is still considered to be an appropriate destination for missionaries. When Jesus said to his disciples: 'And ye shall be witnesses unto me in Jerusalem ... and unto the uttermost part of the earth' (Acts 1:8), he left an instruction that missionaries have chosen to follow as faithfully as possible. For this reason, a representative of the Southern Baptists suggested that it was good public relations to maintain a missionary presence in Punta Arenas, despite the heavy costs.

Peter Dooley came because the South American Missionary Society needed an experienced schoolmaster to run the British School attached to the Anglican Church in Punta Arenas. From the way he describes his call, Peter Dooley seems to have been a little put out by the way God 'hoiked us out from Cheadle in Cheshire and dumped us here in Chile'. And yet, in response to a number of events which they interpreted as indications of God's will, the Dooleys decided to take up a post which has little or nothing of the romantic image of missionary work. Indeed, they are doing very much the same things as they did at home in England. The British School at one time provided a Protestant education for the children of British settlers and missionaries in the region. Today it has outlived that function and serves the children of the upwardly mobile Chilean middle classes. Although Spanish is now the language of instruction, and although, except for the Dooleys, the staff and pupils are exclusively Chilean, the school has remained relentlessly British. The 720 fee-paying boys and girls wear traditional British school uniform and at morning assembly, as well as the Chilean national anthem, they say the Lord's Prayer in English and sing 'God Save The Queen'. Peter Dooley does not think this unreasonable, as the school aims to give the pupils an awareness of British values and culture. Since his school is a mission foundation, Dooley is well aware of the implication that British values and Christian values are the same thing. He acknowledges that an education at the British School has snob value. Children are certainly not sent to him for religious instruction: most of them are nominally Catholic. On their parents' part there is no expectation or fear that there will be any overt attempt to turn them into evangelical Anglicans. In any case, Dooley does not see success as something that can be measured in numbers of converts: he tries to awaken people to Jesus through his life and witness.

In comparison to its recent history, mission in Tierra del Fuego is a bland, suburban affair. Although the pioneer missionaries are still remembered, there is little sense of the disaster that so rapidly overcame the Indians and little awareness that the same dreadful sequence of events that led to the disappearance of the Fuegians is still unfolding in other parts of Latin America today. In Bolivia, the Yuqui Indians are seriously threatened. They were one of the few remaining groups of indigenous peoples in South America who, until recently, managed to retain their culture and nomadic life in the forest despite the encroachment of settlers, logging teams, government patrols and missionaries. According to a recent report on the BBC World Service *Assignment* programme, 124 Yuquis still roam the forest. This is just a tiny rump of the population of several thousand that flourished there when the tribe was first contacted by the New Tribes Mission in the 1950s.

In *The Story of the New Tribes Mission*, Ken Johnston describes how the missionaries attracted the Yuquis by means of 'gift trails': they placed gifts at an abandoned Indian campsite and along the trails leading back to their base. Eventually, a small number of Indians came cautiously to the missionaries' clearing to receive more gifts. As these contacts continued, the missionaries built a house both to shelter their generator and radio and to provide a hideout for one of the missionaries who, in case of trouble, would shoot into the air or start up the generator to scare the Indians off. The missionaries had good reason to be nervous, just as the Yuquis had good reason to be suspicious. Ever since the 1940s, the Bolivian government had been encouraging people from over-crowded highland regions to settle in the rich tropical jungles of the Eastern Andes foothills. According to International Law, the land belonged to the Indians by customary right, where for centuries they had lived by hunting and fishing and gathering wild fruits and honey, but the colonists neither knew nor cared about the rights of people they regarded as little more than animals.

As the Indians were forced off their land, they retaliated by stealing from the colonists' gardens. In defending their crops, the Bolivians did not hesitate to shoot and, as the violence escalated, they set up a vigilante commission with the expressed purpose of exterminating the Yuquis. It was at this point that the New Tribes Mission saw their opportunity. In order to save the souls of the Yuquis, their bodies must first be rescued; and, as the missionaries realised, if the Yuquis remained in the forest, they would certainly be wiped out, body *and* soul. The Yuquis must therefore be encouraged to take refuge in camps set up by the missionaries where they would be introduced to a settled way of life and, above all, where they would hear the gospel. For the surviving small band of Yuquis this presents no choice at all. Whatever happens, they face the end of their culture and of their traditional way of life. Representatives of the New Tribes Mission argue that there is no alternative for the Yuquis and that despite our romantic notions about 'the noble savage', the nomadic lives of the Yuquis are spiritually and materially impoverished. One missionary has declared that even before they came into contact with the outside world, the Yuquis were often on the brink of starvation, and that they lived in constant fear of the spirits.

According to anthropologists who have studied the Yuquis and other tribes of the Guarani language group to which they belong, these judgements are based on a total misunderstanding of their tribal culture. Their life-style is an example of perfect harmony between nature and society, while what the missionaries interpret as the tyranny of the fear of demons is an expression of awe and respect for forces beyond their understanding that is no different from the awe and respect expressed by Christians for their God. Nowhere have relations between anthropologists and missionaries been more acrimonious than in Latin America. In recent years, human rights groups too have battled to save tribal societies from the unwelcome attentions of the missionaries. Both Catholics and Protestants have been fiercely attacked, but the heaviest criticism has been directed at the New Tribes Mission and, to a lesser extent, at the Summer Institute of Linguistics. In most cases, the controversy has centred on the missionary strategy of removing tribes from their traditional lands and bringing them into missionary settlements where they are indoctrinated with Christian teachings and reduced to a state of helpless dependency. It is even claimed that extreme coercion has been used: on more than one occasion Survival International has called upon the missions to cease their activities and respect tribal religion and culture.

These appeals have fallen on deaf ears. The New Tribes Mission argues that, but for its efforts, tribes like the Yuqui would simply be decimated by settlers. In the hundred and fifty years of Spanish rule, the Indian population is estimated to have fallen from ninety million to four million; and, according to New Tribes thinking, every one of the eighty-six million who died went straight to Hell. They are determined to reach the remaining Indians 'in time'. Moreover, the New Tribes, Summer Institute of Linguistics and other fundamentalist missions dismiss all opposition or criticism as simply manifestations of the Devil at work in man. This argument does not do justice to their case. While anthropologists and human rights groups have campaigned to protect the land rights of the Indians, governments have shown little inclination to establish or enforce those rights, and the harassment of the Indians has continued. Even if their attempt has been fatally flawed, the missionaries have at least tried to do something, only to find that their efforts have been condemned and that they are urged to leave the Indians alone. Yet after four hundred years of persecution, Indian numbers are now so small, their groups so fragmented and their territory so compromised that it is virtually impossible to create 'human zoos' where they can be isolated and left alone. The tragedy with the Yuquis today, as with the Fuegians yesterday, is that there are no exits save for the one that leads into the mission compound or the one that leads to the grave. Experience suggests that whichever road they take, the final destination will be the same.

The work of the New Tribes and other missions must soon be drawing to a close. Even in the vastness of Amazonia there can be few if any tribes remaining that have not been contacted and exposed to some kind of missionary influence. But rather than give up and leave, the missionaries are now turning their attention to the 'evangelised non-Christians' – nominally Catholic – who constitute the majority of Latin America's 420 million people. Latin America has always been the backyard for North American missionary zeal and the efforts have never been more intense than at present. According to one calculation, every hour of every day, 400 Latin Catholics are being converted by aggressive evangelicals, most of them independent Pentecostals or fundamentalists. Much of the financial support comes from the USA. The Southern Baptists alone have 1400 representatives throughout Latin America. Faced with evangelical onslaught, the Catholic Church in Latin America looks distinctly vulnerable. There is a dangerous shortage of vocations, resulting in huge parishes served by over-worked

Managua Cathedral is adorned by a huge portrait of General Sandino, the patriot who lent his name to the left-wing Sandinista government – a piquant new symbol of Latin American politics.

priests. In Brazil, although the Church claims over one hundred million members, only 12 per cent bother to go to mass. There is the additional difficulty that since the Second Vatican Council, the Church has been deeply divided between traditionalists and those who support the new 'liberation theology'. This division is inevitably reflected in the mission field.

Liberation theology starts from the premise that the Kingdom of God is not only a future reality but something that is present here and now. Salvation lies in this world as well as in the next. People will never believe the Good News of the gospel if it is blatantly contradicted by what they see and experience. Thus it falls upon Christian missionaries to throw themselves wholeheartedly into the struggle for social justice, to the point where the poor know beyond any doubt that they will risk all in the struggle against economic and political oppression. One thing the Second Vatican Council did was to bring Catholic thinking on mission much closer to that of mainstream Protestants. Few Catholic missionaries today would disagree with the definition of mission formulated at the Nairobi Assembly of the World Council of Churches in 1975: 'The Gospel always includes ... the responsibility to participate in the struggle for justice and human dignity, the obligation to denounce all that hinders human wholeness and a commitment to risk life itself.' Liberation theology, it is claimed, simply follows the example set by Christ himself: 'He has sent me to announce the good news to the poor, to proclaim release for prisoners and recovery of sight for the blind; to let the broken victims go free' (Luke 4: 18–19).

When this definition of mission is put into practice in the politically volatile atmosphere of Latin America it can have explosive consequences. In the past decade, in the Central American republics alone, over 400 Catholic priests, friars and nuns (including one archbishop) have met with violent deaths. Many were missionaries. Their martyrdom was unavoidable: according to Father Dan Driscoll, a Maryknoll missionary from the United States, they could not, and should not, have remained on the sidelines. Dan Driscoll has spent twenty years in Latin America, first in Venezuela and now in Nicaragua. When the Sandinistas began their campaign against the Samosa dictatorship in Nicaragua, the rank and file Catholic priests largely disregarded the Catholic hierarchy which opposed the revolution, and sided firmly with the Sandinista rebels. Since the Sandinistas have formed a government, they have cemented the alliance by appointing several priests to serve in ministerial positions, despite the disapproval of the Church hierarchy. It has been a difficult time for Dan Driscoll and other like-

American nuns pray over the bodies of four of their compatriots kidnapped and murdered by right-wing terrorists in San Salvador. In Central America missionaries still face the possibility of martyrdom for their faith.

The Pope and politics. Above, in front of an SLN poster, Nicaragua. Below, on the platform with Pinochet.

minded American missionaries as they have had to watch the Reagan administration actively support the Contra rebel army in its attempt to overthrow the Sandinista government which they believe has the legal and moral right to rule. Father Dan says that his most painful duties ever have been to perform funeral rites for young government soldiers killed in action against rebels supported and supplied by his government: 'As I celebrate mass over that casket, I know where the bullets came from that killed him. I hold his mother and I wipe away her tears and I know that it was the government of my country that caused those tears.'

Father Dan believes that the only answer to Latin America's problems is a radical restructuring of power. As a missionary, he sees his task as accompanying the people in their struggle, supporting the new co-operatives, consoling the bereaved, encouraging his flock to defend the revolution and, while the armed conflict continues, celebrating mass in honour of departing and returning soldiers. Above all, his mission means opting for the poor. This means that he will refuse to co-operate with any government which does not serve their interests. He is a great protester and regularly joins hundreds of Christians and others in a vigil outside the US Embassy in Managua in protest against US aid for the Contras. Father Dan assumes that his activities are well documented in CIA files and not just for what he is doing in Nicaragua. He continues his protests when he returns to the United States on leave, travelling the country on speaking tours, trying to break what he sees as the stronghold the political right has over Central American policy.

For Father Dan, the idea that you can be a missionary today in Latin America and not be politically involved is unthinkable. If any scriptural authority is needed, missionaries like Father Dan can find inspiration in the Epistle of James, Chapter 2, 14–17: 'What good is it my brothers if a man claims to have faith but has no deeds: Can such faith save him? Suppose a brother or sister is without clothes and daily food. If one of you says to him "Go, I wish you well, keep warm and well fed" but does nothing about his physical needs, what good is it? In the same way, faith by itself, if it is not accompanied by action, is dead.' According to liberation theology, if faith in action means entering the political fray and acting in opposition to established governments, then there is biblical authority for so doing. Many evangelicals disagree: they argue that Christians should submit to temporal powers because that is God's will. It is argued that, in adhering to this principle, North American evangelical missionaries have become a tool of neo-colonialism in Latin America. According to Catholics, there is clear evidence of a conspiracy by the US government to oppose liberation theology, which is regarded as dangerously left-wing, by promoting the conservative evangelical cults. The conspiracy is said to stem from 1969 when Nelson Rockefeller reported to President Nixon following a visit to Latin America. Rockefeller feared that because of the growth of liberation theology, the Catholic Church was no longer a trusted ally of the US and no longer guaranteed social stability on the continent. The evangelicals, on the other hand, preached a message that firmly supported the status quo. Whatever the truth of the conspiracy theory, there is plenty of evidence that *evangelicos* (a word used in Latin America to describe all Protestants, Bible Christians or Pentecostals) do tend to support right-wing regimes.

Nick Pino is Field Director of the Assemblies of God in Chile. Before Jimmy Swaggart's fall from grace, he acted as the TV evangelist's tour manager during a Chilean crusade. Sicilian by birth and brought up in Argentina and the United States, he is as unlike the missionary stereotype as it is possible to be. In his leather jacket and dark glasses, with his Italian-accented American English, he is more like a popular image of a Mafia boss. In fact, he is the highly successful leader of a church-building project called *Impacto Chile*, and he is proud that its success is partly due to the support he has received from the military government of General Pinochet: 'Pinochet likes the evangelicals because he himself is a Godly man and he doesn't like the way the Catholics have organised opposition to him. He also knows evangelicals can deliver ten per cent of the vote.' Pino believes in strong rulers, both in government and in Church. People need telling what to do; choice just paralyses them. He himself personifies the no-nonsense approach and says that whereas until recently, missionaries were regarded as tourists, they are now held in respect. The secret of his success lies partly in bringing teams of volunteers from Assemblies of God churches in the United States to Chile on two-week stints. They pay their own expenses and give their labour free. Pino has no qualms about bringing in Americans on a project that could have provided badly needed employment for Chileans. He points out that some local labour is used and his materials are locally obtained. To get his churches built as cheaply and quickly as possible he has become a missionary wheeler-dealer. As a 'fixer for Jesus', he says that he 'buys from the Jews and sells to the Scots and still makes a profit'. Nick Pino has had three private meetings with General Pinochet and yet he still insists that he has no involvement in politics. Pinochet is well aware of the political influence of the million-strong Pentecostal vote. He regularly visits the Evangelical Cathedral of Santiago for the annual thanksgiving service. In 1974, when he inaugurated the new cathedral sanctuary, it marked the first time a Chilean head of state had ever attended a Protestant service.

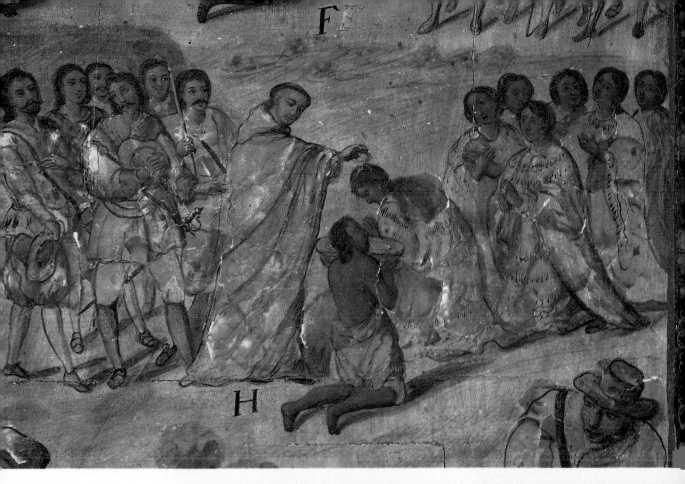

The Christening of South
America, now and then.
Right: Catholic priest
preaches to the Embera
people of North Western
Amazonia.

Above: Brother
Bartolomeo de Olmedo
baptising the Indians,
by Miguel Gozález.

Left: Ruined El Carmen
church, Guatemala.

Above: People's art,
a Christian mural in
Valparaiso, Chile.

Right: Page from the Codex
Azcatitlan, an Indian
artist's impression of the
work of Franciscan friars.

Previous page: A Catholic church beneath the Urubamba mountains, Peru.

Images of 'the Last Catholic Continent'.

Left: Peruvian Indians at mass, Chincheros.

Right: The ornate object of peasants' devotion, a Mexican altar dripping with gold.

It may also have been Pinochet's way of showing Roman Catholics his displeasure at the political activists among them.

Pentecostalism, which is experiencing a veritable explosion in Chile, can be traced back to one American missionary, Willis C. Hoover. In 1909, Hoover, who was an Episcopalian, heard of the Pentecostal movement that was sweeping the United States and felt drawn to this religion of ecstasy and prophecy and speaking in tongues that contrasted so strongly with the formality of his own Church.

The fervent and uninhibited worship that is characteristic of Pentecostal churches worldwide has caught on with Latin Americans. The people clap their hands as they sing, urge on the preacher with loud 'Amens' and frequently take to the floor in energetic dance. The same enthusiasm goes into their street preaching which is largely responsible for their rapidly growing congregations. Although it was an American who brought Pentecostalism to Chile, its amazing growth is largely an indigenous affair and owes less to foreign missionary activity than is the case with other evangelical groups.

In seeking to explain the advance of Protestant missions in Latin America, the fact that Catholic liberation theology is condemned as Marxist is only part of the story. In many areas, evangelicals and 'revolutionary' Catholics are both gaining adherents from the ranks of the traditional, nominally Catholic masses. Harriet Skinner, an English anthropologist, recently made a study of the impact of liberation theology at grassroots level on a single parish in highland Ecuador. She concluded that it has indeed motivated and influenced developments and had greatly improved the socio-economic position of the Indian population in relation to the dominant mestizos, those of mixed Spanish and Indian blood. She also noticed the progress of the evangelicals among the Indians. The increase in missionary work and the growth of converts had been possible because the local Catholic Church, under the influence of liberation theology, had become far more tolerant of Protestant incursions. The evangelicals introduced strict moral codes and emphasised the importance of the home. There was a new interest in education and many more children from evangelical Indian villages were now entering secondary school. This amounted to a new sense of self-respect, a departure from the Indians' traditional subservience and their emergence as a 'modern' and 'civilised' people.

In talking to an evangelical convert of eighteen years' standing, Harriet Skinner learned that the greatest attraction for him had been to hear the scriptures in his own language, Quichua. At that time, the Catholic mass was still given in Latin and the priest stood with his back to the congregation. No one but the priest could read the Bible.

A Catholic burial ground, Huancayo, Peru.

Young people on the annual pilgrimage to the Templo Votivo de Maipu in Chile. Despite these demonstrations of support, the Catholic Church in Latin America is losing ground to a determined missionary onslaught from North American evangelicals: in Chile alone, there are now a million Pentecostals.

Then the evangelicals translated the New Testament into Quichua and broadcast it on the missionary radio station. Today church services and religion meetings are held completely in Quichua and include many Quichua hymns set to traditional tunes accompanied by guitar or local bands. Although the Catholics have followed suit, they are unable to compete with the Protestants on another important matter: celibacy. Without the rule of celibacy, evangelical Churches have encouraged Indians to become pastors. Thus, unlike the Catholic Church whose priests are all mestizos or foreign missionaries, the Indian evangelicals run their own churches with a minimum of outside help. Yet far from being inactive, the evangelical missionaries are putting a great deal of effort into running radio stations.

Ecuador is the home of the oldest and one of the largest of all missionary radio stations. HCJB The Voice of the Andes began to broadcast on Christmas Day in 1931, using a 250-watt transmitter and a studio in a tumble-down sheep shelter. It remained on the air for half an hour. Since there were only six radio receivers in Quito, which was the limit of its signal, its audience was insubstantial.

Today HCJB is one of seventy missionary radio and television stations world-wide. It has a staff of 600 missionaries and an annual budget of $10 million. It broadcasts nineteen hours a day in thirteen languages, in addition to its Quichua language programmes. Clarence Jones, the founder of HCJB, began his broadcasting career as a trombone player in a brass quartet that accompanied an early radio evangelist in Chicago. In those days, many preachers issued warnings to their congregations to beware of radio as a tool of Satan. Clarence Jones soon recognised that radio could become a powerful tool for propaganda of all kinds, including the Christian variety. The possibility of using it to reach the Quichuas presented itself when he teamed up with Reuben Lawson, a young missionary who had been trying, without much success, to contact the Indians. They were convinced that the way to evangelise Ecuador was by setting up a radio station. The missionary establishment dismissed them as mad, but the sceptics failed to foresee that broadcasting would revolutionise communications. With the development of the mass-produced transistor receiver, a set that cost £35.50 in 1965 was available ten years later for £5.00. Little wonder that by 1974 the number of radios in Africa, Asia and Latin America had soared to 130 million.

The radio missionaries had not been slow to respond to these new opportunities. HCJB has long since expanded its audience beyond the Quichua and Latin America, beaming its Good News as far as Japan, the Soviet Union and the South Pacific. To provide power for its ten transmitters with a cumulative output of one million watts, the station has constructed its own hydroelectric power station, high in the Andes, generating enough electricity to supply a city of 200 000 people. This may sound extravagant, but HCJB has extravagant plans for using it. In Ecuador, the sights are set on the year 2000. In its prospectus, 'The World by 2000', HCJB states its intention to provide every man, woman and child on earth with the opportunity to hear the gospel on the radio in a language which they can understand. Two other major evangelical radio missions, the Far East Broadcasting Company and Trans World Radio, are involved in this global plan. Between them, they intend to double the number of languages in which they broadcast, bringing the total to 246 by the year 2000. In pursuit of this goal, Trans World Radio has just opened another one-million-watt transmitter in Monte Carlo.

While it is true that evangelical broadcasts in the vernacular have been effective to some degree, it is almost impossible to gauge with any certainty who is listening and how they respond. This will not deter HCJB from stepping up its efforts to Ecuador as well as the rest of the world. Like the Catholics who follow the teachings of liberation theology, its message is directed largely at the under-privileged for the simple reason that the poor are the bulk of the population. Like the Catholics, the evangelicals in their way are opting for the poor.

Other missionaries in Latin America have quite deliberately taken a different course and are opting for the rich and powerful. This age-old mission tactic of getting to the leadership first worked in the initial evangelisation of Europe, then in the Pacific and eventually in Africa. Now Southern Baptist missionary Manny Manferd and his wife Becky are trying it in the Chilean capital of Santiago. Manny is a very unusual phenomenon: a Christian missionary who also happens to be a Jew. He is an accountant, but as well as looking after Southern Baptist finances in Chile, he also has a dedicated passion for souls – in particular the souls of the ruling class. The Manferds have turned their home into a mission station devoted to the salvation of colonels' wives and bankers' widows. How they reached this apparently inaccessible group of wealthy women is a tale of ingenuity and patience. Becky advertised her intention to give lessons in handicrafts and in English conversation. Nothing was said about the Bible. Ten years later, she can proudly boast that despite a terrible beginning when nobody came, 3000 women have now attended her classes and many of them, she believes, have taken the gospel away with them. Biblical texts are introduced into the conversation lessons – not the most subtle method, but Becky claims that it works. As well as English, classes are held in flower arranging and handicrafts. So successful have classes been that they have overflowed into adjoining outbuildings and Becky has had to recruit former pupils as teachers. Manny believes that in Chile it is more difficult to reach the wealthier classes than to reach the poor as they are less open about their physical and spiritual needs. He is also concerned about the high cost of providing churches in middle-class areas where the expectations are greater: 'For sixteen thousands dollars we have a church – it's not much of a building, I admit – but it meets the people's needs ... but in the rich part of town it's going to need pews and a carpet and an attractive environment. It's going to take maybe a quarter of a million dollars.' In the long run, though, Manny feels that the wealthy may be a more cost-effective investment than the poor as they can influence those beneath them: 'The gospel may not sift upwards but it may sift downwards. Our hope is to get to the upper class and to the leaders'.

Manny rejects the suggestion that politics could be part of his Christian mission and does not accept liberation theology and its insistence on political commitment: when it comes to politics, the missionaries consult the Lord. Above all, Manny and Becky insist that what they are doing is totally *non*-political. In reply, Father Dan Driscoll might have repeated the anecdote about a Brazilian Bishop who was accused of being political. The Bishop remarked that in the days before liberation theology changed his thinking, he used to bless banks and dine with the rich and with the military, 'and no one accused me of being political. Now that I am defending the right of the poor, I am attacked for being political. The truth is, I was always political. I just changed sides.'

8   The Blood of the Martyrs is the Seed of the Church?

Yet more, O my God, more toil, more agony, more suffering for thee.

St Francis Xavier

Manila, Philippines. A delegate called it the nearest thing to a spiritual nuclear power plant. More than forty intercessors prayed in shifts around-the-clock during the ten day Second International Congress for World Evangelisation that began July 11 1989. Prayer warriors supported an estimated four thousand evangelical leaders from more than one hundred countries. Each intercessor committed to pray at least six hours a day in a designated hotel room. Almost immediately results were visible. Thai and Laotian participants, who had been delayed, arrived on time. Soviet representatives were granted visas. Major technical problems were resolved...

That was just one of the press releases that flooded out of the 'media relations' office of Lausanne II. In 1974, 2700 evangelical leaders had gathered in Lausanne where they heard, among others, Dr Billy Graham proclaim his belief that 'World evangelisation is now a possibility before the end of the century'. Fifteen years later, at Lausanne II in Manila, 4000 delegates were once again focusing on the year 2000. The Congress theme, 'Proclaim Christ until He Comes', was a reminder that, for many, AD 2000 is much more than a special birthday. Predictably, there was a fair measure of mutual congratulation on progress made and a slightly nervous cheer for what is claimed to be a major breakthrough for Christianity in Asia. Nervous because the gains are apparently being made by Pentecostals and Charismatics with whom the evangelicals have, at best, an uneasy alliance. It may in fact have struck some of the delegates that there was a certain irony about holding the event in Manila; or perhaps it was located there deliberately to focus attention on the magnitude of their task. Despite gains in South Korea, the Philippines is still the only major Christian country in Asia. The missionaries were successful there for the same reasons they were successful in Africa, Latin America and throughout the Pacific basin. Roman Catholic priests entered the Philippines on the arm of the Spanish conquerors and found there numerous vulnerable tribes adhering to their traditional religions. In these circumstances, the Church scored another extraordinary success.

Elsewhere in Asia, Christian progress has been slow, even negligible. Wherever missionaries have encountered other great religious cultures such as Buddhism, Hinduism or Islam, the people have remained quite resistant and sometimes downright hostile. Moreover, because of high birth rates in those Asian countries, the number of Christians may actually decline as a proportion of the whole. David Barrett predicts that the total number of Christians world-wide will increase by less than 1 per cent by the end of the millennium. Despite these sober calculations, in evangelical circles there seems to be a revival of triumphalist attitudes that informed the work of people like Lars Dahle a century ago. Dahle was a Norwegian futurologist who worked out a mathematical formula which enabled him to predict categorically that the entire human race could be Christian by the year 1990. This assumed that the religious cultures of Asia were suddenly going to collapse: in view of the historical evidence so far, the likelihood of this happening is remote. The fact that missionaries have failed to make mass conversions in Asia does not make their stay any less interesting. On the contrary, it is a tale of extraordinary obstinacy and persistence in the face of every kind of adversity.

It begins with the spread of Christianity through the Roman Empire into Egypt and Syria; from here the apostle Thomas is believed to have gone to India as the first missionary in the first century and to have founded the Church of the Thomas Christians. The next great missionary thrust to the East came when the Nestorian Christians spread from Syria, first into Persia and then, in the seventh century, along the trade routes into China. The Emperor permitted the Nestorians to establish monasteries but it seems that their adherents never numbered more than a few thousand, although the Church did survive 200 years before it fell victim to Taoist and Buddhist persecution and declined into oblivion. The modern missionary movement in Asia began with the founding of the Jesuit order in 1534. Within a few years, its members had taken the Catholic faith to the limits of the known world. Among the founder members was Francis Xavier, a Basque priest who stands out as one of the greatest missionaries of all time. After spending seven years revitalising a moribund Church in Portugal's Indian possessions, he set his sights on Japan, a country about which few facts were known. When he landed in Kagoshima in 1549 he realised that he was not dealing with simple, uncultivated people but with a civilisation that was in some respects superior to his own. He was impressed by their good manners, sense of honour, sociability and thirst for knowledge and recognised that it would be vital to send missionaries of the highest quality, men who would be able to adapt their message and their methods to the customs of the Japanese. This was a thoroughly unorthodox approach at a time when it was generally assumed that everything non-Christian was valueless

Matthew Ricci, left, *a missionary in advance of his time, believed in retaining the best of the Eastern cultures in which he worked and he urged his missionaries to adapt to local customs and adopt native dress.*

and had to be destroyed before the correct Christian structures could be installed.

One characteristic of Japanese thinking proved to be both a curse and a blessing to Xavier's efforts: contrary to Western tradition, religions were not, and are not, regarded as mutually exclusive. Xavier learned that the Japanese were perfectly happy to listen to the Christian message and even to attend mass, but could see no reason to abandon their traditional Shinto and Buddhist beliefs in order to do so. Nevertheless, from the strategic standpoint, the timing of Xavier's arrival in

Japan was fortunate. During the Sengoku Period, there was no strong central authority and the country was torn by strife among 250 daimyos, local rulers who had total control over their own fiefdoms. Some of them saw great advantage in building up foreign contacts, not least because opportunities for trade gave them access to firearms. The disunity also meant that if the missionaries were persecuted by one ruler, they could quickly move on. Xavier remained in Japan for more than two years and put in place a plan for the evangelisation of the people that was initially very successful. He had realised that in order to gain converts, it was essential first to win over the local rulers. Once one had been converted, others quickly followed suit and in some instances not only the ruler but all his subjects were baptised at once.

The next milestone was the arrival in Japan in 1579 of the Italian Jesuit Alessandro Valignano. There was already a community of 150 000 Christians in Japan, and they so impressed Valignano with their lively faith and enthusiasm that he had visions of a totally Christian nation in the north of Asia. To help realise this dream, he set about founding seminaries, colleges and a novitiate for training Japanese priests. The first ordination took place in 1601; by that time there were estimated to be 300 000 baptised believers in the land. The missionary effort had gained such momentum that it must have seemed irreversible. But while the Church had been growing, profound political changes had occurred that did not bode well for its future. By the beginning of the seventeenth century Japan had been unified under the Tokugawa shoguns. The missionaries were now unable to seek the protection of local rulers and were entirely at the mercy of new overlords. The first intimation of trouble came when the missionaries managed to displease Hideyoshi, one of the powerful generals who had helped unite the country. Hideyoshi had appeared to be on intimate terms with the Jesuits but, on 24 July 1587, after a bout of drinking, he flew into a tantrum and ordered the missionaries to leave the country: 'Japan is a country of the Gods of Japan and for the padres to come here and preach a devilish law is a most reprehensible and evil thing ... Within 20 days, they must return to their own country.'

Although the order was not immediately enforced, it was the beginning of the end of the brief and brilliant flowering of Christianity in Japan. A further decree, much fiercer in tone, set in train a ruthless persecution that continued until all overt vestiges of Christianity had been destroyed. The new edict was the work of Hideyoshi's successor, Ieyasu, the first of the shoguns. His action was triggered by a growing suspicion that the missionaries were the advance guard for the Spanish

'Ana-tsurushi' or hanging in the cess-pit was a torture reserved for the priests. They were tortured by the Tokugawa not as a punishment but to force them to apostasise.

King; and it may well be that the seeds were planted by English and Dutch Protestants who now frequented his court and looked for any opportunity to do the Papists down. What is more, the unquestioning obedience of his Christian subjects to their foreign religious teachers was quite unacceptable to him.

When the second decree of expulsion was promulgated, a number of missionaries left Japan but many remained and tried to continue their ministry in hiding. All of them were hunted down and put to death. In *The Christian Century in Japan*, C.R. Boxer has charted the systematic destruction of the Church under Ieyasu and, more particularly, under his successors. Iemitsu, the third shogun, took pleasure in devising brutal methods in order to exterminate the Christians. Whole communities were put to the test. They were forced to trample upon a *fumie*, a small plaque bearing a carved image of the Virgin and Child, and those who refused were executed. Crucifixion was the usual fate, but, in a cruel refinement, the victims were crucified upside down on the shoreline. As the tide came in, they slowly drowned. Another common form of execution both for missionaries and Japanese Christians was by burning alive, with up to 150 000 people coming to witness the spectacle. Glorious martyrdoms of this kind did not best serve the purpose of the Tokugawa; what was needed to discredit the missionaries was apostasy. In order to make them recant their faith, execution was preceded by torture carried out with such precise cruelty that resistance usually proved impossible. Most devilish and successful among the torments they devised was the *ana-tsurushi*, or hanging in the pit. According to Boxer's description, the victim was tightly bound and then suspended head-down in a pit containing filth and excreta. So that the rush of blood to the head did not cause the victim to become insensible, the forehead was cut with a knife just sufficiently that the bleeding relieved the pressure. Some survived more than a week but most victims died within a few days. Many Japanese recanted their faith.

The missionaries held out until 1652. But then, after six hours of insufferable pain, the leader of the mission, Christavao Ferrcira, gave the signal for apostasy. It seems that altogether seven missionaries, all Jesuits, gave way under torture; all but two of them later revoked their apostasy and died the martyr's death. During the twenty-four years of the great Japanese persecution, sixty-two European missionaries were put to death together with thousands of Japanese Christians. It was to be more than 200 years before the Japanese would again open their doors to missionaries but even then, they did not open their hearts. Despite fervent evangelism by all denominations of the Protestant and Catholic Churches over the past one hundred years, the number of

Christians remains stubbornly below one per cent. According to accepted wisdom, the Church grows strongly when it feeds on the blood of its martyrs and there are convincing examples of missions that flourished despite – or even because of – persecution. In Asia every country tells a different tale. In Japan, the Church was struck a blow from which it never recovered. In China, there is growing evidence that the period of persecution that followed the Communist revolution has stimulated the growth of a small but truly indigenous Chinese Church; whereas in Thailand, Christians have generally been tolerated and even welcomed although the missionaries have never managed to gain momentum.

The first Protestant missionaries to enter Thailand were the American Congregationalists who arrived in 1831; they pulled out eighteen years later without having baptised a single convert. The American Presbyterians showed more fortitude and stayed for nineteen years until they at last brought their first Thai Buddhist into the Christian fold. The indifference with which the Christian message was heard, although the missionaries themselves were welcomed, remains a puzzle even today. Daniel McGilvray's memoir, *A Half Century among the Siamese and the Lao*, published in 1912, provides some clues. When McGilvray arrived in Bangkok in 1858 the Presbyterian Mission had very few converts to show for its first twenty-five years, there was squabbling with other missions, money was short and, because of ill-health, so was manpower. The missionaries had great difficulty learning the Thai language and even greater difficulty in understanding the culture. Furthermore, they felt neglected by those at home who were much more excited by events in China which was just opening up to missionary endeavour. The only encouraging development had been the accession to the throne of King Mongkut who was quite friendly towards the missionaries. He had learned English from American Protestants and Latin from the French Catholic Bishop of Bangkok and saw the missionaries as a useful source of education for his people.

Daniel McGilvray had grown up in the United States, the son of a Scotsman who had rigid ideas of family discipline and piety. He describes Sunday routine as follows: 'A sunrise prayer meeting, breakfast, a prayer meeting at nine, a sermon at ten, an intermission and then another sermon. The sermons were not accounted of much worth unless they were an hour long'. There seems no doubt that in rejecting his father's brand of devotion, McGilvray developed a flexibility and tolerance that were invaluable in the difficult conditions of the Siam mission field.

Unlike most of his missionary contemporaries, some of his closest friends were Buddhist abbots and monks and he had a thorough

The young prince (a son of King Mongkut of Siam) is attended by a personal slave who must approach on his knees. It was King Mongkut who first made missionaries welcome in Siam. He had no time for their religion but he valued them as educators.

understanding of their faith. He also had a boundless curiosity about all aspects of Siamese culture and set himself the task of learning the language. After six years in Bangkok, McGilvray felt ready to attempt what was to be his life's work: to bring the gospel to the Northern Thai. At that time, the six northern principalities were ruled by feudal princes, each virtually sovereign but owing allegiance to the King of Siam. The most important of these was Chiang Mai and it was there that he determined to establish his mission. Despite a long and arduous journey to reach Chiang Mai, he was full of confidence. From the moment they reached the principality, McGilvray and his little band were celebrities, especially as they were the first-ever permanent

Western residents. For months they lived as in a goldfish bowl, in a little house without walls, surrounded by gawping crowds. While his young wife and children found this curiosity nerve-racking, McGilvray saw it as so many opportunities to proclaim the gospel.

Despite the problems, McGilvray felt that he was making progress. In order to establish his mission he had sought the permission of Chiang Mai's ruler, Kawilorot, and for a while it seemed that the prince was supportive. But as McGilvray began to win converts, the ruler's attitude changed. His suspicions were perhaps aroused by learning that among the first Christian converts were men and women of position and influence, including a member of the royal family. To a feudal despot like Kawilorot, Christianity may have seemed to pose a threat to the old order and to his own power; and he was probably right. His reaction was to accuse two of the Christian converts of refusing to perform their feudal duties and to have them executed. Although the killings proved to be an isolated incident and Kawilorot died soon after, he had struck a shrewd blow at the infant Church. Shaken but undeterred, McGilvray was convinced that the church would be nourished by the blood of martyrs. However, far from leading to further conversions, the killings had the effect of scattering the Christians. Before the oppression began in 1869, McGilvray had been able to stir up interest in Christianity among community leaders and the intelligentsia. Four of his first seven converts were drawn from the middle and upper classes. After 1869 most of the converts came from the margins of society, outcasts accused of witchcraft or poor people who had benefited from missionary charity or medicine. There was another damaging consequence of the martyrdoms: fearing an all-out attack on the mission, McGilvray had appealed for protection from the Bangkok government. This the King was happy to grant for it gave him an excuse to intervene and encroach upon the jurisdiction of the local ruler. Thus, without intending to, the missionaries became allied with the growing power of Siam. This privileged position became evident as the missionaries themselves became substantial landowners with opulent homes and retinues of servants. The gulf between the increasingly powerful missionaries and the now powerless converts grew ever wider until the relationship became essentially one of patronage.

McGilvray was well aware that many of those who came to his mission were only seeking medical treatment. Far from resenting this, he deeply regretted that he was neither a qualified physician nor a surgeon. What little medicine he knew, was self-taught and he had to do the best he could. He was able to relieve much suffering with the help of quinine, which was a boon in a country where malaria was rife.

His 'missionary medicine' was regarded with wonderment, especially when all native potions had failed. Goitre was another common illness which had proved incurable. McGilvray learned that potassium iodide provided an almost certain remedy, and quickly gained a reputation as a healer who could cure any disease. However, judged by modern standards, some of the treatments he prescribed were so drastic and so apparently mistaken, that one wonders how the patients survived. After twelve years' work, forty converts had been gathered into the Chiang Mai Church. Many of those who were not beneficiaries of missionary medicines were victims of witchcraft. Among the Northern Thai there was a widespread belief in demonic possession; and accusation of witchcraft was a common device for getting rid of envied rivals or disagreeable neighbours. If the accusations held, the unfortunate individuals and their families were driven out of their homes and off their lands and became utterly destitute. When it became known that the missionaries had no fear of demons and were prepared to offer a sanctuary many of the outcasts gratefully accepted the gospel and promised to obey their teachings.

As McGilvray travelled extensively through Northern Thailand, he discovered another fruitful area for evangelisation among the Hill Tribes, a nomadic group of peoples who wandered throughout the mountain region between Siam and Burma. Since they were not Buddhists but animists, and since they did not fall under the jurisdiction of any of the princes, they were likely to be a softer target for the missionaries than the Thai. McGilvray had neither the time nor the manpower to launch a major crusade, but he did identify them as a likely future mission field, and in that he proved to be right.

Daniel McGilvray died in Chiang Mai in 1911, aged 85. In the course of the fifty-three years he spent in Thailand he recorded a number of lasting achievements. He introduced both quinine and vaccination and his pioneering medical work was the beginning of five hospitals and a leprosarium. He opened the first Christian schools that quickly grew into an entire educational system with primary and secondary schools and a university. However, despite his determined efforts he was not able to establish any kind of mass movement towards Christianity. After forty-four years in Chiang Mai, he managed to achieve 4000 converts.

The period of persecution and the martyrdoms of the early days convinced the Thai that there was a social price to be paid for converting to Christianity. This was the result of the conflicting demands of the Church and the feudal overlords, particularly when it came to observing the Sabbath. When Christians were ordered to work on Sundays, the Church expected them to refuse even though they knew

Missionary preaching in Chungking, China, in the 1920s. China is no longer open to missionary endeavour but public worship is tolerated and there is evidence of a vigorous 'house-church' movement.

the consequences were imprisonment, beatings or even death. Faced with this impossible choice, most people decided to avoid the decision altogether. Given this confrontational attitude on the part of the Mission, some of the ruling classes believed that the foreigners were trying to create a new power structure in which the missionaries would be the patrons. The suspicion grew to the point where straightforward evangelism became almost impossible and all the Mission was able to do with any degree of freedom was medical and educational work. So, in the end, the Thai realised that they could benefit from the missionaries' good works without making any great commitment to the Christian faith. This has not changed greatly since McGilvray's day.

In Asia, the missionaries never enjoyed the same freedom as they did in Africa. Large parts of the continent – Japan, China, Thailand, Korea – never fell within the European empires and, with the exception of the Philippines, even in those countries that were conquered and colonised, the missionaries were not granted the freedom they enjoyed elsewhere. French Indo-China was virtually closed to Protestants and plans to establish a mission were turned down. In British India, no missionaries were allowed to enter for some time. The East India Company fought long and hard to keep the missionaries out, arguing, 'The sending out of missionaries into our Eastern possessions is the maddest, most extravagant, most costly, most indefensible project which has ever been suggested by a moonstruck fanatic.' The Company was terrified that the already delicate and dangerous relations between its Hindu and Islamic subjects would be greatly exacerbated by the preaching of Christianity and might lead to rebellion. Judging by the tensions that led up to the Indian Mutiny, the judgement was not far wrong. At the time, rumours circulated of a British plan forcibly to convert all India to Christianity. After much campaigning in England, India was opened up to both Catholic and Protestant evangelism in 1833, albeit with great misgivings. The Catholics already had several enclaves in India, established by the Jesuits in the seventeenth century, when they had enjoyed almost as much success as they had initially in Japan and China. Yet, by the end of the British Raj, after one hundred years of uninterrupted missionary effort, neither Protestants nor Catholics had made great headway with the Indian masses. Converts from Islam were few and for the most part the new Christians were once again drawn from marginal groups – untouchables, hill tribes, Anglo-Indians – who had little to lose and much to gain by adopting the foreigners' religion. In India, the missionaries faced a twofold disadvantage: not only was Christianity regarded as alien but it was identified in Hindu and Muslim eyes with the rule of a foreign power. Much missionary effort foundered on the rock of Nationalist sentiment.

9 'And some fell on stony ground'

In this day and age, we do not need converts to Christianity or Buddhism ... our common enemies are materialism, militarism and consumerism. Buddhist and Christian should join hands in working for peace and social justice.

S. Sivaraksa, *A Socially Endangered Buddhism*

The fortunes of Christian missionaries to Asia have in many areas declined substantially since the end of the nineteenth century. A hundred years ago, missionaries flocked to China, Indo-China and Burma. Today, those doors are tightly closed, and even the Indian subcontinent is far less welcoming than it used to be. In Indonesia, too, the stirring of Islamic fundamentalism is giving Christians cause for unease. Missionaries have had success in South Korea and Taiwan but in the larger mission fields evangelism has either been banned or has failed to make much impact. Today, fewer than 5 per cent of the people of Eastern Asia are Christian.

For 200 years Japan remained entirely closed to Christian penetration. Even when missionaries were once again admitted in 1859, they found themselves facing an uphill task. Christianity was still a prohibited religion punishable by death and the penal laws were not finally rescinded until 1889. However, when Catholic missionaries returned to those parts of Japan that had suffered religious persecution under the shoguns they discovered tiny groups of Catholics who had managed to survive. These *Kakure-Kirishitan* (Christians in hiding) had secretly passed their belief from generation to generation with almost no literature, no priesthood and in total isolation from other Christians outside Japan. They had evolved their own brand of Christianity and, even up to the present, have resisted all efforts to draw them back into the mainstream of Catholic orthodoxy. This should perhaps give pause for thought to the large missionary community that labours, with very little reward, throughout Japan today. Despite a huge investment of manpower and money and decades of effort, the number of Christians remains around one million in a total population of over 120 million. In explanation, missionaries point out that for them the modern history of Japan could hardly have been more unfavourable. Their reappearance in Japan coincided with the

Only the façade remains of this magnificent church built in Macau by the Portuguese. Despite 400 years of missionary endeavour, Asia is the continent with the lowest percentage of Christians.

accession to the throne in 1867 of the Emperor Meiji and the beginning of a period of rapid industrialisation and Westernisation. This willingness to absorb outside ideas and systems did not extend to religion, even though the new Constitution gave the Japanese freedom of religious belief. The Meiji government made Shintoism the national religion with the Emperor as its highest priest. Before long, devotion to the Emperor became Emperor-worship which in turn developed into ultranationalism and intense patriotism; this eventually precipitated the Japanese involvement in the Second World War. But Christians and Christian missionaries faced severe problems of conscience long before that. The new orthodoxy demanded that whatever one's private religion or ideology might be, every citizen should believe in the national destiny expressed through the Emperor and guided by Emperor-worship and state Shinto. In 1911, the government issued an ordinance that all schoolchildren should attend Shinto shrines and participate in their ceremonies. Refusal to do so was heresy. The authorities argued that this did not conflict with freedom of religion since attendance at the shrine was a gesture of respect of ancestors and not an act of worship. Many missionaries and Christians were unable to accept this and found themselves in conflict with both the law and the majority of the Japanese people. Christian teachers in public schools were challenged about their beliefs and ran the risk of being stigmatised as unpatriotic. As time went on, all Christians were attacked politically and socially as 'un-Japanese', and some were even imprisoned on the grounds of questionable beliefs and lese-majesty. After the Second World War, the Emperor renounced his divinity and the new Constitution guaranteed freedom of thought and belief, but even today Christians are still regarded with suspicion for being in some way 'different'. Paradoxically, however, not only does Christian Mission continue but Christians themselves enjoy an influence quite out of proportion to their small numbers. Some of Japan's most admired schools and universities are Christian foundations; and Christian welfare organisations such as orphanages and clinics have done valuable pioneering work. The missionaries have felt sufficiently encouraged to continue their endeavours in the hope that one day a mass movement will sweep the land. Although exact figures are hard to come by, there could be as many as 4000 missionaries in Japan, the largest single group being the Catholics with 900 workers. There are numerous Protestant societies, some of them very small; among the largest are the Southern Baptists with a workforce of 205 and the Overseas Missionary Fellowship (OMF) with 120.

The Overseas Missionary Fellowship was formerly known as the China Inland Mission and, like several societies now working in Asia, was founded specifically to bring the gospel to China when its doors were opened to Western influence in the latter part of the last century. The China Inland Mission was founded 125 years ago by Hudson Taylor. Sickened by the complacency of the church he attended in England, he set about gathering workers for mission to China. The Mission grew to over a thousand missionaries before they were forced to withdraw with the Communist take-over of China in 1951. OMF still has over a thousand missionaries in Eastern Asia, but they are now scattered over nine countries. Its large operation in Japan and Korea is headed by Bill Fearnehough who, with his wife Sheila, has been in Japan for twenty-five years. Although much of his work is now administrative, in the past he and Sheila were solely involved in the difficult task of church planting. This is a jargon term that, outside missionary circles, is easily misunderstood. In its initial stages, it has nothing to do with church building but rather with forming the nucleus of a Christian community that may one day grow into a congregation that may one day be housed in a purpose-built church.

Bill Fearnehough is adamant that the main reason why OMF is in Japan is to establish churches which can grow to become independent and self-supporting, run by Japanese. Even to attempt church planting in Japan is a daunting task for which the missionary will need years

James Hudson Taylor, founder of the China Inland Mission, with his wife in Chinese dress. Until the Communist take-over in 1949, China was one of the most active of all Christian mission fields, vigorously contested by Catholics and Protestants.

Bill Fearnehough discourages his Japanese converts from visiting the Shinto shrines. This effectively cuts them off from all the major festivals and many family activities – part of the high price of being a Japanese Christian.

of preparation. As a young man, Bill Fearnehough was quite unprepared for mission work of any kind and for several years was involved
in the family-owned engineering business in Sheffield. But instead of a
comfortable life in a spacious house in one of the city's more affluent
suburbs, he and his wife obeyed the missionary call and found that
their home was to be a tiny Japanese apartment. Once in Japan,
their first major obstacle was the language which, for some aspiring
missionaries, proves to be the end of the road. Bill admits that it can
take five years and even longer before the missionary feels at home
counselling a Japanese on a one-to-one basis. An added difficulty is
the strict verbal etiquette that demands that all persons are addressed
according to their status: 'Just when you think you've mastered the
verb "to go", you discover it is only used in that form to the dog!'
Having acquired the minimum language skills, the Fearnehoughs were
ready to plant their first churches. They were sent to the island of
Hokkaido in Northern Japan where the OMF effort was concentrated.
They quickly discovered that even the most superficial relationships
were hard to establish. Among Japanese men, most social contacts are
made at their place of work or at the bars where they assemble in the
evening while Japanese women are still confined to the home. There
is very little opportunity for any kind of casual encounter with
Japanese, let alone the sort of meeting where religion might be
discussed. One device employed by most missionaries is to wander the
streets and shopping malls handing out Christian leaflets. The response
to this approach is extremely small: Kenneth McVetti of the Evangelical
Alliance Mission (TEAM), which has a huge publishing operation in
Japan, has estimated that it takes 36 000 tracts to get *one* person inside
a church. The Fearnehoughs came to a similar conclusion when, in the
early days, they handed out their tracts and then spent ten months
without a single person turning up to a church service. 'We used to sit
around in our front room with the chairs set out and the hymn books
ready and week after week, nobody came ... I must admit it was pretty
tough ... and then, one day, a woman came into our front room and
looked around and said "Where's the church?" and I couldn't help
saying "You are the church".' That experience is more the rule than
the exception. Progress is always slow – a score of churches have been
established in Hokkaido but rarely do the congregations exceed fifty
and are often much smaller.

One of the lessons the Fearnehoughs have learned is that the best
way to establish contact with the Japanese is through the women.
Japan is not a country where missionaries can attract adherents by
offering education or medicine or material goods. In almost every other
mission field, however poor the missionaries may be, they will be much

better off than the local population; but in Japan their life-style is likely to be modest in comparison to their Japanese neighbours. However, the missionaries do have two things that Japanese women often want: a knowledge of English and of European cooking. With plenty of time on their hands, Japanese housewives can often be tempted to respond to advertisements or leaflets offering English lessons or cookery classes. Sheila Fearnehough has used these classes as a means of winning the confidence of the women; as the friendship develops, she introduces a period of Bible study into each session. This is not a new approach: it was used as long ago as 1954 by Stella Cox, a veteran missionary of thirty-six years in Japan. She tells how she began showing women 'how to make Western delights like three bean salad or apple cake while sharing the gospel. Are the women really interested in the Gospel? Not necessarily. They listen to be courteous but keep coming to learn cooking. Some find it a convenient time to take a short nap. Regardless, the seed sown comes up in time and it rejoices my heart ... The publication of my book, *Aunt Stella's Easy American Cakes* has helped sow the seed in so many hearts.'

Bill and Sheila hope that in this way they will eventually evangelise entire families. It is almost the only way to reach Japanese men who are sometimes persuaded by their wives to take English lessons and the concomitant Bible class. Conversion is likely to be a long and laborious task and, at the end of the day, there are frequent disappointments. All missionaries in Japan have learned to have modest expectations of success. They know that any Japanese turning to Christianity will have to pay a heavy social price. There is the danger of encountering hostility and even ostracism from family and friends and there is the certainty of cutting themselves off from the mainstream of Japanese life where conformity is all-important. As a convert to Bill's brand of evangelical Christianity, it will be particularly difficult for the Japanese male. He will be forbidden to take part in the heavy drinking sessions that traditionally cement the social bonds between work-mates, or in the stag parties to the red light districts of the larger cities. Nor will he be allowed to attend the thirteen annual festivals at the Shinto shrines. The shrines play an important part in all aspects of life. The Japanese visit them regularly, for everyday activities such as success in examinations or blessing a new car, and for major festivals marking the beginning of spring, the Emperor's birthday, the gathering of the harvest and many others. At Hokkaido's main festival in June, more than one million people visit the shrine. Bill Fearnehough accepts that attendance of the shrine and observing the festivals is an integral part of Japanese life but he is uncompromising in his belief that Christian converts should turn their back on their own culture. Bill

A young couple bring their new car to the Shinto shrine to be blessed.

said there were no circumstances in which he could condone attendance at the shrine 'except perhaps as a tourist'. Such an unbending attitude is likely to cause maximum hardship among people who place great store in conformity and in belonging to a social group. Nearly 1400 years ago, when Pope Gregory the Great sent Augustine to England, he advised that traditional habits and customs be turned to the service of God as a means of winning the people. For today's evangelicals, there is no such spirit of accommodation; total severance from the old life is part of being 'born again'.

Bill Fearnehough takes the view that Japanese Christians are more than compensated for detaching themselves from their social groups by joining the fellowship of the church community. Japanese churches develop into exceptionally close-knit groups whose members not only pray together but play together. Financial support of the church is provided by the congregation and many Christians give one-tenth of their income directly to the church. One of the reasons Japanese congregations have not grown much beyond thirty to fifty persons is that this seems to be the maximum number which permits the close social interaction they seem to value so much. Bill Fearnehough is aware of the danger that churches may become rather like exclusive little clubs and fears that this could limit future growth.

The OMF takes a hard line on alcoholism and has set up a residential rehabilitation centre for between ten and twenty male alcoholics in Sapporro. Anyone joining an OMF Bible class is expected to forgo alcohol completely. Bill Fearnehough recognises that there is no scriptural authority for prohibition and that it may adversely affect Church growth yet believes that it is justifiable because of the social problems with alcoholism in Japan. The rehabilitation centre offers institutional life and strict Christian teaching – it is very reminiscent of similar establishments elsewhere, above all of Salvation Army hostels.

Far away to the south in Tokyo, Father Neyrand, an elderly French Catholic priest, is carrying on a missionary enterprise of a different kind. His mission field is the red-light district of Shinjuku. Every evening, he walks from the metro station to Kabuki-cho where the neon signs that beckon from every high-rise proclaim the presence of more than two thousand bars within four city blocks. Inside one of the gaudiest of these buildings, Father Neyrand enters a lift plastered from floor to ceiling with pictures of pouting hostesses and topless barmaids. Arriving at the fourth floor, he steps out into his mission headquarters. Ten years ago he opened a bar here as the only way he could devise of meeting the 'salarymen' or middle managers on a sufficiently sustained basis to bring them the gospel. Almost all of his customers are regulars who drop in for a few drinks after work before going home to the suburbs. While the Fearnehoughs try to reach the men through their wives, Father Neyrand approaches them via the bottle. The 'Pub' has at least been popular enough to pay its own way and Father Neyrand also feels that from the mission standpoint it has been effective, not only because he has actually baptised a number of his clients but also because of the comradely atmosphere in the place. Many Christians would disapprove of a missionary selling alcohol, whatever the reason; but everything has been done with the approval of the archdiocese and even the Archbishop himself sometimes drops in for a drink. For Father Neyrand the bar is simply a way of making a bridge between the Church and everyday life. In Europe, such bridges are unnecessary because the Church is woven into the fabric of life, but in Japan it is completely separate. The 'salarymen' bring many of their anxieties and problems with them to the bar where the priest does his best to give advice and comfort. 'To say that Christ is important is all very well, but what does he bring people? That's where I might use the Japanese word *ikigari*, which you might translate as "the meaning of life" . . . that is the route by which I present Christianity'. If his customers show any interest, he will invite them to his Bible circle or to mass, and everyone will be asked to the big party at Christmas. In this way, he has baptised thirty converts over the ten years. The slow rate of progress does not dishearten him: it simply takes time.

One regular customer is the distinguished novelist Shusaku Endo who met Neyrand in France when both were young men. They renewed their friendship years later after the Second World War, when Father Neyrand came to Japan as a missionary. Endo has been called the Japanese Graham Greene. In that he is a Catholic novelist and his books reflect his own inner conflicts and anguish about his faith, the comparison is an apt one. Much of his work concerns Japan's failure to adopt Christianity despite its success in absorbing other foreign ideas and customs. Endo's conclusion, expressed notably in *Silence*, the story of Christian Mission in the seventeenth century, is that Christianity will never be transplanted into 'the swamp' of Japan unless and until it can truly and radically adapt itself to the prevailing social, cultural and spiritual traditions. The Christian God is presented all too often as a strict and demanding father figure, most unsympathetic to the Japanese. In his bar, Father Neyrand is trying to practise what Endo preaches in his books. Instead of attempting to uproot the Japanese from their culture, he is hoping that Christ can set them free *within* their culture. Only then will the Japanese cease to think of Christianity as 'the foreigner's religion'.

This rather derogatory image of Christianity was one of the findings of a survey carried out by the J. Walter Thompson Company's Market Research Bureau. The committee that commissioned the survey was chaired by Father Jose M. de Vera, Professor of the Department of Journalism at Sophia Catholic University in Tokyo. Father de Vera confessed that the results of the survey left him even more puzzled than he was before. He pointed out that not only are there 908 Catholic schools in Japan, including twelve universities, with a total of 300 000 students; not only are there 33 Catholic hospitals, 51 children's homes and 146 day nurseries; there is now the evidence of the survey, which on the positive side described Christianity as bright, modern, active and a defender of high moral values, yet still the number of Catholic converts each year is only numbered in thousands.

While the slow growth of the Church continues to be a theological and cultural puzzle to the missionaries, Father de Vera has hope of better things to come. The increasing number of people who ask for baptism before dying is considered to be a sure sign of the 'delayed effect' of evangelisation efforts, although Father de Vera admitted that it might equally be regarded as taking out a last-minute insurance policy. An increasing number of young people are asking to be married in church even though they are not Catholic. However, a story in the French press suggests that this may be more a matter of changing fashion than changing faith. One of Japan's most popular television soap operas featured a picture-book wedding in a French village, whereupon an enterprising travel agency began promoting a package which included a wedding ceremony in the particular church. When it was discovered that the couples were not Catholics, a ban was placed on such weddings, and, in 1986, a similar ban ended the practice of Japanese tourists being married in Catholic churches in Guam. At one time, Father de Vera also opposed the marriage of non-Catholics yet has come to the view that the young couples whom he marries are looking for something religious in their lives, and that this is justification enough. Despite his guarded optimism, Father de Vera does not foresee any mass movement to Christianity. He recalls approvingly a Protestant missionary who described Japanese Christianity as a bonsai: 'very small, very beautiful, very cultivated ... You don't know whether it can be taken outside to face the storm'. Whether Christianity in Japan will ever again have to 'face the storm' is a question that all missionaries from time to time ask themselves. What they fear more than anything would be a revival of the nationalism that gave rise to the state Shintoism which would stigmatise Christian nonconformity not just as foreign but as unpatriotic. Bill Fearnehough admits that this is a possibility all Christians are aware of and that they are making every effort – even lobbying members of the government – to make sure that religious freedom is preserved.

It would be very easy to dismiss these fears as paranoid were it not for the recent personal histories of many missionaries working in Asia. The mass expulsion from China scattered men and women all over the East, to whatever countries still permit Christian evangelism – and to some countries that do not. Some of them settled in new mission fields, only to be thrown out for a second or even third time. Such was the fate of the Morse family who, for the time being, have come to rest in Northern Thailand, in the town of Chiang Mai. Drawn from four generations, the family has become in itself an entire mission organisation. It is headed by Eugene Morse who has recorded in his memoirs *Exodus To A Hidden Valley* the extraordinary saga of the Morse family wanderings that started almost seventy years ago. Eugene was only four months old when his father, J. Russell Morse, left the United States to establish a mission station on the Tibetan borders of China, an area so remote that it took four months on horseback to cover the final stages of the journey. Eugene and his brother Robert grew up speaking Chinese and Tibetan, just two of the languages they speak better than English. In 1929, the Morses were ordered to leave China because of the outbreak of civil war. They escaped by trekking through trackless jungle across the border into Burma. During the Second World War, the Morses found themselves totally cut off from the world on the China/Burma border and in a unique position to help the Allied war effort. J. Russell Morse and his sons set up an intelligence network among the hill tribes to search for allied pilots who often came down in the treacherous mountains known as 'The Hump'. The next upheaval came in 1949 when the Communist take-over of China forced the evacuation of all missionaries. The Morses moved their operations to the Putao area of Northern Burma where, for fourteen years, they worked among the Lisu tribal people. Their major achievement was the introduction of thirty-four varieties of fruit trees that laid the foundation of a prosperous fresh fruit and bottled juice industry that survives to this day. Another lasting benefit has been widespread literacy. None of the tribal languages had ever been written down until Robert mastered five of them well enough to give them alphabets and orthographies and the beginnings of a literature, invariably the Gospels.

The idyll was destroyed following a military coup by General U. Ne Win in 1962 that resulted in the expulsion of all missionaries. Rather than desert their Lisu friends, the Morse parents, two sons and their wives, an adopted Tibetan daughter and assorted offspring set off with 5000 tribespeople into the unknown. The plan was to walk to the Indian border 70 miles away – not only did they make the journey, but they eventually discovered a 'hidden valley' near the Indian border, where they settled, out of reach of Ne Win's troops, for the next six years. Before long, rumours began to circulate of a white patriarch who had established his dynasty deep in the jungle where he ruled over a secret kingdom. In 1972, the secret was out and the Morses were finally rounded up by Burmese troops and escorted out of the country. The following year, they arrived in Thailand and based their mission in Chiang Mai. Their reason for choosing Chiang Mai was determined by the presence nearby of an estimated 20 000 Lisu.

The Morse family history is an extreme case of the pressures faced by Christian missionaries; and although they now appear to be firmly established in Thailand, they are well aware that for them nothing is ever permanent. In Asia there are few countries where missionaries can feel completely confident of an uninterrupted future for their work. Even the Thais are sensitive on the subject of missionaries and if evangelism is not carried out in a tactful manner, their tolerant attitude may change. At present, in a country where 97 per cent of the population is Buddhist and 2 per cent Muslim, there are obviously very few Christians. Accurate figures are hard to come by but an estimate of 250 000 Catholics and 50 000 Protestants is one that circulates among Buddhists; missionary statistics put the figures somewhat higher. Whatever the truth of the matter, Christians offer no threat at all to the

Buddhist majority. There are large numbers of missionaries who, like the Morses, are working among the hill tribes. As the tribesmen are neither Buddhist nor ethnic Thai, national sensibilities are unlikely to be upset. It may well be, in fact, that the Thai government is making use of the missionaries to help pacify its sometimes unruly and independent-minded subjects.

If the Thai government does one day decide the missionaries must go, it will not be because of people like the Morses. They are well integrated into Thai society and several of the children have intermarried with Thais or members of the minority tribes. They are sensitive in their dealings with the Buddhist majority and careful not to give offence. That cannot be said of some of the other evangelicals. Sulak Sivaraksa is a Buddhist intellectual who was educated in Christian schools and who has a high regard for some aspects of the Christian faith. He is, however, severely irritated by evangelical literature that describes Thailand as 'the territory of Satan'; that declares '99 per cent of Thais are in bondage to demons'; that condemns Buddhism as 'idolatry' and 'a religion of hopeless escapism'; and which insists that 'without Christian revelation, there is no relationship with God'. As Sulak points out, this is the everyday language of a certain kind of mission literature, which is deeply offensive to Thai Buddhists. The main culprits are the 'new wave' of over 800 evangelicals, but at the same time Sulak is confident that their arrogant, judgemental approach will be counterproductive and without any lasting impact. That is just one Buddhist's opinion but one cannot help feeling that if Sulak is wrong and if the missionaries did start to make any significant progress among the mainstream Buddhists, Thai tolerance might be short-lived. After all, Buddhism is the state religion: the King is spiritual as well as temporal leader. Any real threat to Buddhist predominance might well be seen as a threat to the state itself. It was a former Prime Minister of Thailand who declared that any Thai subject who renounced his Buddhism ceased to be truly Thai.

10   The Greatest Challenge

One hears this name [Mohammed] in the bazaar and in the street, in the mosque and from the minaret, sailors sing it whilst hoisting their sails, coolies groan it to raise a burden, the beggars howl it to obtain alms; it is the cry of the faithful in attack, hushes babies to sleep as a cradle song, it is the pillow of the sick, the last word of the dying; it is written on the doorpost and in the hearts, as well as, since eternity, on the throne of God; the best name to give a child, the best to swear by for an end of all disputes.

Anon.

In 1947, the dream of one of the greatest Muslim poets, Dr Muhammad Iqbal, was realised. He had longed for a separate Muslim homeland within the Indian subcontinent. With partition it was achieved: Muhammad Ali Jinnah led his country to independence. The state was to be called Pakistan, meaning 'Land of the Pure' in Urdu. In 1958 a new capital city was created, named 'Islamabad', meaning 'Citadel of Islam'. Islam itself translates from Arabic as 'submission to God'. The signs were clear. In planning the new capital they would demonstrate that the Islamic faith was at the centre of everything and encompassed all aspects of personal and national life. The most imposing building would be the Shah Faisal Mosque, the biggest mosque in the world, with a prayer hall big enough for 15 000, and a marbled courtyard with space for 85 000 more. Built in the most dramatic of sites, against the foothills of the Himalayas, it resembles a gigantic eight-sided Bedouin tent made of white marble, suspended between four concrete minarets. Attached to the mosque is the International Islamic University, to which students come from all over the Muslim world. To Muslims, the mosque celebrates the fact that Islam is at the very foundation of the state. To the non-Muslim minorities, it appears to sound a warning: challenge Islam and you challenge the Republic itself. For the Christian missionary this is the stoniest ground.

Barely a mile from the mosque, Graham Burton holds a Christian service under a tree. There is no Protestant church building in the capital, so Burton and his tiny congregation worship in the open air. The small group of Christians are drawn from the poorest class in Pakistan. They live in the *bastis*, or shanties, in rough mud houses

The might of Islam.
The Shah Faisal Mosque,
Islamabad, built for
100 000 worshippers,
inspired by the shape of a
Bedouin tent. Islam is
firmly planted at the centre
of Pakistani national life.

hidden behind high walls and in river valleys, away from the view of passing diplomats and government personnel. Burton, an Anglican missionary from England, has set himself a difficult, some would say foolhardy, task: to build the first Protestant church in Islamabad. At first he used his own home as a temporary church, then, despite much opposition, managed to negotiate a site for the new building. He had to promise to build the church as far as possible from the city's many mosques. Then, in the spring of 1989, Salman Rushdie's *Satanic Verses* was published. It caused repercussions throughout the Muslim world and in Islamabad there were fierce demonstrations. In this tense and volatile atmosphere, Burton's church site was attacked by a group of Islamic fundamentalists. Building had barely started, but the foundations were damaged and a tent was burnt by the demonstrators. Work on the church was immediately and indefinitely suspended. Armed police moved in to protect what remained. In the history of relations between Islam and Christianity, it was a tiny incident, but it powerfully symbolised the uneasy, unequal relationship between the two great missionary religions in Pakistan.

Christians make up just 1.5 per cent of the population, while more than 95 per cent are Muslim. Many Muslims and Christians are tolerant of each other and urge peaceful coexistence. Both religions, however, have their extremists, whose fundamentalist reading of their own holy books makes them believe they have found the answer for all. Both Christianity and Islam claim to be universal religions, and each has a sense of world mission. Their claims are incompatible. Pakistan is just one of the frontiers on which the two great religions clash head on as they have done for over a thousand years in the continuing battle for the hearts and minds of the people.

Islam is the fastest-growing religion in Europe: six million Muslims live in the continent. Christian missionaries once travelled many thousands of miles to the Muslim mission field, now they believe that this mission field has come to them. For evangelical Christians there is no greater missionary challenge, and no greater threat, than Islam. There are an estimated 850 million Muslims world-wide. That, the missionary statisticians have calculated, makes two out of every eleven people in the world Muslim. For those bent on reaching the world with the Good News of Christ by the year 2000, such statistics are profoundly disturbing. More and more missionary attention turns to Islam and the appeals for volunteers for the Muslim mission field are urgent, even desperate. Many agencies are involved including Manarah Book Ministries which organises the distribution of Bibles in the Arab world: 'God's word must reach the Muslims of the Arab World ... Their message of darkness is reaching far and wide! Shall we lag behind – we who have God's message of light and salvation?' In the US, 'Frontiers' mission agency declares: 'Muslims. It's their turn! It is our goal to see 2000 unstoppable missionaries planting churches among 200 Muslim people groups in the next 20 years.' An anonymous Cyprus-based organisation looks for volunteers to help mail Gospels into the Arab world while Friends from Abroad seeks teams to spread the gospel among Asians in Britain. The recruitment drive is fierce but their successes among Muslims are few. In Morocco, for example, one missionary who worked for the Frontline mission reported that there were only about 300 Christians in a population of 26 million; more missionary graves in North Africa than Christian converts. Despite the very real sense of failure, the unquenchable optimism that typifies evangelical missionary endeavour is sustained. In the words of Patrick Johnstone, an evangelical author, 'The cracks in the seemingly impenetrable wall of Islam can be widened by prayer!' To the evangelical community, prayer is seen as a genuine and effective tool with which to combat Islam.

Pakistan is one of very few Muslim countries in which Christian missionaries are openly tolerated, and indeed, freedom of worship is enshrined in the constitution. Yet many people in the religious minorities claim consistent discrimination against them because they are not Muslim. But Pakistan remains at pains to prove itself tolerant, and while the mission societies complain that visas are becoming much harder to obtain, about a thousand missionaries continue to live and work there.

Historians argue about when the first Christian missionary arrived in the Indian subcontinent. Many believe that St Thomas the Apostle travelled to the southernmost tip of India, on his way passing through the valley of Taxila in the kingdom of Gandhara, a Buddhist state ruled by the Parthian dynasty in what is now northern Pakistan. A third-century romance, *The Acts of Thomas*, tells a tale of Thomas in India. In the story the Lord asks Thomas to travel to India to spread the Good News. But Thomas has no wish to go. The Lord arranges for Thomas to be sold as a slave to an Indian merchant. Thomas is taken to India and ordered to build a palace for the King Gundaphorus. The Apostle chooses to build the King, not a temporal palace of brick and marble, but a spiritual home in heaven, by giving to the poor all that the King has given him to build the palace. When the King demands to see his new palace, Thomas answers: 'Thou canst not see it now, but when thou departest this life, then thou shall see it.' Thomas is flung in jail. But God intervenes to release his Apostle, and the story ends happily as King Gundaphorus is baptised. Is there any truth in the romantic tale? While there was indeed a king called Gondophares, one of the greatest Parthian kings, who ruled in the first century AD in the north of present-day Pakistan, no one knows whether he received the itinerant Christian at his court. Even if St Thomas did make his way through the Taxila valley, his fleeting visit made no impact on the Buddhist state. He left no fledgling Church behind him, and there is no evidence that the conversion of Gondophares is anything more than wishful fancy.

It was the Islamic empire, not Christendom, that was first to establish its grip on what is today Pakistan. In so doing the Muslim invaders condemned Christianity to more than a thousand years of obscurity in this part of the world. When Islam came to Pakistan, it spread from both the north and the south. In 711 an Arab expedition under Muhammad bin Qasim established authority over the coastal hinterland as far north as Multan. Three centuries later, Mahmud of Ghazni extended his empire into the provinces. The new Islamic rulers chose Lahore as the cultural centre of the Punjab. In due course the Ghaznavid kingdom gave way to three centuries of rule by Muslim sultans based in Delhi. Then, in 1526, Babur, a descendant of Gengis Khan, defeated the last Delhi sultan and established the Moghul Empire. This ushered in the golden era of Islamic culture in Pakistan, spanning the reigns of the great emperors Akbar, Jehangir, Aurangzeb. These great emperors extended and consolidated their empire, and left a legacy of magnificent mosques, forts and gardens.

When the Christian missionaries arrived in the Indian subcontinent in the nineteenth century, despite the best efforts of the British East India Company to keep them out, the Moghul Empire had run its course. But if the political map was still being redrawn, the ink on the religious map had dried, indelibly. Islam was firmly established in North-western India, but as the century progressed, missionaries pushed deeper inland. In 1833 American Presbyterians arrived in the Punjab. Among the earliest of their missionaries was Charles Forman, after whom was named the Forman Christian College in Lahore, one of the premier educational institutions in Pakistan. The Church Missionary Society extended its work rapidly, reaching Amristar in 1852, and Peshawar on the north-west frontier three years later. But their numbers were small: by 1851 there were just 339 ordained missionaries in the whole of India, 600 if their wives were included, and they were spread through a country with an estimated population of 150 million. Their numbers alone determined that their impact would be limited. The Indian Mutiny of 1857 represented a further set-back: a contributory factor in the uprising against the colonial government was a rumour of plans forcibly to convert the entire population to Christianity. When violence flared, thirty-eight missionaries died in the fighting. No distinction was made between the representatives of Christ and the agents of Queen Victoria. This fact has been at the centre of the history of mission in Pakistan. In the eyes of the people, the missionaries have been firmly, fatally aligned with colonialism.

This legacy burdened the missionaries in the nineteenth and twentieth centuries as they strove to win the confidence, the trust and ultimately the soul of the Muslim population. Nowhere did they set themselves a more thankless task than in the mountainous strip bordering Afghanistan that today constitutes the North-Western Frontier Province of Pakistan. Its capital, Peshawar, is a walled frontier town where the Indian subcontinent meets Central Asia, a rich melting-pot of races and cultures. To modern visitors Peshawar appears to have leapt straight from the pages of the Old Testament with its labyrinthine streets and glittering bazaars. In 1849 the British occupied the city, overthrowing an unpopular Sikh regime that for thirty years had steadily destroyed and demoralised the city. Peshawar became a garrison town, as for the next seventy years the British waged a series of inconclusive wars against the Pathans. At this point the only formal Christian presence was the army chaplain, the Reverend Worthington Jukes. He was under strict instructions only to minister to the occupation forces, within the cantonment, but he decided to try to reach the local Muslim population. The descriptions of the Peshawar populace in

A Shinto priest, Northern Honshu, Japan.

Above: Techniques to convert the Orient: a missionary in China, 1850s, distributing tracts.

Right: Early-seventeenth-century Japanese screen, depicting two Portuguese Jesuit priests.

Overleaf left: The Buddha of Grahi, an idol to evangelical Christians. In the words of the nineteenth-century missionary hymn, 'The heathen, in his blindness, bows down to wood and stone!'

Overleaf right: Temple of the Golden Buddha, Bangkok.

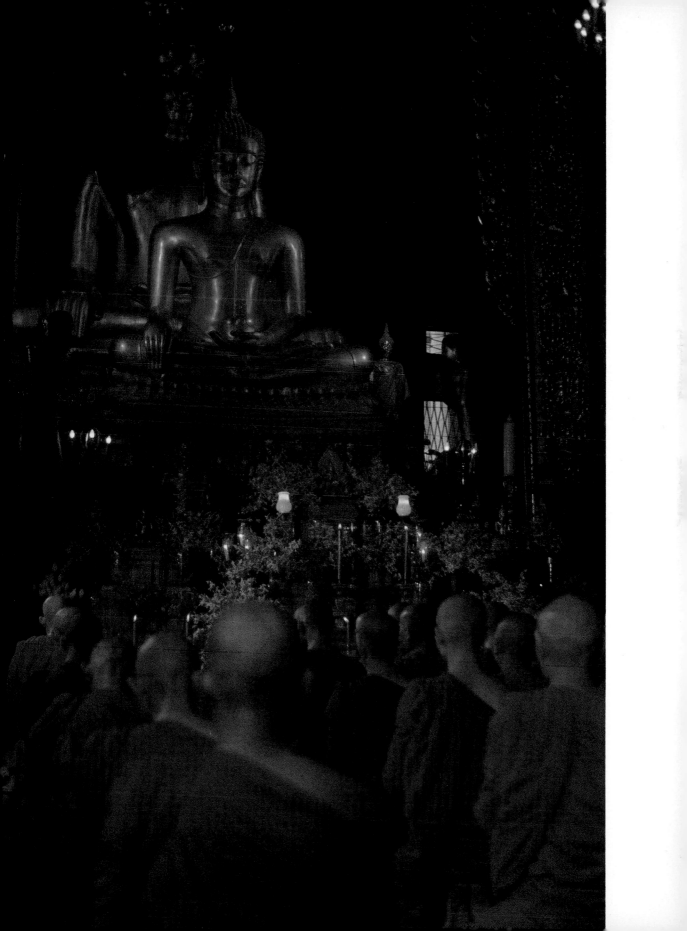

Right: Buddhist priests take a stroll on the shore of the Choa Phya River during the Chak Phra Festival, Songkla, Thailand.

Below: Portrait of a Shinto priest at the Tofukuji Temple, Kyoto, Japan.

missionary accounts did not augur well for his efforts: 'The people of this city were at that time, as they are still, the most turbulent, fanatical and bigoted of all the peoples who are under Britain's rule in India.' In order to overcome the prejudice against the British Jukes dressed like a Pathan in turban, baggy breeches, a flowing robe and a bushy beard.

Local people were forbidden to enter the cantonment, where the only church stood. So Jukes organised the building of All Saints Church in the very heart of the walled city. The church was designed like a mosque so that the local population might recognise it as a place of worship. Only a cross mounted on the minaret identified it as Christian: the cross was pock-marked with bullet holes where a Muslim, incensed at its presence, shot at it. A century after Jukes left Peshawar the Afghans are no nearer embracing the Christian faith. All Saints Church still stands today amid the bustle of the bazaars, but the spiritual church Jukes hoped to build has never risen above its foundations.

Ten years before Jukes arrived, Isidore Loewenthal, an American Presbyterian missionary, had been buried in the cemetery for Europeans in the cantonment of Peshawar, shot by his own nightwatchmen who mistook him for a thief. He had spent just seven years on the mission field but in that time he had learnt the Pushdu language of the Afghans and had translated the whole of the New Testament. Loewenthal's ambition was to 'open up the Afghan people to Christ'. His call came when a Christian military officer, Captain H. Conran, donated $7500 to the American Presbyterian mission for use in evangelistic work among the Afghans. In 1856 the mission decided that Loewenthal, himself a convert from Judaism, was the man for the job. It was an impossible task. The English officials were rigidly opposed to any Christian teaching which might further inflame the feelings of the colonised Muslim peoples. In Africa the colonial forces were busy harnessing the missionary efforts to the pacification and 'civilisation' of the local population; in India, by contrast, they were doing their best to keep the missionaries at arm's length. In banning missionaries from Peshawar, one Commissioner swore that no missionary would cross the Indus river while he was in office. A few months after making this bold declaration the Commissioner was stabbed to death. His successor, Sir Herbert Edwardes, felt differently – 'to permit the Gospel to shed its rays in the dark places of the earth would bring blessing and not disaster' – and encouraged the Church Missionary Society to begin work in the city.

Lonely monument to a minority faith, a church overlooking the busy traffic on the Choa Phya River, Bangkok.

The local population could have been forgiven for having difficulty in distinguishing between the British military man and the missionary. The first batch of three missionaries included Major Martin, who had

Dr Theodore Pennell, an Anglican medical missionary to the North-Western Frontier Province, travelling dressed as a sadhu, or mendicant pilgrim.

only recently resigned his army commission to begin Christian work. Loewenthal arrived soon after. He obviously found the local population bewildering, a people both warlike and deeply religious: 'The Afghan is fierce and bloodthirsty and is never without weapons. There is hardly a man whose hands are not stained with blood ... Like all Mohammedans they are excessively sensual ... and yet the surface of all Mussulman life is thoroughly religious. God, if not in all their thoughts, is certainly in all their words.' He was confused by the highly visible role religion played in their lives. Here was not a pagan, irreligious people, but a people with a highly defined sense of God, who spent more time in prayer and worship than many missionaries. Superficially religious they might be, Loewenthal decided, but there was 'the lamentable absence of a sense of sin and of the necessity of a Saviour, the only basis of real religion'. To convey the basics of 'real religion' Loewenthal entered into innumerable discussions with the Peshawar mullahs. He became known for his skills as 'a disputant with Mohammedans'. Yet he was assailed by a sense that the hours spent in theological debate with the mullahs were fruitless. All the talking did not result in conversions, and that was Loewenthal's only real criterion for success.

The careers of Jukes and Loewenthal in Peshawar clearly indicated that this was not fertile ground for Christian Mission. Yet the warning did not dissuade others from following them. Theodore Pennell, an English missionary doctor of the Church Missionary Society, was one who found the lure of the North-Western Frontier irresistible. He ventured south of Peshawar to Bannu. Whereas Jukes and Loewenthal came expressly as evangelists, Pennell was a doctor with medical as well as spiritual ambitions. He felt that this gave him a considerable advantage over his colleagues as a doctor would be able to break down native suspicion and prejudice. Like Loewenthal, Pennell had learnt the hard way that words did not have the desired effect. In his autobiography *Among the Wild Tribes of the Afghan Frontier* he recounts one medical visit to an outlying village. No sooner had he unpacked his medicines and begun prescribing than the Mullah arrived, 'with his Quran under his arm and his rosary in his hand, and with a very sanctimonious and superior kind of air. He has come to see that the faith of the flock is not endangered, and is followed by a number of his talibs, or students, whose great desire is to hear a wordy battle between the Padre and the Mullah, and to see the former ignominiously defeated.'

Since the missionary rarely had any idea of the rules of the 'battle' which the mullahs were fighting on their home ground, the Christian frequently ended up the object of ridicule. Pennell soon discovered that he was safer in his hospital ward. Here he had a captive audience to which he could explain Christian principles.

Blood-feuds and revenge killings were commonplace among these people of the mountains. This not only provided Pennell with a regular supply of wounded patients, but also a perfect springboard for his Christian moral tales. In one such incident, a man was brought in with both his eyes slashed by a knife. There was nothing that could be done for him, but they kept him in hospital for a few weeks, 'that he might hear the story of the Gospel of goodwill and forgiveness'. All the while the blind man insisted he wanted revenge, so Pennell told him the story of 'The Christian's Revenge'. Above each bed at the hospital were framed cards denoting the name of the benefactor of each bed. Above the blind man's bed was written, 'Conolly Bed, in memory of Captain Conolly, beheaded at Bukhara'. Captain Conolly, an English officer, had been imprisoned by a Muslim ruler, Bahadur Khan. After a long captivity and much hardship, Conolly was told that he would be spared if he renounced his faith and became a Muslim. He refused, and was executed. In 'revenge', Conolly's sister asked Pennell to dedicate a bed to the memory of her brother. Pennell was quite sure that this story of Christian forgiveness of one's enemies had set many an Afghan thinking.

Pennell became convinced that medical mission was the way to overcome Muslim opposition. He believed that the mission dispensaries were an effective means of influencing the life of the village: 'They exert an extraordinary Christianising, civilizing, and pacifying influence on the tribes in their immediate vicinity.' He urged the missions to sponsor a rash of dispensaries all over the frontier. Not only did this present the best opportunity to Christianise and pacify the people, but it gave the missionaries a chance of 'familiarizing them with the more peaceful aspects of British rule'. No matter how enlightened the missionaries were, they were all still tainted by the colonial connection.

The hospital founded by Theodore Pennell in the dusty market town of Bannu in 1893 is still in operation a century later. Now called the Pennell Memorial Hospital, it has grown into a well-known centre for medical treatment and preventive health care. The buildings have deteriorated, but the queues of sick men and women are as long as ever. By 1989 the Medical Superintendent was a Pakistani, but there were still four women missionaries on the hospital staff. One of those is Dr Ruth Coggan, daughter of the former Archbishop of Canterbury, who in 1970 joined the hospital as an obstetrician and gynaecologist. Another is Alison Foote whose own parents were married in the little church attached to the hospital. All four missionaries are highly dedicated to their work, and although some people accuse them of old-fashioned paternalism in their working practice, no one doubts their determination to surmount the difficulties of being professional women in an area where Islam is observed so strictly. The women adhere to a principle of Christian service, in which they hope their faith will speak through their dedication to their patients. There are few remaining traces of overt Christian activity in the hospital. At the start of each day a Pushdu hymn is sung on the wards while pockets containing Christian tracts hang in the waiting rooms for those who can read. Occasionally one of the missionaries will offer a prayer for a patient at the request of a relative.

Further down the frontier on the edge of tribal Waziristan is the unknown, unremarkable town of Tank. There is another mission hospital in Tank, and here the evangelistic effort is more pronounced than at Bannu. There are many more missionaries on the hospital staff, and expatriates fill the most senior positions. Two members of staff are specially employed to conduct bedside evangelism and share their testimony with the Afghans as they lie on their charpoys, awaiting operations or recuperating from illness. The 'Jesus' film of Christ's life is regularly shown in the evenings. The little hospital chapel is the only church in the town and the hospital ward is one of the only places where the Bible is read in Pushtu in a public place.

Some of the staunchest Muslims in Pakistan live in and around Tank. The hospital staff are aware of just how sensitive the Christian side of their work is. The hospital director explained just how high the stakes are: 'If a man heard that his wife had become a Christian in hospital, he'd have no compunction about shooting or poisoning her. The men often go off to work in Saudi. Their vigorous young wives sometimes come in after they have left, pregnant. They come to sound us out to see if we will do an abortion which we won't because morally we don't feel we can. But it's a difficult decision because we know we are sending them back to capital punishment. If they can kill their wives for getting pregnant, they can certainly kill them for apostasy.'

Apostasy is a life and death issue, and the apostate must expect to face it alone. The hospital staff are neither permitted nor do they have the time to follow up the evangelistic work done on the wards. When a patient leaves the hospital all contact with the missionaries abruptly ends. If that patient was converted while at the hospital, he or she plunges straight back into Muslim society, isolated and vulnerable. At best he could expect to be ostracised by his friends and family, at worst he might be killed. Yet even against that background, the hospital staff continue to attempt such evangelism.

In reality they know that most patients will take the medical care and ignore the message. Even if the Pathans had the inclination to convert, which very few seem to, the price would be too high. The truth is that, despite years of effort, the missionaries have not succeeded anywhere in Pakistan. Ron Pont is the headmaster of the prestigious Edwardes College in Peshawar, a missionary of considerable experience, who worked as a surgeon in Iran until he and his wife were expelled during the revolution in 1979. The long years spent in Islamic countries have not altered his view that final salvation is only attainable

Young Muslims relax in central Lahore, at a monument built around a copy of the Quran.

through Christ, but his youthful dreams of seeing a mass movement to Christianity have dissolved. In Pont's view: 'These days I try and act in a Christian way rather than lead people to Christ ... I don't believe Christians will get anywhere by chipping away at the edges of Islam. It's a great monolith ... If any Muslim did choose to convert and I'd be very hesitant to ask anybody to consider the step, then I'd stand in awe of his bravery. He'd be a hero in my mind.'

Dave Davies, who has spent a lifetime in Pakistan and now leads the American TEAM mission, admits that such heroes are very few and far between. Looking for signs of progress he points to a greater openness among Muslims in the cities to read the Bible, but he admits that people simply are not prepared to change religion. This creates particular problems for him as his evangelical mission organisation in America expects results: 'Some churches send out reports asking "How many did you convert, how many did you baptise, how many churches did you plant?" If you keep sending back the answer zero, they begin to wonder.'

Missionary experience in Pakistan has been so disappointing that some missionaries have ceased to think in terms of winning Muslims to Christ at all; they look instead for areas of shared belief on which to establish dialogue with the Muslim community. Yet the majority of those in Pakistan still pray for a great movement to Christianity, as has happened in sub-Saharan Africa, in South Korea, or in the Philippines. The reasons why their prayers have remained unanswered are rooted in the nature of Islam, and in the Muslim experience of Christianity through history. For most Westerners the Crusades mean little more than tales of knights and forts, and the derring-do of Richard Cœur de Lion against the heretics in the Middle East. To many Muslims, the Crusades remain the indelible proof of Christianity's implacable hatred of Islam. 'Civilisation' was considerably further advanced in the eleventh-century Islamic world than in Western Europe. The university mosque of Cairo, the Al Az'har mosque, was founded in 970, two centuries before the earliest European universities of Bologna, Paris and Oxford. But Christian Europe was ready for war, a religious war, in which all death would be to God's glory. 'We shall slay for God's love', said one popular slogan. 'A Christian glories in the death of a Muslim because Christ is glorified,' wrote St Bernard. On 15 July 1099 the Christian Crusaders streamed into Jerusalem: 'With drawn swords our people ran through the city; nor did they spare anyone, not even those pleading for mercy. If you had been there, your feet would have been stained up to the ankles with blood. . . . The horses waded in blood up to their knees, nay up to the bridle. It was a just and wonderful judgement of God.' The Jews who had taken

Victorious football team of the London Mission High School, Bangalore, with the Mysore Cup, and the Revd E.P. Price.

shelter in the synagogue were burnt alive. To commit such atrocities in God's name turned the Christian gospel on its head. The Christians at once became the bloody aggressors. For many Muslims, that is how they have remained: the Christians will never be able to wash away those blood-stains.

Eight centuries later, when missionaries first arrived in Pakistan in significant numbers, they came with the colonial forces. The faith they brought was therefore interpreted as an enslaving not a liberating religion. Though the missionaries and colonialists perceived themselves as very different, the whole tone of missionary work mirrored the grand ambitions of the British Raj. There is no better symbol of this than Lahore's red-brick Cathedral Church of the Resurrection, built in the Early English style. Consecrated in 1887, this great colonial building was always vastly out of proportion to the potential congregation of Christians in Lahore and now it has become a huge financial liability to the Diocese of Lahore and its Bishop. Next to the cathedral stands the Cathedral School. While the church stands almost empty, the school turns away pupils. The success of missionary education, and of the missionary hospitals, is ironic. Today the very politicians who in parliament press for increased 'Islamicisation' queue up to send their children to the best Christian schools, and are treated in the Christian hospitals.

Many of Pakistan's most prestigious institutions, Forman Christian College, and Taxila Eye Hospital, were founded by missionaries. Though many gratefully accepted the schooling and medical provision on offer, it only served to reinforce the belief that the missionary was little more than a functionary of the British Raj, and indeed, that in the schools and hospitals there was some subtle form of bribery to encourage them to abandon their religion. This is the charge levelled against the missionaries by Professor Anis Ahmad, Chairman of the Department of Religion at the International Islamic University: 'There's hardly one hospital whose purpose is not to propagate the message. Should the Gospel go through with the syringe and the capsule, or with the decent moral fibre of a person?' For their part the missionaries claimed that they did not discriminate between patients or students, whether Muslim or Christian. It soon became clear that in fact the mullahs had little cause to fear that exposure to mission education or hospital treatment would lead to conversion. Many of the most senior politicians in contemporary Pakistan, including the Prime Minister Benazir Bhutto, received some schooling from missionaries, yet by 1989 there was only one Christian Member of Parliament, Father Rufin Julius. In any case in 1972 Zulfiqar Ali Bhutto took the decision to nationalise the Church schools, so removing from many missionaries both their power base and their justification for being in Pakistan.

On closer inspection, the real criticism of missionary activity in the schools and hospitals by hardline Muslims is not that they have converted and continue to convert people from Islam. Their true fear is that exposure to expatriate Christians has drawn many Pakistanis into a spiritual no-man's land. Here, between Islam and Christianity, they fall prey to secular socialist and Marxist ideology. Professor Ahmad explains that the consequence of this spiritual 'neutralisation' is to make those who are weak Muslims more susceptible to Marxism and materialism: 'Those who were educated in Christian missionary institutions ... love Marxism better than Islam.'

This is the key to the opposition missionaries face from the powerful Muslim fundamentalist coalition in Pakistan which argues that missionary education has been an obstacle to the process of Islamicisation. It has created an influential body of politicians sympathetic to the goals of Western education and to Western cultural influence.

The reasons behind the continuing failure of Christian Mission are complex. One is the negative historical associations of Christianity, but the rest are to be found in the very nature of Islam. Mohammed, the prophet who founded Islam, died in AD 632. As a religion it was therefore in a position to borrow selectively from both Judaism and

Christianity. In fact, it has a great deal in common with Christianity, in the words of one Christian writer, 'just enough to innoculate it against the real thing'. In Islam, the Four Gospels, the Laws of Moses, the Psalms of David and the Quran, are all recognised as divine revelations. These are four of many revelations God gave to mankind, but the only ones to survive. The Quran, as the last of the four, is the most authoritative. Where the Quran and the Gospels do not agree, it is because Christians through the ages have tampered with the Bible. The Quran, on the other hand, is fixed in its Arabic authorised version, and must not be translated. The Quran mentions Christ as a great prophet, and even acknowledges his ability to work miracles. What no Muslim can accept is that Christ was the son of God, or that he was crucified. The first implies that God had a wife, which in itself is a blasphemous notion. It also raises the concept of the Holy Trinity, which Muslims interpret as three Gods, not one. The second suggests that God, the creator of the universe, would allow his son to die the death of a common criminal, an inconceivable thought to Muslims.

Christian missionaries can engage in theological debate with Muslims with some confidence, but then flounder when they confront Islam as a social and political phenomenon. In Islam there is no separation of Church and State: the faith permeates society. The spirit of Islam is woven into poetry, art and architecture. It is a code for life, a complete political, social and economic system. As one Presbyterian missionary to the Middle East explained, 'a follower of Islam who renounced his religion would in effect be tearing up his birth certificate, citizenship papers, voting registration, and work permit, and would become like a man without a country'. While to an outsider this might seem harsh, the devout Muslim rejoices in the all-embracing quality of Islam. Professor Ahmad describes it in these terms: 'A person when he breathes, breathes Islam, a person when he dreams, dreams Islam ... When he is away from it he will feel as if you have taken a fish out of water, and how long can the fish survive if you take it out of water?' For a Muslim the consequences of stepping out of the water are severe. He would be a traitor, not just to his family and relatives, but to his country. He would also be quickly discovered, for Islam is a very public faith. It is the public, communal nature of Muslim worship that has perhaps been the best defence against effective Christian penetration. Prayer is one of the Five Pillars of Islam, and five times a day throughout the year throughout the Muslim world, the muezzins call the faithful to prayer. Wherever he is and in whatever circumstances the Muslim takes out his prayer mat, faces Mecca and prays. And at the end of Ramadan, the month of fasting, tens of thousands of men gather in mosques everywhere to say their prayers, in the Eid-ul-Fitr celebration.

If such public displays of faith are not enough to induce a brotherly loyalty to Islam, then there is always the deterrence of the most severe punishment to keep the believers in line. In Islam, apostasy is the most severe of crimes, for which the Koran sanctions capital punishment. In the second Surah of the Quran it warns 'Whoso shall apostasise from his religion, let him die for it, and he is an infidel.' There is little doubt that this has effectively deterred would-be converts through the ages. The solidarity of Muslim society is so important that it becomes the responsibility of the state to punish an apostate for challenging its very foundations. Apostasy is quite simply treacherous behaviour.

Islam – the greatest challenge of them all for Christian missionaries.

Graham Burton is well aware of the possible consequences of conversion for a Muslim. Yet it is a danger that he believes all missionaries in Muslim countries must face squarely: 'You can't be glib about anything you say in that kind of situation. It's sometimes a matter of life and death. Literally.' Despite the dangers into which they may be leading potential converts there are many mission groups which continue to reach out into the Muslim community in Pakistan. Inevitably their activities are discreet. Operation Mobilisation is one such group which throughout the 1980s has placed particular emphasis on Muslim evangelisation. In Pakistan, teams of men and women, living discreetly in team houses dotted around the major cities, carry out street evangelism, distributing Gospel tracts translated into Urdu. Women's teams carry out door-to-door visitation as a means of reaching and befriending Muslim women. The missionaries are mostly young Americans or Europeans, some with official missionary visas, most without. It is highly risky work which treads a thin line between permissible activity and behaviour that is likely to provoke a backlash. But the organisation confidently claims that thousands have purchased its religious material.

A different technique has been developed by a Faislabad-based mission, which hopes to avoid the confrontation without compromising its evangelistic goals. A Bible Correspondence Course is run from the headquarters of the Christian Pakistan Radio Broadcasting Services. The organisers believe that there are Muslims who for social reasons cannot be open about their interest in Christianity, yet who are prepared to enter into discussion by means of a plain brown envelope. All evangelical Christians refer to these 'secret believers' whose numbers will always remain unknown. The courses are carefully structured so as to avoid giving offence, and the Quran is not mentioned. As pupils complete the courses, they are sent Bible portions, a New Testament, and finally a complete Bible as a reward. The organisers stress that they do not offer leading advice on subjects such as baptism: their hope is that the Bible will speak for itself.

No one is more clearly aware of the negative implications of embracing Christianity than the Pakistani Christians themselves. Until a century ago, the poor, down-trodden minority that today make up the Christian population in Pakistan were low-caste Hindus who were employed as general factotums by the soldiers and administrators of the British Raj. Then, at the turn of the century, a series of mass conversions swept through this displaced community. For the missionaries, whose efforts had largely been concentrated on the education of India's élite, this was an awkward surprise. If they were to retain any chance of convincing the well-bred Muslims, Christianity could not

Traditional skills applied to new tasks. Afghans work on a carpet for the Salvation Army, who run their Haripur refugee camp in Pakistan.

A child working in the brick kilns – gruelling and dangerous work. Many are from Christian families, the poorest section of Pakistan's population.

become identified as the religion of the lowest 'sweeper' class. Yet this is exactly what has happened. In modern Pakistan the Christians are interchangeably called the 'sweepers'. Most of the sweepers and cleaners in the cities are in fact Christians. They are regarded as the dregs of society and live in poor mud or brick dwellings where sanitation and sewerage are virtually non-existent. Schooling and health provision are frequently beyond their means. The Christians claim that the Muslims have inherited the caste prejudices of Hinduism. Everything in Pakistan, they claim, is geared towards showing how great Islam is. And when Islam needs a scapegoat, it is to the vulnerable Christian minority that it turns. Bishop Malik, Moderator of the Church of Pakistan, is himself from a family of converts from Hinduism. He explained the Christian predicament: 'We have learnt the art of living under Islam ... We are punished for anything the West does. Rushdie is a Muslim, but they burnt down the foundations of our church. When the Americans bombed Teheran, one of our churches was destroyed.'

While some missionaries continue to tiptoe around the minefield of Muslim evangelism others argue that their rightful place is among the poor Christian community, helping to build its self-respect, and supporting local Christians in their efforts to improve their quality of life. In the slums of Islamabad, Dr Jill Burton, wife of Graham, is developing a network of health clinics and training health workers for the Christian community. It is valuable work in a country where health treatment is based on one's ability to pay. Between 1982 and 1987 eight clinics had been opened. In Peshawar, Father Len Steger has also opted to work among the Christian community. Many of the Christian children in the town work at the brick kilns or in the carpet factories. The children are paid a pittance for long hours of hard labour and they are virtually bonded to their employers. Father Steger is pushing through a major rehousing project on the outskirts of the city, as a means of breaking the spiral of poverty in which so many are trapped. He rejoices in the people he has chosen to work among and is not downcast that the number of Christians is so small.

A Christian wedding in rural Pakistan. Many Pakistani Christians were converts from Hinduism: they still retain much of Hindu cultural practice.

Father Steger's work suggests an alternative that avoids offending the Muslim majority. Most missionaries in Pakistan would say that he had missed the point, which is to bring Muslims into obedience to Christ. Most, but not all. Andrew Knight, a Quaker working for the Anglican Church Missionary Society, is fiercely critical of his evangelical colleagues: 'They still believe they have to be here to witness to Christ. Have they ever really considered what they are converting Pakistanis to? Mission that is still motivated by the notion that you are bringing God is so supremely arrogant. Christ is here already.' Knight is an eccentric in Pakistan's missionary circle and does not share the theological consensus. The presence of evangelical missionaries is itself unusual. No other Muslim country gives them such freedom of movement. Indeed, most Muslims live in countries which are closed to missionaries. As a way of getting round this problem, the missionary community has devised something known as 'tent-making'. Where traditional missionaries are barred from entry, a professional person who is also a Christian may be able to get a visa to work in another capacity. These Christian professionals take every opportunity to share their faith. As more and more countries feel unable to tolerate the proselytising activities of missionaries, 'tent-making' assumes a greater importance. There are even those who predict that in time most missionary work may be conducted in this way.

The strength of the 'tent-making' movement indicates that after a thousand years of unsuccessful, some would say futile, endeavour, Christian missionaries have no intention of surrendering. For them it is a spiritual battle which Jesus Christ must win. As Muslim populations disperse into Europe, their chosen task becomes more immediate. In an Operation Mobilisation campaign in the summer of 1989 called 'Love Europe', thousands of young Western Christians were organised into groups specifically to target Muslims for evangelism. In evangelical Churches in America, congregations are urged to 'adopt a Muslim people group'. History has shown that this is a dangerous route to take. If missionaries continue to venture down this path Muslims are confident they will come to a dead-end. Professor Ahmad explains why: 'Islam has no fear from Christianity at all because it's so confident about ... its relevance to human life ... Christianity can't come and uproot Islam, all it can do is perhaps lose a few good human friends.' From the sound of the missionary rhetoric, which sees the Muslims as God's harvest before the year 2000, there are no qualms about losing a few friends. In response the moderate Muslims suggest a partnership against their common enemies Marxism and atheism. If missionaries do not accept this offer, then Professor Ahmad warns: 'Christianity will be the loser. Islam will not be the loser.'

11 Into Darkest England

In these pages I propose to record the result of a journey into a region which lies at our own doors – into a dark continent that is within easy reach of the General Post Office.

George Sims, 1889

Darwin's On the Origin of Species *caused a scandal on its publication, and earned the author considerable ridicule.*

In 1890, thirty-three years after Livingstone's memorable speech to Cambridge students rallying them to mission in Africa, a new hero threw down a new challenge to would-be missionaries. Follow me, he cried, not to the ends of empire, but to the very heart of empire, to the domestic wilderness of London's East End. William Booth, General of the Salvation Army, was writing *In Darkest England and the Way Out*. For Booth, the metaphor of the Dark Continent of Africa was irresistible. Stanley's popular news accounts of Africa had fired the public imagination: he wrote of dripping, malarial jungle inhabited by pygmies and cannibals. Booth made a parallel with the homely horrors of the East End: 'As there is a darkest Africa is there not also a darkest England? Civilisation, which can breed its own barbarians, does it not also breed its own pygmies?' With relish he extended the analogy between the African arboreal and English urban jungle. Both were harsh environments with innocent victims: 'The ivory raiders who brutally traffic in the unfortunate denizens of the forest glades, what are they but the publicans who flourish on the weakness of the poor? . . . The lot of a negress in the Equatorial Forest is not, perhaps, a very happy one, but is it so very much worse than that of many a pretty orphan girl in our Christian capital?'

Booth was charging imperial Britain with blind and shameful hypocrisy. Zealous young missionaries were leaving in their hundreds to spread the material and spiritual benefits of Christian empire to those overseas, when the heart of that empire was rotting with material and spiritual poverty. His book touched a rich vein of popular sentiment and in the first year of publication it reputedly sold 200 000 copies.

By 1890 the Victorian inner city had been firmly established as a mission field. This was no sudden development. In the course of the nineteenth century Christian England had been forced to face certain uncomfortable truths. Firstly, the fundamentals of Christian doctrine were now firmly established within the parameters of intellectual

debate. In 1859 Charles Darwin had thrown an evolutionary cat among
the biblical pigeons with the publication of *On the Origin of Species*.
Many people were appalled by his assertion that they were distantly
descended from apes, and by the implication that the book of Genesis
was at best metaphorical myth. Darwin was by no means the first
author to challenge the factual basis of the Bible. In 1835 David Strauss
in his *Life of Jesus* suggested that the supernatural events described
in the New Testament were no more than myths created around a
charismatic spiritual leader, while in *The Essence of Christianity*
written in 1841 Ludwig Feuerbach proclaimed God was a human
invention. It was George Eliot who translated both works into English.
There were others, among them the militant atheist Charles Bradlaugh,
who launched a more direct attack on Christian leadership. In a
celebrated and protracted campaign he battled for the right to enter
the House of Commons by affirming rather than taking a Christian
oath in which he did not believe. In 1888 he secured legislation that
permitted affirmation in Parliament and the law courts. It made another
sizeable rent in the already tattered Anglican cloak that had shrouded
the great institutions.

More profoundly worrying than the well-publicised activities of a
few intellectuals was the simple fact that by the middle of the century
the majority of the urban working classes did not go to church. This
was a cause of national embarrassment – Britain was in the process of
transplanting a religious ideology throughout her empire in which the
majority of those at home had already ceased to believe. The signs had
been there for several decades, triggered first by revolution in France
in 1789 which shook the religious foundations of the British establishment. The reverberations that crossed the Channel forced the
British Government hastily to re-examine its own position. One
Member of Parliament, Arthur Young, argued that the Church was
the country's best defence against revolutionary uprisings. In 1798 he
pleaded with Parliament to build more churches and to send more
preachers to where the working classes lived: 'The true Christian will
never be a leveller, will never listen to French politics or French
philosophy.' To make true Christians, however, the churches needed
to be present in the community. With an exploding population this
was becoming an almost impossible task – over the first half of the
nineteenth century, the population grew from 11 to 21 million and,
what was even more worrying, by 1851 for the first time half of the
population lived in cities.

The new cities were not God-fearing places. This was the worrying
conclusion of the 1851 census. The first and last national census of its
kind, it sought to establish the religious health of the nation. On

Sunday, 30 March a census counter was allocated to every church and chapel in the country. Their returns revealed that only 40 per cent of the population were in church that day: a statistic that would stagger today's Christians by its size, mortified those in 1851, as a clear sign that the nation was sliding towards Godlessness. And this in the same year as the Great Exhibition, when Britain boasted to the world of its technical, scientific and commercial achievement. The Churches had been aware there was a problem for at least thirty years. The Church of England had tried to tackle it with a massive church-building programme, aided by regular government grants and special lump sums of £1 million in 1818 and £500 000 in 1824. More than 2500 Anglican churches were built in this period. But there was also a desperate shortage of vicars willing to work in the great industrial cities. In 1858 a House of Lords committee estimated that the Church of England alone was a thousand men short. A Leeds vicar, giving evidence to the committee, explained that only inferior men were going into the manufacturing towns. And Trollope observed that nobody in their right mind would take a town parish when they could get one in the country offering a higher income and a better chance of marrying the bishop's daughter. The 'Society for Promoting the Employment of Additional Curates in Populous Places' was established, but was effectively handcuffed. To improve recruitment the Church of England needed to cast its net over a wider social circle, and this it was reluctant to do. Said one bishop: 'It will be a fatal day to the Church of England when she shall be obliged to recruit her ministry from men of lower education and social position.'

The divisions and prejudices of feudal society still clung to the Churches, reinforcing the all-important divisions of Victorian England. The working-man, it was said, was reluctant to go to church because of his humble clothing. 'God, it is true, does not look at clothes,' said one clergyman, 'But congregations and guardians of the temple do . . . Nowhere do the pomps and vanities of this wicked world assert themselves more strongly than in the House of God.' The *Clarion* magazine reported that one parson in Clerkenwell was holding special services for shabby parishioners 'in a dim religious light, almost in darkness, so that the people cannot see each other's looped and win-dowed raggedness'. The inequalities were expressed in the very seats on which church-goers sat. Most churches were under-endowed and had to raise money by renting their pews to the wealthier worshippers; the poor squeezed into the few free seats set aside for them, usually towards the back of the church, or tucked behind the arches. In census returns from Sheffield, Manchester, Liverpool and Birmingham clergymen reported that they had no seats at all available for the poor.

A Leeds clergyman described a church in which almost all the pews were owned by absentee parishioners. Reporting on the census, Horace Mann commented that this practice alone deterred the poor from attending church; religion had come to be regarded as a middle-class luxury. While the system did have a few supporters, battling to save the middle classes from dirt and fleas, the campaign for free pews grew more vociferous and the practice gradually dwindled and died. But was the pew system at the root of the problem? The organiser of the census was certain that it was not: 'Teeming populations often now surround half-empty churches, which would probably remain half-empty even if the sittings were all free. It is evident that absence from religious worship is attributable mainly to genuine repugnance to religion itself.' There was ample anecdotal evidence to show that the working people viewed religion if not with repugnance then with indifference. Friederich Engels had observed as much in 1844 in *The Condition of the Working Class in England*, and Henry Mayhew, in *London Labour and the London Poor*, recalled a typical conversation with a costermonger. 'What is St Pauls?', Mayhew asked. The answer came 'A church so I've heard. I never was in church.'

Ironically, there was considerable suspicion of the motives of those poorer people who did go to church. This was still the age of parish dole, on which many people depended. But reform-minded Victorians were sure that such handouts led to an unhealthy dependency and assisted a process of 'pauperisation'. They were shocked to discover that some poor parishioners were attending three or four different churches in order to secure charity from each. Both clergy and social reformers like Henrietta Barnett waged war on the practice: such dependency was not just undesirable, it was immoral. 'If one sentence could explain the principle of our work,' she wrote, 'it is that we aim at decreasing not suffering but sin.' In a celebrated incident, Barnett attempted to stop 'dole-giving' in a particular parish of St Jude's in Whitechapel. Her actions prompted a riot. Contrary to her intentions, she was in effect breaking the last meaningful material link between the poor and the parish. The dilemma facing the Victorian reformers was whether the greater sin was to go to church for the wrong reasons, or not to attend church at all.

There had been City Missions for many years, the most famous being the London City Mission, founded in 1835. But these initiatives at first were quiet, unspectacular, and unfashionable. Domestic mission had none of the glamour of work overseas. All this changed with a group of dramatic publications in which the East End of London was depicted as a dark, arnarchic, godless netherworld. To a readership who had avidly read tales of exploration in Africa, here was a world,

A scripture reader in a night shelter, sending the homeless to bed with a biblical homily, by Gustave Doré, 1872.

almost as alien and almost as dangerous, but on the very doorstep: 'In these pages I propose to record the result of a journey into a region which lies at our own doors – into a dark continent that is within easy walking distance of the General Post Office.' The writer was George Sims who, in a series of articles in the *Pictorial World* on the lives of the outcast poor, earned himself the nickname 'Dante of the London Slums'. He was reacting against the flood of interest in mission overseas at the expense of the poor at home. Sims hinted that clouds were gathering, but it was a small anonymous penny pamphlet, entitled *The Bitter Cry of Outcast London*, published a few months later that unleashed the storm. In vivid, emotive language it described a world within a world, an abscess or canker about to erupt. So forceful was the writing that readers believed Victorian civilisation itself was in danger, from within. 'Seething in the very centre of our great cities, concealed by the thinnest crust of civilization and decency, is a vast mass of moral corruption, of heartbreaking misery and absolute godlessness.'

It was taken for granted that there was a causal link between sin and slum-living. Among the facts the pamphlet asked the readership to face were the acts of sexual immorality and promiscuity that occurred among people living in overcramped conditions. This particularly shocked many Victorians: sins that they condemned in savages were being committed in the very heart of the Christian empire. Although the author acknowledged the efforts of the handful of Christian men and women who were already working in the cities, he argued that their efforts were pitifully inadequate: 'We must face the facts; and these compel the conviction that THIS TERRIBLE FLOOD OF SIN AND MISERY IS GAINING UPON US.' Here was both a dire warning and a call to action.

The authorship of the pamphlet was disputed at the time, but there is now little doubt that it was written by the Reverend Andrew Mearns, Secretary of the London Congregational Union. He began with what he perceived was the root cause, non-attendance at worship: 'One street off Leicester Square contains 246 families, and only twelve of these are ever represented at the house of God.' Although the mass infidelity of the working classes had been known since the census, revelations of religious apathy still had the power to shock. Mearns's new contribution was to urge state-financed slum clearance as essential in assisting the missionary effort. Social intervention was to pave the way for Christian evangelism. Mearns, like Livingstone, had come face to face with acute poverty, and had had to recognise the limitations of Christian conversion as a force for change. But Mearns was not passing the responsibility entirely over to government. He also threw down a challenge to Christians to open their eyes and hearts to the misery of the working classes. He warned that urban missionary life was full of danger – the air laden with disease-breeding gases, robbers and muggers loitering on every street corner. He conjured up a world of gin-palaces and squalid tenement courtyards, inhabited by thieves, prostitutes and drunkards. For the would-be missionary, he gave the repugnant squalor of the city a tinge of dangerous glamour. The pamphlet ended with the simple appeal to missionary fevour: 'Whom shall we send and who will go for us?'

At a time when an appetite for social reform was growing among the educated classes, *The Bitter Cry* contained just the right recipe. A few weeks after its publication the headmaster of Harrow School, the Reverend Montagu Butler, used it as the basis of his sermon at St Mary's, Oxford, pleading that its call would be answered. In the years that followed, many of the brightest and the best were arrested by the idea of domestic missionary service. For well-to-do Victorians 'heathen England' became a fashionable subject of conversation. Many made the expedition into the mysterious territory to the east, as if going on an adventure to an African mission station. For the charitable housing reformer, Octavia Hill, to venture into the depths was a murky spiritual journey: 'by gradations imperceptibly darkening as we advance, we arrive at the classes who are at open war with society and professedly live by the produce of depredation or the wages of infamy'.

With popular attention turned to focus on this domestic mission field, a new batch of missionaries took their first tentative steps into the darkest East End. In 1886 the Reverend Osborne Jay was destined

'The terrible flood of sin and misery is gaining upon us.' Slums in the East End.

for Shoreditch; his first impressions as a domestic missionary were unpromising: 'I saw on all sides of me poor, weary, tired, erring straying beings, whom I could only call human because God had originally intended them for such. Women, sodden with drink, fighting and struggling like wild creatures; men, bruised and battered, with all the marks and none of the pleasures of vice upon them ... the very children, with coarse oaths and obscene jests, watching, like wild beasts, for anything, dishonest or otherwise, which might come their way.' And as for the religious life of Shoreditch? 'Nothing', said a clergyman who knew the locality well, 'will ever rouse the people of that part, save the last trump, and then they will respond too late.' The Christian middle class put its mind to this newest, most difficult missionary challenge and the result was a clutch of initiatives to different working-class professions. The principle was laid out in an article in the Christian magazine *Quiver* entitled 'Class Missions: Leverage to Higher Levels'. The cities were full of humble workers, yet despite their station they had the same capacity for good and evil. The article pointed out that they too experienced human feelings and that '... A hymn sung in a coal yard will at times draw tears to wash white streaks down a black face.' Herein was the answer, the key to uplifting the working man: 'Experience shows that the ideal Christianity is the best lever to raise all classes to higher levels of true citizenship.'

The London City Mission chose to exercise its leverage on the dockers, the casual labourers and the 'coalies', but its overtures were not always immediately embraced. 'When a missionary first asked permission to visit the coal depot at St Pancras Goods Station, the manager attempted to dissuade him on the ground that the men were too depraved for any hope of doing them good.' In this mission field, the missionary had to take his chance to preach and hand out tracts, 'Whilst men sleep, the great enemy is active. To contest the ground with him the servants of God have to be abroad at all hours of the night.'

It was not just male manual workers who were at risk from temptation. The acting profession for women was regarded as one small step from prostitution and suicide among actresses was not uncommon. In 1876 the Reverend Courthorpe Todd founded the Theatrical Mission. Vulnerable and lonely in their long periods without work, actresses were taken in by Revd Todd and encouraged 'to lead holy lives'. There were occasional successes. Revd Todd recounts bumping into one of them, little Jessica, while out walking in Shaftesbury Avenue: 'You will not remember me,' said a pleasant voice; 'but I shall be ever grateful to you for leading me to the Saviour nearly twenty-two years ago, when I was a little fairy in a pantomime.' It was the plight of the flower-sellers, often no more than 10 or 12 years old and working up to fifteen hours a day, that induced John Groom to found the 'Watercress and Flower Girls Christian Mission'. The Earl of Shaftesbury, President of the Mission, firmly outlined the Victorian charitable principles on which it should be run: to help the girls to help themselves and to train them to 'usefulness, self-dependence and trust in God'. The Mission also ran a home for crippled girls of good character, where they were given the means to make an honest livelihood, making artificial flowers. The missionaries involved in the process of uplifting these various classes of people reflected on a double achievement. Not only were they leading the humble to good Christian lives, but they were having an impact at the very heart of the empire, whose beneficial effect might flow out to be felt by millions.

The young Christian gentlemen of Oxford and Cambridge decided on a mission not to a particular class of workers, but to an area. In essence it was a strategy of Christian gentrification. Edward Denison, the leader of the movement, began a trend for Oxford graduates to spend part of the vacation in the East End. A number of 'settlements', the most famous of which was Toynbee Hall, were established throughout the East End. University volunteers staffed the settlements: it was hoped that the presence of gentlemen would rub off on the local community. They were primarily educational institutes, small academic oases in a desert of illiteracy. Samuel Barnett, vicar of St Jude's in Whitechapel, continued to prick the conscience of Oxford, urging privileged students to accept their social responsibility towards the less fortunate classes.

Toynbee Hall, opened in 1884, was not a conventional mission. In fact, Barnett disputed that it was a mission at all as his overriding passion was not to proselytise, but to build bridges between the classes. Another settlement, known as Oxford House, was opened in Bethnal Green, more missionary in its approach. Many more followed: a non-sectarian Women's University Settlement in Southwark in 1887; Cambridge House in Camberwell Road in 1897. The staff of the settlements ran education programmes, alcohol-free men's clubs, sat on public health committees and pushed for urban reform. Two Congregational settlements, Mansfield House and Browning Settlement, became deeply involved in social reform: Mansfield House provided the first 'poor man's lawyer' in 1891, and the campaign for old-age pensions was launched at Browning Settlement in 1898. The settlements were unrepentantly middle class in their approach and one American visitor described Toynbee Hall as 'essentially a transplant of university life in Whitechapel ... not so distant from the dreamy walks by the Isis or the Cam. But these things are not so much for the sake of the university men as of their neighbours, so that they may breathe a little of the charmed atmosphere.'

How many of the outcast poor took the opportunity to fill their lungs with the rarefied air of Toynbee Hall? Barnett himself was modest in his claims for its success, admitting that such a small group of men could not make much impression on a population of half a million. Yet he did feel that the settlement had brought an increase in goodwill. In this way the English middle class might gradually hope to uplift the unfortunates around them immersed in degradation and poverty.

Not far from the site of Toynbee Hall was a burial ground. In 1865 the Quakers who owned the cemetery had allowed a tent to be pitched there for the purpose of holding revival meetings. It was here that a fiery preacher by the name of William Booth began in earnest his mission to London's poor. In missionary instinct he was opposite to Canon Barnett: emotionally he was a working man and spurned the gentlemanly tactics and goals of the middle-class reformers. Christ came to the world to save it, he believed, not to civilise it. His mission was fuelled by a fearful urgency. Canon Barnett might not expect to make a mark on the public opinion of half a million people, William Booth had nothing else in mind. To him, the only reform that ultimately counted was the reform of the soul. The stage had long been set for the emergence of a domestic missionary hero. For the poor East End Christian at least, William Booth was the man. With his unorthodox, provocative, populist approach, Booth turned the mission world upside down. He began his professional life as an apprenticed pawnbroker, but it soon became clear that what he was really fitted for was not to pawn but to preach. His first substantial appointment was to the Bethesda Chapel, Gateshead, in 1858. So successful was Booth's salvation-based message there that the chapel earned the nickname 'The Converting Shop'.

Father and son, William and Bramwell Booth, together turned the missionary world upside down.

'Hallelujah lasses', Salvation Army officer cadets in training at Tring, 1889.

Booth and his missionary army were quick to realise that conventional approaches had failed: extraordinary times, it seemed, required extraordinary tactics. His first London auditorium was the Whitechapel tent. Booth had no doubts that this was where he should be: 'I was continually haunted with a desire to offer myself to Jesus Christ as an apostle for the heathen of East London.' And the heathen came forward in considerable numbers to express their conversion by kneeling on a penitent-form at the front of the tent. When bad weather eventually destroyed the tent, Booth and his followers, now called the Christian Mission, moved to new premises in Professor Orson's Dancing Academy. When it rapidly outgrew the academy, Booth rented the Oriental Hall, Poplar, dirty and comfortless, just the sort of place, as he put it, 'in which to catch drunken navvies and train them to be martyrs'. This was no idle boast. Booth had the knack of appealing to the working man and woman. Among his first and most loyal converts were an Irish boxer, Peter Monk, who took on the role of bodyguard, and a one-time chimney sweep, Elijah Cadman, who became a senior and respected Salvationist. Then there was Sarah McMinnies the Saved

Elijah Cadman (left), a former chimney sweep and militant Salvationist, and Dr Reid Morrison (right), who weighed 33 stone and was a Salvation Army attraction as 'the Christian Mission Giant'.

Barmaid, and Happy Hannah the Reformed Smoker. They were just a few of a growing collection of ex-drunkards, pugilists and prostitutes who responded to the fresh, blunt expression of the gospel message. Booth was certain that these people would be more effective missionaries to their own kind than any number of well-meaning charitable gentry from the West End. Booth's message was well tuned to his rough-and-ready audience and his preaching always drew crowds. The whole purpose of his mission was to reach people where they were, not in churches, which most of them would refuse to enter. But the approach was a dangerous one. His missionaries, who became his Salvation Army officers, were not universally beloved; the publicans, in particular, soon realised that these evangelists could be bad for business. Skirmishes and scuffles inevitably interrupted many meetings. 'On the way to the hall we were baptised with tea slops; winkle shells were also thrown at us from the same upstairs window.' The bonnets worn by the lassies of the Salvation Army were designed large, black and strong, not for aesthetic reasons but as protection against missiles thrown in the streets. In just one year, 1882, some 669 Salvationists were violently attacked. It was a point of principle not to give way to harrassment. The only acceptable response to violent attack was the rejoinder 'God bless you'. Elijah Cadman boasted of one encounter in Hackney: 'We were set upon by a band of ruffians shouting, howling and pulling us about. Some of the sisters were very roughly handled indeed ... but we stood our ground ... They pelted us with all sorts of things, and flour in abundance. I was as white as a miller. We had a good meeting, and one man professed to be saved.'

Booth enjoyed provocative gestures. When a supporter recommended all-day preaching, rather than conventional evening meetings, he argued, 'The gin palaces are always open. The emissaries of evil are always at work, why should the ambassadors of Christ wait for the evening?' As a tactic, this unashamed fighting spirit proved immensely popular. Booth was trying to break loose from 'all the trammels of custom and propriety which may in any degree have hindered or hampered us in the past'. This he did with considerable success. The brass bands, or Hallelujah bands, first used to drown out hostile mobs, became regular features of Army meetings. Tea was provided at Bible readings, transforming predictable scripture sessions into 'Jam and Glory meetings'. Prayer-meetings were out: 'knee drill' was in. In March 1878 two young evangelists, Rachel and Louise Agar, went to preach in Felling-in-Tyne. The local printer, William Crow, who was preparing a poster to announce their arrival, suggested the wording 'Two Hallelujah Lasses' as a way of attracting attention. Even Booth was initially unnerved by such a racy billing but the response was so overwhelming that his doubts were swept aside. The approach was derided by some and envied by others. Something of the same energy was behind the 'Pleasant Sunday Afternoon' movement, initiated in the non-conformist Churches. With its motto 'Brief, bright and brotherly' the PSA Society set out to break the dreary convention of Sunday morning church services, and erase the memory in the minds of many working men of Christianity as an 'unpleasant' experience. Sunday afternoon events, often for men only, were held, with sacred songs, a few prayers and readings. The movement had a certain success, but was continually under suspicion. Pleasure and religion: how far could you go before one corrupted the other?

Booth concluded that the end – eternal life – justified the means. In 1877 a 'Great Salvation Fair' was held at the People's Mission Hall in Whitechapel. It was promoted with all the colour and flair of a music hall entertainment. Among the banners proclaiming the virtues of 'The wines of Kingdom', and offering rewards to help the Master recover his 'Lost Property', was an invitation to hear preaching by the Christian Mission giant: Dr John Reid Morrison, also known as 'The Hallelujah Doctor', weighed in at 33 stone. He spoke for many of his colleagues in justifying his participation in this bizarre Christian show: 'I am willing to become a fool for Christ's sake.' Booth frankly admitted that the heathen masses needed to be enticed to salvation since they would not embrace it of their own free will: 'When we go fishing, we bait our hooks with the most enticing bait we can find. If one bait does not take, then we try another, and another, and another, and if they won't take any, then ... we go down and hook them on.' But there were many criticisms of this form of fishing for souls. One letter to the *East London Observer* complained about the 'disorderly mob' which disturbed the local people with their singing. One Wesleyan wrote that their services were a travesty of music hall entertainment, another said that they would be guilty of rank blasphemy if they understood the meaning of what they uttered. Lord Shaftesbury concluded that the Army was a trick of Satan, who had failed to make Christianity odious and was now trying to make it ridiculous. The missionary leadership expected, and rebutted, such attacks: 'We in the army have learned to thank God for eccentricity and extravagance, and to consecrate them to his service. We have men in our ranks who can rollick for the Lord ... Thank God for the dare-devil! ... They have helped to keep us free from the shackles of respectability. They keep us passionate.'

As the band of evangelists grew in confidence and numbers, so the military metaphor for their mission evolved. These were jingoistic times. The Reverend Baring-Gould's rousing military anthem 'Onward Christian Soldiers' had become hugely popular since its composition in 1865. The great American evangelist Moody led a crusade to London ten years later, with the theme 'Hold the Fort'. The Archbishop of Canterbury, Archibald Campbell Tait, had expressed his view that the whole population must be armed in the cause of Jesus Christ. This was the kind of emotive language that Elijah Cadman loved. He had begun to use hoardings and bellringers in the towns of the north to issue warlike declarations on sinfulness. On Good Friday 1878 in Whitby, the posters announced: 'War is declared! Recruits are wanted!' His colleagues liked this new militant approach. Later in 1878 they held a War Congress where the Salvation Army proper was born. William Booth was its first General. Most important, it was to be run with the full measure of military discipline, in a way not dissimilar to the Jesuits. The basics of the military system were to be incorporated into the new gospel army: authority and obedience above everything; proper use of everyone's ability; full training; and the combined action of all.

The heady rhetoric could not cloud the fact that this was by all accounts a very small army, just eighty-eight evangelists throughout England. Its influence was none the less considerable and breathed life into the domestic missionary movement. With its audacious tactics it challenged the dreary paternalism of many churches and broke evangelistic conventions for good. Others sought to recreate the Army's formula: within four years the Church of England had formed the Church Army. Church and Salvation Armies competed for the most belligerently titled journal, the Salvation Army with its *War Cry*, the Church Army with *Battleaxe*. The blood-curdling titles announced in no uncertain terms that evangelical Victorians were back on the offensive. By 1883 *War Cry* had an English-language circulation of 350 000.

Though many were carried along by the tide of evangelical jingoism, there were others who resented what they saw as Booth's attempt to usurp mission. The Reverend Osborne Jay was just one of the critics. Although he too was an East End missionary, his experience had led him to different conclusions. Christ's love, he believed, could equally be expressed in good secular work, not only through the flamboyant approach of the Salvationists. He openly criticised their missionary tactics, doubting whether they would be of any lasting benefit to the mass of suffering poor: 'To force religion down people's throats is like attempting to cook your turkey before you have caught it.' Jay attempted to catch the unchurched working class by means which were as unorthodox in their own way as Booth's. He began a boxing club, open only to parishioners, for a penny a week. Here they could also play cards and dominoes, bagatelle and cribbage; bad language and drink were forbidden. Around the boxing ring grew an unusual inner-city mission station: the gymnasium was in the basement, then the hall

Above, the Church Army Flying Squadron, 1911.

Below, demonstrating the latest missionary techniques at the Church Army annual conference, London, 1911.

228

for mothers' meetings or boxing bouts, above this Jay's own rooms, and right at the top, the church, made with Roman mosaic, Carrara marble and best Munich glass. Jay believed he had created a holistic mission in one building where the outcast poor could receive lessons in the most important aspects of civilised life. From these lessons might grow morality and religion, and finally, it was hoped, the boxers and the bagatelle players might end up as regular visitors to Revd Jay's church.

There has always been a tension between those missionaries who believe that the diffusion of 'better principles' must precede any meaningful conversion, and those who put their faith in the primacy of salvation. In this the East End was no different from any other mission field in the world. The theological differences between the two approaches were intensified by the envy with which the new breed of home missionaries were regarded. The Salvation Army had captured the public imagination for home mission. Jay, like many others, felt that he had been 'left long years to fight unaided and alone with the strong cohorts of the mighty armies of black bannered sin'. Suddenly the British public had found its conscience and General Booth, a relative newcomer, was cashing in on it. In reality by 1890 there was little ground between the two camps. The manifold problems of the East End were too great and too complex for belief in simplistic solutions to last for long. Booth himself was forced to realise that his form of evangelism could only be a partial solution. In 1890 the publication of *In Darkest England* was greeted with the charge that he had turned a Socialist. Booth himself described the book as a scheme of social salvation. According to the *Methodist Times*, General Booth had at last discovered that men had bodies as well as souls, and that Christianity must save society as well as individuals. In part, Booth's conversion to social action *was* a recognition of defeat. Those attending Army services in London in 1887 numbered about 54 090. While much larger than any other evangelical Church of the day, this was still no more than a drop in the godless ocean. Flamboyant evangelism alone was clearly not enough to turn London around and Booth had become convinced that poverty was a grave impediment to salvation. In the late 1880s a new string of slum posts and night shelters were opened. Salvation remained the ultimate goal, but social work opened a whole new social stratum, the very poorest, to the evangelical message.

Whatever the reasons, by the time Booth wrote *In Darkest England* he had accepted that urgent social intervention was needed as well as religious effort. He mapped out a grand, hopelessly impractical scheme to redeem the domestic jungle. It included a City Colony, a Farm Colony and an Overseas Colony where the destitute would be lifted

Above, *Captain Taylor, a blind Church Army officer, preaches at a labour home, Tufton Street, Westminster.*

Below, *soup and salvation: a Church Army soup kitchen, 1912.*

up, taught industry, morality and religion. A programme of mass emigration would give the poor a new start overseas. He appealed for £100 000 to finance his plans: the money rolled in, and he won the support from the mainstays of respectable society, *The Times* newspaper and Queen Victoria. But there were many critics as well, from the Charity Organisation Society, to T.H. Huxley, the constant scourge of the evangelicals, who argued that intemperance, harlotry, even starvation, were lesser evils than the subjugation of 'the intellect of a nation to organised fanaticism'. Public support flared, dwindled and died. None the less the social wing of the Salvation Army was established: and it would be for its mission halls, soup kitchens, hostels for the homeless, rather than its outrageous displays of evangelism, that the Salvation Army would later become famous world-wide. What the Salvation Army had discovered in London's East End, Christian missionaries had been discovering throughout the world. Most people needed a reason to give their allegiance to a mission, and for most people the gospel alone was not reason enough. Education, health provision, old-age pensions, all would in time be provided by the secular authorities. As leisure opportunities widened in England and the working people became more involved in politics, the Church grew less and less important in most people's lives. If the focus of the Salvation Army's work shifted to take this trend into account, Booth's missionary zeal remained unimpaired. In his last public address at the Royal Albert Hall on 9 May 1912, he concluded with undiminished vigour that 'while there remains one dark soul without the light of God, I'll fight – I'll fight to the very end'. Although the Army was by this time established in twenty-two countries, the golden age was over. It would gradually expand, but was soon destined to become just one more evangelical sect among many. Booth had without doubt kindled in many people a fervour for mission at home, but it proved a lot easier to ignite than to keep ablaze.

Times were changing to the detriment of Booth's cause. As the first foundations of state welfare provision were laid, the last real material link between parish church and parishioners was severed. The ominous threats that sinful, squalid London was on the verge of collapse came to nothing. Politics and new leisure opportunities were competing successfully for the attention of the working man. The Salvationist was losing his captive audience to the Labour politician, the trade unionist, and the manufacturer of the bicycle. Even the novel approach of the Army itself grew familiar, tired and finally began to bore people. As the nineteenth century gave way to the twentieth, it became clear that not even General William Booth had been able to achieve his dearest aim, to reach the heathen masses with the gospel.

Unusual seventeenth-century illuminated manuscript of third Moghul Emperor Jahangir with Indian rendering of Christ.

Below: Reading the Quran, Lahore.

Right: Muslims face Mecca in prayer, Kano, Nigeria. For Christian missionaries, Islam, itself a missionary faith, is the most pressing challenge: in the words of Dr Keith Parks, Director of the Southern Baptist Convention: 'Does your heart ever bleed for Mecca, the heartbeat of Islam?'

Left: A young Muslim in the doorway of Wazir Khan Mosque, Lahore.

Right: A fresh coat of paint for the Virgin Mary, outside the church of the Immaculate Conception, Panjim, Goa.

Overleaf: 1.1 million people gathered in Yoido Maza, Seoul, Korea in June 1973 for the largest known Christian gathering: a clear sign of the changing demography of Christianity.

237

JOHN JACOBS AND THE **POWER TEAM**

WORLD "WINNING THE BATTLE" TOUR

10th—13th JUNE 7·30 pm
Tickets £2.00 from SPORTS CENTRE

EVERTON PARK SPORTS CENTRE
GREAT HOMER STREET · LIVERPOOL 5·Tel: 051-207 1921

Luis Palau

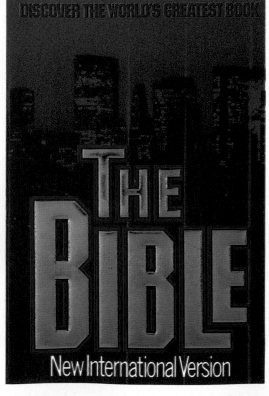

DISCOVER THE WORLD'S GREATEST BOOK

THE BIBLE
New International Version

12 Coming Full Circle

God is raising up an army to fight another battle, a battle for Europe. Europe the missionfield. Europe the battlefield. Will you join this army?

Floyd McClung, International Director of Youth With A Mission

In the Smithtown Gospel Tabernacle, Long Island, New York, 250 American Christians have just received the last stage of their missionary induction course. The sessions have been designed to prepare them for the demanding challenges they are likely to meet, to simulate disastrous situations that might occur, and to pray for the mission's success. The course complete, the missionaries are ferried in coaches to John F. Kennedy Airport. Another band of eager missionaries is leaving for the mission field. Their destination is neither Lagos nor Lahore, neither Rio de Janeiro nor Bombay. They are heading for Frankfurt. On 22 July 1989 the American mission team along with 3000 other Christians from around the world arrived in Offenburg, where many of the world's best-known evangelical leaders had gathered. It was the beginning of an audacious missionary offensive entitled 'Love Europe'. Over the next three months this huge volunteer army set out in an ambitious attempt to evangelise Europe.

Some weeks earlier, the crusade veteran Billy Graham had spearheaded 'Mission 89' to London. It was the most sophisticated, most expensive and most effective Christian crusade of its kind ever in Britain. Meanwhile the Argentinian evangelist, Luis Palau, Graham's heir apparent, had been leading a unique mission to the Welsh, called 'Tell Wales'. For six weeks, Palau preached throughout Wales, culminating in a week of mass evangelism in the Cardiff Arms Park sports stadium. In France, the Church of the Nazarene was mid-way through 'Thrust Paris', part of a campaign to boost the evangelical Church in major cities of the world. In the midst of France's revolutionary bicentennial fever, evangelicals held their own celebrations: 'Rev 89', a mass vigil dedicated to the 'true revolution' which had yet to come, Christian revival in France.

It was a remarkable summer, a convergence of some of the most powerful forces in modern mission. They all said the same thing: the continent that had done so much to shape the religious map of the world had lost its direction. In the words of Luis Palau, Europe had become 'an embarrassment to Christianity', a continent of what the German theologian Kierkegaard called 'baptised pagans'. In short, Europe, for centuries the cradle of Christian Mission, had itself become a mission field.

The evangelicals debate the precise definition of the European condition. Some say it is a 'post-Christian' continent. Some dispute that it has ever been truly Christian. Others, like Floyd McClung, International Director of Youth With A Mission, define secular Europe as a 'pre-Christian society' on the brink of a great revival, another reformation. In the meantime, he claims that Europe 'sits in a spiritual pig-pen'. For Floyd McClung the emotive metaphor is no over-statement: there is a fear that if Europe continues to turn its back on God, the time may come when God will turn His back on Europe. McClung's belligerent rhetoric echoes the appeals of the other great revivalist commanders, the Wesleys, George Whitefield, Dwight Moody, William Booth: 'Europe is not only a missionfield it's a battle-field, a spiritual battlefield. And I believe that the battle that is being fought for Europe today is far more important than even the great battle that was fought 40 years ago in World War Two. And once again we need an army of ordinary people, young and old.' Volunteers *are* enlisting for this army, mustering around the standards of their generals, Floyd McClung, Billy Graham, Luis Palau, George Verwer and Tony Campolo. It is a committed, well-financed missionary force. In the face of all the odds, their belief in their ability to win and their determination to do so are absolute.

The missionaries believe that Europe is in danger of being swamped by a tidal wave of secularism. They vigorously deny that this is the inevitable and ultimate destiny for all Christian nations. Tony Campolo, an American born-again sociologist, says that, on the contrary, it is religious renewal in Europe which is inevitable. And it is inevitable because there is such a popular craving for it: 'Spiritual hunger is everywhere. ET is such a religious film. Look at what ET does. He dies and is resurrected. And why is he resurrected? Because of a power from beyond. Where have you heard that story before? Rudolf the Red-nosed Reindeer: the despised, the rejected, the scorned becomes our saviour. We need a saviour.' The evangelists argue that the need for the mystical and the miraculous is so great that if it is not filled by Christianity it will be filled by something else. That, Tony Campolo fears, may be the occult: 'On British breakfast TV, Good Morning Britain, they give me ... the astrologist as though it's part of the news ... England accuses us of being mad because we have

Dereliction and decay in the established church. As few as 4 per cent of Britain's population are thought to attend church regularly.

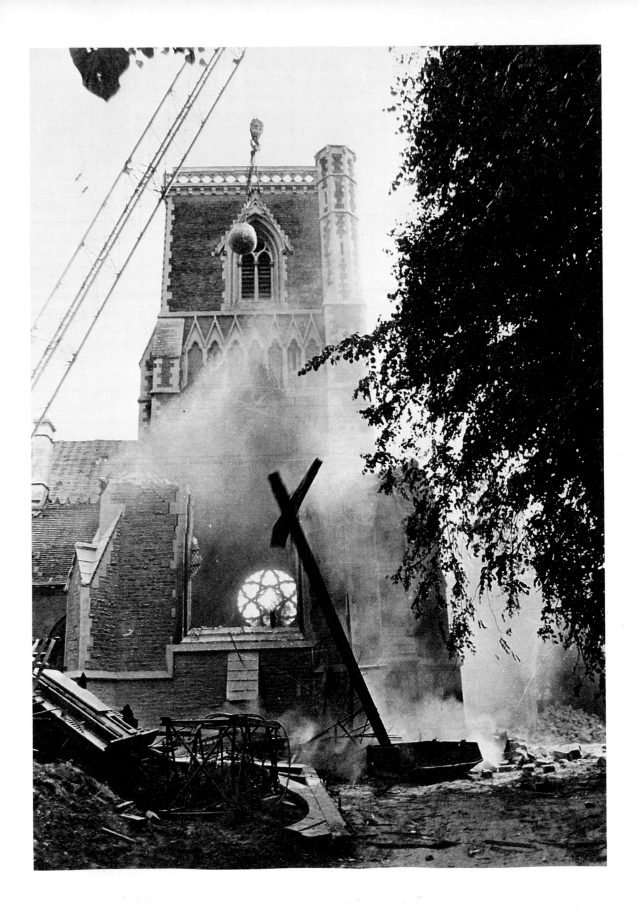

televangelism, but we're not nearly so crazy as to have horoscopes on TV.' A frequently quoted statistic in European missionary circles is that there are more spiritualist healers in France than medical doctors. Eastern religions and the human potential movement groups like Est and Insight are also growing in popularity throughout Europe. For evangelical Christians there is always the spectre of Islam. Volumes of anecdotal and statistical evidence have been amassed by the American societies to prove how deeply the continent is shrouded in spiritual darkness. Europe as a whole is characterised as materialistic, hedonistic, secular, apathetic, pessimistic and fearful. Each country is a slightly different blend of these ingredients.

When Booth published *In Darkest England* godlessness in Britain was presumed to be a contagion confined largely to the urban working classes. It was here that missionary activity was directed. Although there were notable exceptions, the middle classes remained, if not God-fearing, then at least church-going folk. A century later the picture had completely changed. The disease had spilled into middle-class suburbia and even the life-blood of the Church, the rural parishes, had been infected. On census Sunday in 1851, some 40 per cent of the population went to church. A century later it was nearer 10 per cent.

The statisticians quibble about just how low the figures are for practising Christians in Britain. Some argue that consistent church attendance is as low as 4 per cent. By 1986, a fifth of London's 2870 Protestant churches had congregations of less than twenty-five; three-quarters had less than a hundred members. The Church of England's Redundant Churches Department is having to assess a growing number of churches that are unable to attract a viable congregation. Churches all over Britain lie abandoned and derelict. In London particularly, church conversion has become big business. Disco lights illuminate the stained-glass windows of one central London church, renamed the Limelight Nightclub; in Barnsbury, Bromley-by-Bow, Ealing and High-gate, developers have turned Victorian churches into exclusive apartments; the London Symphony Orchestra rehearses in Holy Trinity, Southwark; St Mary's, Lambeth, has become a museum of garden history. In Wales, the Presbyterian Church is converting 300 churches into homes for young married couples struggling to buy a first house. Elsewhere, churches are being used as furniture warehouses, carpet discount stores and restaurants.

But concern over Britain's spiritual welfare is nothing compared to that over France. According to the American missionary David Barnes, despite the richness of their culture, the French 'are as ignorant of the things of God as the uncivilised natives of one of the world's darkest continents'. A mere 0.22 per cent of France's 54 million population are evangelical Protestants. Although 94 per cent are baptised Catholics, a mere 2 per cent regularly attend church. Despite the huge influence of the Catholic Church, the Unevangelised Fields Mission have declared France a mission field. A profile of France by the UFM revealed that the country was home to two and a half million clairvoyants. It also divided French characteristics into positive and negative groups. Among the positive 'French Frills' were: super skiing, delicious cheeses, love and loyalty to family life. Among the 'French Flaws': there are 7-year-olds who no longer believe God exists; the French are angry,

Church conversion is big business. St James's, Hatcham, New Cross, London, is now the Laban Centre for Dance.

intimidated people lacking a good and well-balanced self-image; and many people believe there are no principles worth dying for. The UFM have compared the French with the Americans, concluding that the French have 'an inner spiritual decay' which shows itself in their attitude to law and morality, which often goes against biblical principles. Robert Evans, American founder of the Greater Europe Mission, is one of the many evangelicals who have recommended a cure for these French ills. In a book entitled *Let Europe Hear* he asserted that the French are in need of salvation whether they admit it or not. As a nineteenth-century missionary might have reflected on an African tribe, he wrote: 'Since most of the homes of France do not have the Bible, her people show little sense of sin ... Only ignorance of the gospel among the French (not any biologically inborn stubbornness) keeps them from the unmerited blessings we enjoy in Bible-saturated lands.' He concluded optimistically, 'There is nothing wrong with France that Jesus Christ cannot put right.'

Whom do the missionaries hold responsible for the present spiritual condition of France, Britain and the rest of benighted Europe? Evans has no doubts as to the chief culprits. Like most evangelical Protestants, Evans does not believe that the Roman Catholic Church is truly Christian. Since Rome so effectively dominated much of Europe, and since the impact of the Reformation was only partial, the missionaries argue that many countries of Europe have never had a chance to hear the Good News at all. In evangelical missionary terms Catholic Europe is 'virgin territory'. Atheistic Marxism has also hastened Europe's spiritual decline, and along with Catholicism has been the continent's most destructive gift to the world: 'Together Rome and Moscow exercise a terrifying power over half of the human race. Both exclude and reject the gospel of salvation through faith in Christ. Are they really sisters under the skin? To the extent that they are the progeny of the same evil one, yes. Because Europe gave them birth, suckled them, and looses them upon the world, that continent qualifies today as one of the world's most needy mission fields.'

Chief among the remaining suspects for Europe's dark condition is the established Protestant Church. It is accused of working too hard to be relevant and to avoid offending the cultured community. It has ceased to believe in conversions, and has become a moral influence rather than a religious one. In short, the Church failed because it compromised the essence of the gospel. In the view of the evangelicals, people have left the Church because of the lack of relevance of its message and the lack of conviction shown by its ministers. For many, this enemy within is personified in Britain's David Jenkins, the Anglican Bishop of Durham. The entire fabric of the Church has ceased to have relevance and has become a caricature of Christianity with its old cathedrals, stained-glass windows and organ music. Luis Palau's solution is dramatic: 'Probably the best thing that could happen is for all that real estate to be sold out for high rate apartment buildings and start from scratch. Because it's people that matter to God, not buildings, not institutions ... if we had to raze all the buildings ... in a way it would be the greatest thing that could happen. Think of all that real estate and how useful it could be!'

In the dock alongside the established Church are the European intellectuals who first denied the deity of Christ and then the existence of God. From Voltaire and Rousseau onwards, they stand accused of passing on their humanism, rationalism, existentialism, Marxism, all of which the new missionaries regard as so many heresies. And to Luis Palau no man bears a greater burden of the guilt than Jean-Paul Sartre whose negative philosophy he sees reflected throughout Europe. Statistics suggest that the Second World War might also have accelerated Europe's rejection of Christianity. At the outbreak of war church attendance in the United States and Great Britain was comparable. By the end of the war six million Jews had died in concentration camps. Yet God was not seen to act. Hitler and Nazism were manifestly evil. If God existed, then why, people were entitled to ask, had He permitted such evil to flourish?

In their goal to re-evangelise Europe, the missionaries have set themselves a monumental task. They come without the incentives and leverage of material prosperity, which missionaries to Africa, South America and Papua New Guinea were able to wield with such success. The story they come to tell does not fall on fresh or open ears. In a post-Christian society it has lost its tarnish: Kalevi Lehtinen likens the difference between pre- and post-Christian Europe to the difference between a virgin and a divorcee, 'one of them has ideals, hopes, dreams and expectations; the other has frustrations, bitter memories, a bad aftertaste and apathy. Post-Christian Europe is like the divorced woman, divorced from Jesus Christ.' He pinpoints the problem at the core for this newest of missionary armies, a loss of idealism based on an inability to believe. Asking Europeans to believe in a world of God and Satan, seems to be asking them to deny their own intelligence. More importantly, the tools of the missionaries' trade, the carrot and stick of salvation and damnation, have lost the power to frighten. But in the end, for Lehtinen and others like him, so total is their conviction in the persuasive power of the gospel message that they believe that somewhere along the line the presentation must have failed. Perhaps Europe has not had the opportunity to confront the real gospel. The effort of the missionary to Europe goes two ways: into devising new

ways of presenting the gospel that will penetrate the indifference and apathy, and into making sure that when the message gets through it is in their terms the right one, of personal salvation through a personal relationship with Jesus Christ.

No missionary has better captured the winning combination of presentation and message than Billy Graham. In a lifetime of mass evangelism, he has communicated his message to more people than any other missionary in history. Over four decades, the Graham team have perfected the stadium crusade as a means of making maximum impact on British society. His crusades represent a triumph of strategy based on a solid, unchanging fundamentalist message. Perhaps the greatest achievement of all has been to get himself, and by implication his evangelical message, embraced and endorsed at the highest levels by the British religious and political establishment. In 1955 two million attended Billy Graham's meetings, with an estimated 40 000 responding to his invitation to accept Christ. In 1966 almost a million people heard him at Earls Court. At the end of his 1984 crusade, his statisticians calculated that 96 982 people had registered public Christian commitments. In 'Mission 89' a galaxy of satellite link-ups were employed so that, in addition to the regular crowds, on huge screens all round Britain more of the population than ever before could catch the Billy

Pat Robertson, evangelist and American Presidential candidate, is in the forefront of Christian media evangelism with his Christian Broadcasting Network.

Graham experience.

Amplification, telecommunications and advances in satellite broadcasting allow the modern evangelist to communicate with larger and larger numbers, but the mass crusade to Britain is not a twentieth-century creation. Estimated gatherings of 20 000 listened to the eighteenth-century evangelist George Whitefield preach unaided from a portable pulpit in Blackheath, London. His unorthodox open-air rallies scandalised the clerical establishment of the day. Dwight L. Moody, the greatest evangelical figure in nineteenth-century America, visited London in 1875 and 1884. The press were quick to ridicule the 'illiterate preacher' who believed he had something to offer imperial England, but far from scandalising his audience, Moody electrified it. And while commentators derided him as a charlatan and his crusade as hopelessly un-British, the crowds flocked to see him. Over four months in 1875 Moody addressed an estimated two and a half million people, at a series of meetings in Islington's Agricultural Hall. He returned nine years later and an average of 9000 people went to hear him each day. Doubtless many people went to hear him more than once, and most who attended were probably Christians already. It was still a great achievement, suggesting that mass evangelism could work in Britain.

The numbers that cram the stadiums are indisputable, but what, the analysts ask, is the lasting impact of such missions? Do they bring the evangelicals any nearer their goal of winning the country for Christ? Or are the great missionary drives just temporary staging posts on the road to secularism? Certainly Moody's celebrated visits did not prevent the spread of the moral jungle that Booth believed to exist in 1890, any more than Billy Graham's crusades of 1955 and 1966 were able to forestall the anti-establishment backlash of the 1960s. Short revivals do often follow the campaign of a popular evangelist, but historically these have merely served briefly to staunch the flow of people out of church, before it begins again. The modern missionary to Europe has higher ambitions, to turn the river of desertion right around, so that it begins to flow in the opposite direction. This is the long-term aim. In the short term, the goal is to ensure that 'God-consciousness sweeps a city'. In other words, to devise ways of making a Christian event the talk of a predominantly secular city. The strategists believe that if this can be achieved, they have created an atmosphere with the potential to have a real impact on society: existing Christians have an opportunity to step into the limelight and focus their own evangelistic efforts, and national Church leaders receive a boost of morale. Best of all there is an increased chance of reaching the most prized converts of all, those who will not go near a church.

Billy Graham learnt early the lesson of what was possible with effective planning. His first mission to Britain was in 1946 as part of a four-man Youth for Christ team. The national press ignored him. However, an Anglican clergyman, Tom Livermore, commented that Graham had the attribute essential in a mass evangelist, 'tremendous appeal to the ignorant and unlettered and the rougher element of the boys and girls'. By 1954, at the age of 35, his preaching power and film-star looks had made him the best-known preacher in the United States. He was tempted across the Atlantic for a second time, to lead a crusade in central London. One day out of Southampton docks, Graham was given the news that a Labour Member of Parliament was trying to bar his admission to England on the grounds that he was interfering in British politics under the cloak of religion. A prayer calendar had been discovered at his headquarters in Minneapolis with a picture of London. Under it was the sentence: 'What Hitler's bombs could not do, socialism with its accompanying evils shortly accomplished.' Graham's supporters argued that it was the work of a subordinate and that in any case 'socialism' meant 'secularism' in their lexicon. The move to bar Graham failed, but in a swift stroke it put an end to his anonymity. The press dogged his footsteps and a huge crowd greeted his arrival at Waterloo Station in London. The barrage had not been planned, but for the crusade team it was providential. Billy Graham was on the map.

In an article in the *People* newspaper Graham was dubbed 'Silly Billy'. It continued, 'Being bulldozed into loving God by ecstatic young men who talk about him with easy familiarity is something which makes the biggest British sinner shudder.' The charge was essentially the same one that had been levied at Moody a century earlier: Graham's style was un-British. But the cynicism of the press, its veiled anti-Americanism and its deep-rooted assumption that in the areas of spiritual life Britain had nothing to learn from an American, were not matched by the public response. For three months Billy Graham consistently packed Harringay stadium with crowds of 12 000. The mission hired long-distance telephone lines to relay the sermon to theatres, concert halls and churches throughout Britain – a technique the BBC had used to relay speeches by Lloyd George. By the end of the crusade no one could ignore Graham. The Lord Mayor and the Archbishop of Canterbury, Geoffrey Fisher, were among the crowd of 12 000 at Wembley Stadium for the mission finale, the largest religious congregation ever seen in Britain. When Graham made his invitation at the end, thousands came forward.

Conclusive proof that Graham had been given the British seal of approval came when he was granted a private audience with Sir Winston Churchill. And the Royal assent followed in a sympathetic and encouraging letter from Queen Elizabeth the Queen Mother. Here was no Southern hick preacher: Billy Graham had the stamp of respectability. Graham was back again in 1955, this time to Glasgow. The headline in the local newspaper on 9 March read simply, 'Glasgow belongs to Billy'. The early hostility of the media had been replaced by a bemused incomprehension at his success, and even signs of fondness. Britain had embraced Graham as the acceptable face of American evangelism. Graham for his part had accommodated his approach to the British cultural environment, leaving behind the loud suits and ties and moderating his aggressive delivery at the microphone. By this time the mission had been extended into 'Operation Andrew', which established the principle that every Christian should bring a non-Christian to hear Billy Graham. On Good Friday of that year, Britain's only television channel was given over to Graham's sermon. Graham was not afraid of the secular media: and the BBC for its part loved Graham. The American evangelist was 'good television'.

Over the next decades the strategy was refined, but the elements remained the same. 'Mission 89' was the most sophisticated crusade ever seen in Britain, the culmination of years of planning. A subsidiary of the Saatchi and Saatchi advertising agency was brought in to run a clever campaign based around anagrams of the word 'Life', which developed over the weeks leading up to Graham's arrival. By the first night of the crusade, Graham's picture could be seen in tube stations, on hoardings, in places of work and in house windows all over London. Graham had been interviewed on several major radio programmes, and on Britain's most popular television chat show, *Wogan*. Thousands of counsellors had been trained to follow up on the 'inquirers', who came forward in their thousands each time Graham invited the crowds to commit their lives to Christ. Their work ensured that the impact of the crusade was felt long after Billy Graham had returned to Minneapolis.

London was, as always, fertile ground for Graham, but while he preached to huge crowds, Luis Palau was tackling the stonier ground of Wales. The scattered and divided population of a rural society was not conducive to mass rallies. So Palau and his 'Tell Wales' team adapted their strategy. On a blustery day in June 1989 at Welshpool Football Ground, Luis Palau rose to preach. Around the base of the stand were gathered a group of Welsh sheep farmers who had come to watch the sheep-shearing skills of the New Zealander Godfrey Bowen, a former world champion sheep shearer. Bowen, a born-again Christian, had invited Palau to give an evangelistic message after his display. Palau took the theme of the lost sheep, of which he contended there were far too many in Wales. By his standards it was a tiny crowd, measured in tens, not thousands, and several people drifted away as he began to preach. But Palau and his supporters were happy: they had completed another stage in their ten-week campaign to 'Tell Wales' about the gospel. Their plan to target the sheep farmers had been a qualified success.

There is a heavy irony in each mission Palau leads to Europe, for it was British missionaries who first converted him as a 12-year-old schoolboy in Argentina. Palau has returned to Britain several times since, to show the country where it has gone astray. He feels that Europe itself has become a mission field, second only to the Islamic world. In his eyes there is a particular urgency about the re-evangelisation of Europe: 'I say it's either back to the Bible or back to the jungle – a moral jungle, an ethical jungle, which is already beginning to encroach on society more and more ... if we deny God, turn our backs on Jesus Christ and act like the Bible was a big joke ... we could go right back, other Empires have fallen, Europe could also fall because there is no reason why God should buttress it and protect it. If you turn your back on God, God turns his back on society. The result is decay and demoralisation and depression.' This urgency determines Luis Palau's technique. Time is running out and there is still so much to do and for Palau, the way to reach the uncommitted masses is through the big cities, as they influence the nation. To have any chance of making an impression on a city, Palau, like Graham, has first to grab its attention. In Cardiff his answer was simple and effective: his picture, and the caption 'Try listening to Luis Palau', appeared on buses all over the city. This was complemented by a series of radio and television appearances and a sustained newspaper advertising campaign. To accusations that the media and his message did not mix Palau retorted: 'I think St Paul would have been the champion of the media. Paul went to the market place. Today the market place is radio, television and the press. Paul went where the battle was on, and the battle today is in the media. He couldn't have done it without the media today.'

It is all part of what Palau calls 'an impact package ... You've got to hit society from the top to the bottom'. Hiring the Cardiff Arms Park stadium, with a capacity of over 50 000, was a key element of the strategy as it raised both curiosity and expectation. In the event it seemed like a gesture of extreme over-confidence: only four or five thousand people came each evening, leaving most of the stadium empty. A comparison between the meagre gathering to hear Palau and the huge crowds that come to watch a rugby game was inescapable. Palau's team remained optimistic: the small turn-out only symbolised the profundity of spiritual need in Wales.

Palau himself was more open about the disappointing response which he saw as indicative of the hardened resistance to the gospel throughout Europe. The team decided to change its strategy. Mass evangelism in the stadium can be effective, but it is not precise, and makes the same approach to a wide variety of people. So evangelism by 'affinity group' was devised, the idea being to target particular groups of people such as executive women, or business men, or bankers. Christian women would invite a non-Christian woman to a lavish lunch, or a Christian business man would sponsor a table at a hotel and fill it with non-Christian friends. After the meal Palau would deliver a short, sharp address. There and then he would invite the non-Christian half of the audience to commit their lives to Christ. Not only would this enable him to reach a prize pool of converts, influential middle-class business people who were unlikely to come to his open-air gatherings, but it would give him the chance to target his message more effectively. As a strategy it has echoes of nineteenth-century evangelism, where missionaries targetted a working group such as the dockers or the flower-girls and preached to them as a group in the tea-breaks. In other respects it is a very contemporary approach which capitalises on the habits and expectations of the primarily middle-class target groups. For Palau a long series of affinity groups proved the success of the 'Tell Wales' campaign. In the dining-room of a plush Cardiff hotel he addressed 300 women, professionals and wives of professionals. He spoke of the fears he suspected they might have, such as divorce and widowhood, their concerns for their children, and explained that a personal relationship with Jesus was the only way to complete peace of mind and total security. It was an effective sermon. As it ended the women were asked to make a commitment, and indicate whether they had done so by ticking a card. More than a hundred cards were collected. The formula was repeated over lunch the next day with a large group of business men in a sports hall. This time Palau's message addressed the pressures in business life, political instability, family responsibilities and extra-marital affairs.

Palau has also introduced the principle of targetting into his stadium crusades. The penultimate night of his mission week at Cardiff Arms Park was designated youth night. He delivered an uncompromising message about teenage sex and sexuality, warning his audience about the moral consequences of promiscuity: 'I'm telling you thousands have a hard and a dirty conscience here in Wales, and you're headed for trouble and disaster, because thousands are breaking the laws of God's purity for their life.' Having exposed the nerve-ends of guilt, his tone became more positive, showing the crowd a way out: 'You know ... sex is ... a beautiful gift from God for young people, and for people of all ages ... when you practise it in the plan of God which is one man and one woman married in Jesus Christ'. Finally he made the beseeching, anguished appeal: 'Don't let the world destroy you, don't let sin stomp all over you, don't let the devil take you away ... Young girls, 12, 13, 15, 17, come beautiful girls, if Jesus isn't your Lord make him your Lord tonight ... Oh if only I could walk up there and grab you by the hand and say come on man give yourself to Christ. But it is better that I don't do it, Jesus Christ is there and he's calling you by the Holy Spirit ... Please come.' Several hundred young people, some in tears, made their way down to the pitch where a battery of counsellors stood to receive them.

With the vigour and passion of a revivalist preacher and the nous of an experienced politician. Palau brings his message to bear with relevance on each group that he addresses. To Palau, this precision and flexibility constitute the beauty of the strategy, and this is why he sees in it the future of mass evangelism: 'You can go to a group of leadership wives of industrialists and politicians, they know world events, they are well-read people. You can refer to Christina Onassis, you can refer to Elizabeth Taylor, you can refer to Joan Collins and they're into that world; then you go to Bolivia, switching to another part of the world and you're talking to peasant women ... now you're talking tortillas, potatoes and clothing.' Palau has used this strategy in countries as different as America and Bolivia, but nowhere has it been more effective than in Europe. Throughout the continent, missionaries are targetting affinity groups, by age, by profession, by wealth. In this way they hope to break through the impasse of apathy and indifference, and to permeate every level of European society with evangelical Christians.

In June 1989 the first ever European Christian Sports Congress was held, on the shores of Lake Traun in Austria. The financial sponsors included Athletes in Action, an American evangelistic organisation that uses athletics and sport as a means to reach people with the gospel. The conference had two aims: firstly to target athletes, a vulnerable and lonely group of professionals, and secondly to devise ways of using existing Christian athletes as missionaries. The debate was thorough, asking whether faith in Jesus Christ automatically led to athletic success. The delegates discussed ways of reaching top athletes, often isolated in an effort to keep away the media and the fans, ways of giving the Christian message in press interviews, and of maximising the opportunities for evangelism at major sports meetings. They outlined how one could turn oneself into 'an athlete for God', and glorify God in one's performance. It was a model of the new missionary method, targetting at its most precise and comprehensive.

The business, military and political élite have fallen into the sights of Campus Crusade for Christ. Among the many branches of this huge American organisation is a group based in London known as Executive Ministries. The group seeks out evangelical Christian couples in the upper echelons of European society who must be willing and able to make a substantial financial commitment. Suitable couples agree to host and to pay for an exclusive dinner engagement for up to as many as a hundred guests. A venue is chosen and gilt-edged invitations are sent out to the couple's non-Christian friends and acquaintances. Campus Crusade's involvement is not mentioned on the invitation – at this stage it is portrayed as a personal invitation between the host couple and the guest. Executive Ministries provide a speaker at the dinner, usually a senior man in military or business circles, who will make an address on a topic such as 'The ten commandments for the business community'. Afterwards the speaker will offer the obligatory invitation to the audience. Those who express a commitment to Christ are asked to fill in confidential cards. This is where the task of the host couple ends, and the missionaries step in. Any who have expressed an interest in knowing more about Christ will be followed up for Christian counselling. Rather like the nineteenth-century missionaries to the South Seas who aimed to convert an island chief, knowing that in so doing they would convert the island, Executive Ministries believe that if they can convert some of the most powerful men and women in Europe, the impact will be felt throughout society.

At the opposite end of the social scale, Paula Shields has made her missionary goal the redemption of prostitutes. This is more conventional missionary territory. Shields travels regularly to Amsterdam to minister to the women of the red light district. She became a missionary in 1982, fully expecting and hoping to go to Africa, 'because that's where missionaries go'. Instead her Episcopal Church in Seattle sent her to Europe. In 1984 she travelled to Amsterdam and found herself in a meeting of Christian women who had formerly been prostitutes. The group met in a building called the Cleft which had become a drop-in centre for prostitutes established by the evangelical Youth With A Mission. Its position was deliberate. As Floyd McClung put it: 'The Cleft is as deep into "enemy territory" as it is possible to go, right at the core of the Red Light District. To us it symbolises the rock in the wilderness which Moses struck, and from which God caused water to come streaming out.' By the time Paula Shields arrived in the wilderness, Lura Garrida, another American missionary, was already well acclimatised. The women Lura was working among were Spanish-speaking, attracted from South America and the Antilles; the money they earned was sent home to their families. High above the sex shops and brothels of the red light district rises the ornate tower of the Oude Kerk, Old Church. Consecrated more than six hundred years ago, it is Amsterdam's oldest and biggest church. To the evangelicals, Oude Kerk, isolated in a sea of sin and depravity, stands as a perfect symbol of the old established Church. For the prostitutes who ply their trade in its shadow, it is as close as many wish to get to Christianity. Youth With A Mission had other ideas, and slowly and discreetly began to make contact with the women.

In a deserted car park underneath the metro station at Gaasperplas, where the women live, a Pentecostal church called Pinksterge Meente had been built. It was to this church, 'the Underground Church' as they called it, that several of the prostitutes were invited, and here that Paula Shields first addressed the women. She calls her meetings 'Healing of the Soul seminars', using the facts of her own unhappy life to relate to the hurts and unhappiness of the prostitutes. As a child she was sexually abused by a teenage neighbour, her parents divorced and she was abandoned by her own husband. She preaches an uncomplicated gospel of healing, a God of forgiveness who penetrated the hard protective shell built over years of rejection, sorrow and guilt. The implications for a prostitute of becoming a Christian are considerable, as they are giving up both their source of income and their family which depends on them for support. It is partly for this reason that she refuses to condemn the prostitutes, 'I believe the Holy Spirit is the one that convicts people of their sins', nor does she ask that they leave their work. She leaves all that to the workings of the Holy Spirit. The women testify that it is only with something as dramatic and total as

Christian conversion that they can escape the considerable financial attractions of the work: 'You need a power beyond your own to bring you out of this.' The mission to the women of the red light district has mushroomed. The former prostitutes often feel a considerable duty to pass on the Good News, and join the evangelistic force. To the missionaries involved, the red light district of Amsterdam symbolises Satan's grip on Europe, the frontline of battle between good and evil. The growing congregation in the Underground Church is for them a sign that the battle is beginning to go Christ's way.

If Europe has become the new Dark Continent, then the inner city is the Whiteman's Graveyard. Malaria, yellow fever and the prospect of an early death struck fear into the heart of many nineteenth-century missionaries to West Africa. Few prospects are more daunting to a modern missionary than to suffer ridicule, abuse and indifference on the streets of a European city. Stephen Wilson is one of the new breed of missionaries, in many respects as courageous as their predecessors. His chosen mission field is Paris, and in few places can the prospects for an evangelical Protestant be more bleak. Each Thursday afternoon, Wilson and his small team of Americans and native French leave their headquarters in Belleville, the Chinese quarter, carrying a twelve-foot wooden cross through the streets. In a city used to street theatre and buskers, the little band, their cross and a large banner proclaiming 'Dieu aime Paris', still manage to prompt a response in everyone they pass – blank curiosity in some, jeers in others. Their destination is the Georges Pompidou centre, the epitome of creative, secular, decadent Paris. The piazza in front of the building is a mecca for street performers from all over the world. There, amid the fire-eaters, reggae musicians, anarchists, and mime artists, Steve Wilson's group sets up the wooden cross. The piazza is a theatrical and political market-place, and Wilson is just one vendor among many. It is never very difficult to attract a crowd as the French seem to enjoy a good argument about religion. And instead of passing round a hat at the end, he hands out Gospel portions instead. At the end of the short message, the Christian group mingles with the crowd, in the hope that some of his words will have fallen on open ears.

On Sunday mornings, Steve Wilson and a small group of Parisians meet for church in a third-floor apartment of a house in the heart of the Latin Quarter. It is in every respect an unusual service. The meeting begins at 11 a.m. and, as the church-goers arrive, they are served with coffee and croissants from tables decorated with linen napkins and vases of red roses. They spend half an hour at breakfast, sitting and chatting among themselves. They are a fashionable group, and include several artists. The service itself is brief, uncomplicated and evangelical.

The pastor is Steven Johnston, a missionary from America. This church is simply his answer to the problem of Paris. To most Parisians church means the dark, cold, forbidding formality of the Catholic Church; Johnston's approach is designed to tempt them back to Christianity. He talks about 'welcoming structures': if the right atmosphere is created, warm, relaxed and trendy, he believes there are people prepared to listen to his message even in the heart of the Parisian artistic community.

Stephen Wilson's open-air evangelism: competing for the attention of young Parisians outside the Centre Georges Pompidou.

In the evenings Stephen Wilson meets up with friends on a yellow double-decker bus, the 'Bus for Jesus', parked by the Forum des Halles, a café-lined square packed with tourists and young Parisians. After a short prayer meeting, in which they pray for Paris, the team set off into the streets again in the hope of persuading a few more people that 'Jésus donne la vie'. It is tough, unenviable work, but Wilson carries on with unquenchable optimism, strong in his belief that the battle must be fought against the powers of evil: 'We won't lay down our arms until every nation is bowed and on bended knees before the Lord.'

For France, Wilson accepts that that day may be some considerable time away. But he has pledged himself to the task of bringing the French people to Christ and is prepared to stay for as long as it takes. A vocation that for many would appear to represent struggle and hardship has been anything but dispiriting for Wilson: for him, it is a privilege to be a missionary.

The dilemmas faced by city missionaries like Wilson have changed little since General Booth marshalled his Salvation Army on the streets of London's East End a century ago. Booth was faced with getting to people who never went to church, who spent their waking hours in the gin-palaces and public houses. But it was not enough simply to get to the people: once there, the missionary had to confront the fact that most people did not want to know about religion. Booth's solutions caused considerable consternation at the time, but initially at least they were highly effective.

David Pierce would probably have seen eye to eye with the General. Pierce is one of the most outspoken and unconventional members of

Extreme measures to counter the indifference of Dutch youth. David Pierce, covered in flour and swathed in ropes, rolls on the cobbles of Dam Square, Amsterdam.

Europe's modern missionary army. His uniform alone sets him apart – his hair is long, his jeans torn, he wears dark glasses and a pair of black braces. His headquarters are in Amsterdam on a long red barge, known as Steige 14. Pierce is the lead singer of a heavy metal rock band called 'No Longer Music'. Their music is of the loudest, hardest, and brashest kind, but Pierce's lyrics speak of Christ's love. Each Wednesday the barge becomes a night-club, Pierce calls it 'The Rock 'n' Roll Bible Study', when hundreds of young people come for a few hours of Pierce's own brand of rock 'n' roll, lightly garnished with a little Bible study.

Pierce first visited Amsterdam as a back-packer, fresh from university in America. What he saw appalled him: coffee bars selling drugs openly over the counter, sex shops in the red light district that specialised in child pornography, a popular fascination with the occult, satanism and Eastern religions. The tolerance for which the city was known had done little for Christianity: as few as 3 per cent of the population went to church, and that meant even fewer young people. Pierce, a born-again Christian, became convinced that Amsterdam was in the power of Satan, who attracted the youth of Europe to Amsterdam with freedom, but the freedom was illusory, a trap-door to drug addiction, AIDS and prostitution. The only true freedom was to be gained through a personal relationship with God. He described these young people as the 'lost generation of Europe', a generation without any spiritual values. It was his God-given responsibility to show them where they had gone wrong. All he needed was a means to communicate his unpopular message that would not further alienate young people. He was struck by the power that rock musicians had to influence many of those he sought to convert. Even though Pierce himself had no musical ability, the band was formed. His songs deal with sex, drugs, death, the Devil and the Crucifixion. They appeal for a return to biblical faith and morality, with the threat of death for those who ignore it:

> I sleep with her, all the time,
> Liberation of body and mind,
> Adulterous generation destroying mankind,
> The Bible lays it on the line,
> It's very clear there's not much time,
> To run from God you run to death.

The lyrics are uncompromising, but the music is frenetic, pounding and aggressive, virtually indistinguishable from any other heavy metal music. It is precisely this sort of music that Pierce and many other fundamentalist Christians believe is Satanic. Pierce insists there is a difference between the two. He at least is sure he is not playing the

Devil's music: 'Music in itself is just a neutral medium. What makes it good or bad is the heart of the musician ... If you can worship God with classical music, if you can worship God with black gospel music, why can't you worship God with heavy metal music?' He dismisses accusations that his technique is inappropriate: he is simply trying to rouse the sleeping people in Amsterdam with the noise of his message. In the last resort he turns to the Bible: 'Sometimes the children of Israel would wish of God so loud that the ground would shake. It was like an earthquake. ... Sure you can praise God with loud music.' 'No Longer Music' have played in squatters' camps, in clubs frequented by anarchists, terrorists and drug dealers; and in one bar which had a mural of the Virgin Mary with a noose around her neck on the wall. For the young Christians it is dangerous territory, but they enjoy the heroic quality which it gives their work. They see themselves cutting an open path for Christ through a Dark Continent. For Pierce there is no greater thrill than to be where he believes his Master would be. Ultimately, if Pierce and his missionary band are to have any chance of success among the fashion-conscious youth of Amsterdam, they have to prove that it can be 'cool' to be Christian. Pierce maintains that Christians are already in the radical vanguard: 'Because it's the status quo not to believe in God. It's the status quo to be anti-Christ.'

'Radical' is one of the favourite words of John Jacobs, leader of possibly the most bizarre missionary organisation that exists. Like Pierce, Jacobs set himself the challenge of breaking through Western disinterest in the evangelical Christianity that he believed could save the world. His solution was the Power Team, a group of male body-builders who pump iron for Jesus. In the course of an evening, they break cement paving-stones with their heads, crack walls of ice, and blow up hot-water bottles like balloons. The show is interspersed with yells, 'I declare war on the anti-Christ', 'Death to Satan, death to the spirit of occultism'. At the end of the display the triumphant, triangular men stand among the debris of cement, ice and hot water bottles and invite the audience to accept Jesus into their lives. John Jacobs testifies that he was once in danger of becoming a loser, the one who stuttered, who was bad at lessons and bad at games. That was until God came into his life, and helped make him one of the strongest men in America. 'God gives power' is their message, the power to excel, to fulfil one's potential, possibly even the power to break slabs of concrete. In the summer of 1988 the Power Team enlisted as recruits in the missionary army to Europe. They toured Britain inviting people to come and see 'radical Christians' doing 'radical things' for a 'radical Jesus'. The shock tactics did work for some and at the end of each show there were those who were persuaded to register a commitment. But for many more, the Power Team represented the very worst of American showbiz, which degraded and belittled the Christian message. The critics argued that the Power Team reduced complex theological debate to absurd trials of strength, and simply became objects of fun. In America, the Power Team are a good distance from the mainstream, but they do have their own regular television programme, and their feats of strength are applauded rather than derided. The American audiences can enjoy John Jacobs's exuberance about his faith. It makes Europeans distinctly uneasy.

As in any missionary relationship, cultural differences are at the heart of the mission from America to Europe. In his book *Let Europe Hear* Robert Evans explained the relationship from an American perspective: 'We are living in the American Age ... Western Europe has become increasingly dependent on American leadership of the free world ... What better gift could we impart than the knowledge of Jesus Christ as Saviour and Lord?' Yet many Europeans have no wish to be patronised by a country which was itself evangelised by Europe and feel that to ask a European to embrace a fundamentalist, Bible-based, anti-evolutionary gospel is to ask him to deny the intellectual and philosophical traditions of which he is so proud. Church, the new missionaries say, can be anywhere, in a home, in a football stadium, with improvised prayers, and with simple choruses sung to a guitar. All that ultimately matters is the position of the individual before God. They are asking Europe to be prepared to sacrifice its great Christian structures and traditions on the altar of the personal relationship with Christ. It is a struggle that in the future will be fought fiercely in the airwaves. Prevented from broadcasting on the main television channels throughout Europe, American evangelical organisations have been marshalling their resources to make the most of the communications explosion in satellite and cable broadcasting. As Britain's first satellite channel, Sky Television, began transmission in 1989, audiences were able to watch 'The Hour of Power', a weekly evangelistic programme hosted by the American pastor, Robert Schuller, in which he promised to turn Europe's 'scars into stars'. In Belgium, the Pentecostal Assemblies of God have established their International Media Mission outside Brussels. In a bid to communicate the Christian message to the very young, IMM have devised a Christian puppet show, similar to the Muppets. Recorded in French, the programmes are taken by schools for language learning purposes. The first messages the young students receive in a new language are those of the evangelical gospel. In the heart of the Black Forest in West Germany, the Media Academy at Altensteig has been producing Christian programmes, promoting the gospel of individual salvation. For too long, they claim, the media have

The Revd Robert Schuller in his Crystal Cathedral: 'Finally we have a church where the heavens can do their thing.' Schuller has time on Rupert Murdoch's Sky Channel.

been dominated by men and women of anti-Christian beliefs, secular humanism and even open occultism. But, 'A new day is dawning on the spiritual darkness of Europe.'

In the scramble for the soul of Europe, America is the key player. America has the money that keeps the great wheels of the modern missionary machine turning. But voices from the poorer parts of the world are also trying to make themselves heard. For centuries, missionaries flooded from Europe to South America, to India, to the Far East and to Africa. For the first time a trickle is beginning in the opposite direction. In October 1987 three Nigerian nuns, Maura, Bibiana and Bernadette, arrived in Manchester. They had come to repay the debt they felt that Nigerian Christians owed to the European missionaries. Their reception was neither warm nor joyful, and it soon became apparent to them that the country which had sent missionaries to their homes, was in truth less Christian than their own. It seemed that Britain was embarrassed by, rather than proud of, its missionary legacy. More than once Sister Bernadette sat down next to white people in church on Sunday, only to see them move to different seats. She is philosophical about it and accepts that there are bound to be difficulties at the beginning. Like the missionaries who came to Africa, she and her colleagues will hold out. They may be digging in for a long barren period. For centuries, Europe told itself that other countries needed the Christian civilisation that it could provide. The belief that one has what another needs is at the core of mission. The sisters accept that it will take an unprecedented act of humility before Europe is prepared to accept it needs Christian aid from those it once converted.

Mother Teresa's Missionaries of Charity have already established centres all over Europe. The continent is not blighted with leprosy, nor starvation, but there are other afflictions: homelessness, loneliness, drug addiction and AIDS. On a visit to England in 1989, to the chagrin of the Prime Minister, Mrs Thatcher, Mother Teresa highlighted the plight of homeless people sleeping in 'cardboard city' under Waterloo Bridge in London. It was a simple reiteration that even in its affluence Europe has spiritual and material needs. It was also a reminder that just as Christianity is not the exclusive property of the Western Church, nor is missionary work any longer a monopoly of the rich and powerful nations.

Inner-city Birmingham is the adopted home of Patrick Kalelombe, a Roman Catholic Bishop and a 'White Father' missionary from Malawi. His work aims to recharge the divided, ailing Church in Britain, by bringing black and white Christians together, and infusing them with some of the joy and warmth of African worship. In coming to England, Kalelombe feels he is bringing the Church back to its roots, to a position of human weakness, symbolised in Paul's travels around the Roman Empire. He is a black man in a white country. He has no medicine to offer, no education, no gimmicks, none of the material benefits with which to coerce people to follow him. Those that come to hear him cannot be 'rice Christians': they do not come under any pretence that it will make them more rich, or more powerful, or more intelligent. This, he believes, is how mission should be: Christianity stripped of its temporal robes, as in the days before the Constantinian conversion, when the missionary travelled without the trappings of power, privilege and cultural superiority, armed only with his faith in the crucifixion story.

As the twentieth century of Christianity draws to an end, the missionary story has come full circle, back to Europe's front door. At the threshold stand two types of missionary. One, aggressive and imperialistic, who talks of world evangelisation, of spiritual warfare, and of conquering kingdoms for Christ. He is armed with satellites, computers, aeroplanes, television stations and advertising companies. The other has learnt the lessons of imperial Christianity from the other side, and talks, like Sister Bernadette from Nigeria, in humbler terms: 'I'm working for humanity, no matter what. God has created all of us. Irrespective of who people are, they need our care.'

Largest American Protestant Mission Agencies

Missionaries and reported income for overseas ministries

Mission Income (US $ m)

Southern Baptist Convention, Foreign Mission Board
136.5 $$
1985 Missionaries 3,346 👤👤👤👤👤👤👤👤👤👤👤👤👤👤👤👤👤👤👤👤👤👤👤👤👤👤👤👤👤👤👤👤👤👤

Wycliffe Bible Translators (Summer Institute of Linguistics)
36.8 $$$$$$$$$$$$$$$$
3,022 👤👤👤👤👤👤👤👤👤👤👤👤👤👤👤👤👤👤👤👤👤👤👤👤👤👤👤👤👤👤

Youth With A Mission
Not recorded
1,741 👤👤👤👤👤👤👤👤👤👤👤👤👤👤👤👤👤👤

New Tribes Mission
10.2 $$$$$$$$
1,438 👤👤👤👤👤👤👤👤👤👤👤👤👤👤

Assemblies of God Foreign Missions
56.8 $$$$$$$$$$$$$$$$$$$$$$$$$$
1,237 👤👤👤👤👤👤👤👤👤👤👤👤

General Conference of the Seventh-Day Adventists
70.2 $$$$$$$$$$$$$$$$$$$$$$$$$$$$$$$
1,052 👤👤👤👤👤👤👤👤👤👤👤

Churches of Christ
52.0 $$$$$$$$$$$$$$$$$$$$$$$$
982 👤👤👤👤👤👤👤👤👤👤

The Evangelical Alliance Mission
16.6 $$$$$$$
929 👤👤👤👤👤👤👤👤👤

Christian and Missionary Alliance		Baptist Bible Fellowship	
12.4 $$$$$		12.4 $$$$$	
874 👤👤👤👤👤👤👤👤👤		620 👤👤👤👤👤👤	
Christian Churches/Churches of Christ		**Church of the Nazarene**	
15.6 $$$$$$$		17.6 $$$$$$$	
709 👤👤👤👤👤👤👤		595 👤👤👤👤👤👤	
SIM International		**Baptist International Missions**	
15.1 $$$$$$$		9.1 $$$$	
654 👤👤👤👤👤👤👤		593 👤👤👤👤👤👤	
Baptist Mid-Missions		**Campus Crusade for Christ**	
9.5 $$$$		20.0 $$$$$$$$	
636 👤👤👤👤👤👤👤		574 👤👤👤👤👤👤	

Select Bibliography

ALI, Michael Nazir, *Frontiers in Muslim–Christian Encounter*, Oxford Regnum Books, 1987.

BOOTH, General William, *In Darkest England and the Way Out*, Salvation Army, 1890.

BRIDGES, Lucas, *Uttermost Part of the Earth*, Century Hutchinson, 1948.

COLLIGAN, James P., *The Image of Christianity in Japan*, Institute of Christian Culture, Tokyo, 1980.

CONNOLLY, Bob and ANDERSON, Robin, *First Contact*, Viking Penguin, 1987.

COOPER, Anne, *Ishmael, My Brother – A Biblical Course on Islam*, MARC, STL Books, EMA, 1985.

CRAWFORD, Daniel, *Thinking Black*, Morgan and Scott, 1912.

DAWSON, Revd E. C., *Lion-hearted – The Story of Bishop Hannington's Life*, Seeley and Co., 1889.

DELBOIS, George, *The Mustard Seed – From a French Mission to a Papuan Church*, Institute of Papua New Guinea Studies, Port Moresby, 1985.

ENDO, Shusaku, *A Life of Jesus*, Charles E. Tuttle Co. Inc., 1979.

EVANS, Robert P., *Let Europe Hear – The Spiritual Plight in Europe*, Moody Press, Chicago, 1963.

GARRETT, John, *To Live Among the Stars*, World Council of Churches and the Institute of Pacific Studies, 1982.

GASCGOINE, Bamber, *The Christians*, Cape 1977.

GOLDSMITH, Martin, *Islam and Christian Witness*, MARC Europe, STL Books, 1982.

HASTINGS, Adrian, *A History of African Christianity 1950–1975*, CUP, 1979.

HEMMING, John, *Red Gold: Conquest of the Brazilian Indians*, Macmillan, 1987.

Heroines of Missionary Adventure: True stories of the internal and patient endurance of missionaries in their encounters with uncivilised man, wild beasts, and the forces of nature in all parts of the world, Seeley and Co., 1909.

HURLEY, Captain Frank, *Pearls and Savages*, G. P. Putnam's & Sons, 1924.

INGLIS, K. S., *Churches and the Working Classes in Victorian England*, Routledge Kegan Paul, 1963.

JEAL, Tim, *Livingstone*, Heinemann, 1973.

JOHNSTON, Ken, *The Story of the New Tribes Mission*, New Tribes Mission.

JOHNSTONE, Patrick, *Operation World*, STL Books, WEC Pub., 1978.

KANE, J. Herbert, *Understanding Christian Missions*, Baker Book House, 1978.

LEWIS, Norman, *The Missionaries*, Secker and Warburg, 1988.

LOVETT, Richard, *James Chalmers – His Autobiography and Letters*, The Religious Tract Society, 1902.

MACKAY, Miss, *The Story of Mackay of Uganda, Pioneer Missionary, By His Sister*, 1906.

McGILVARY, Daniel, *A Half Century Among the Siamese and the Lao*, Fleming H. Revell Company; 1912.

MBITI, John S., *African Religion and Philosophy*, Heinemann Educational Books, 1969.

MEARNS, Andrew, *The Bitter Cry of Outcast London*, Leicester University Press, 1970.

MICHAEL, Charles D., *Missionary Heroes – Stories of Heroism on the Mission Field*, Partridge and Co., 1913.

MOORHOUSE, Geoffrey, *The Missionaries*, Eyre Methuen, 1973.

MORSE, Eugene, *Exodus to a Hidden Valley*, Collins and World Publishing Co., 1974.

NEILL, Stephen, *A History of Christian Missions*, Pelican, 1964.

OLIVER, Roland, *The Missionary Factor in East Africa*, Longman, Green and Co., 1952.

OSBOURNE-JAY, Revd A., *Life in Darkest London*, 1891.

PENNEL, Dr T. L., *Among the Wild Tribes of the Afghan Frontier, A Record of Sixteen Years' Close Intercourse With the Natives of the Indian Marches*, Seeley and Co., 1909.

SANDALL, Robert, *The Story of the Salvation Army 1947–68*, 5 Vols., Thomas Nelson and Sons, 1955.

SIMS, G. R., *How the Poor Live, and Horrible London*, Chatto & Windus, 1889.

THOMPSON, R. Wardlaw, *Griffith John – The Story of Fifty Years in China*, The Religious Tract Society, 1907.

WILSON, Samuel and SIEWART, John (Eds.), *Mission Handbook*, 13th ed., MARC, 1986.

Index

Numbers in italics refer to illustrations

A

actresses, 222
Adventists *see* Seventh-day
   Adventists
affinity groups, 253–4
Afghan people, 201–2, *212*
Africa *and see* individual
      countries, 82–91,
      96–7, 101, 108–9, 123
   education, 98, 104–8
   medicine, 27, 109,
      127–8
   numbers of
      missionaries, 123–4,
      127
   polygamy, 91–2, 112,
      121
Ahmad, Professor Anis,
   208, 209, 214
Aidesius, 16
AIDS, in Uganda, 12, *128*,
   128–31
aircraft, 27, 28, *51*, 51–2,
   63–4
airlines run by missions, 53,
   57
alcohol, 62, 91, 183
Alexander VI, Pope, 132
Ali Bhutto, Zulfiqar, 208
All African Conference of
   Churches, 124
America *see* Latin America,
   North America, South
   America, or name of
   country
*American Missions
   Handbook*, 25, 57
*Among the Wild Tribes of
   the Afghan Frontier*, 202
Amsterdam, 255–7, 260–1
ana-tsurushi, *168*, 169
Anglican Universities
   Mission to Central
   Africa, 85
Answers project, 130
anthropologists, and
   missionaries, 146–7
Aouko, Gaudencia, 112,
   121–2

apostasy, 169, 204, 210–11
Apostles of Jesus, 123
Apostles of Johannes
   Maranke, 108
Argentina, and Tierra del
   Fuego, 141–2
Armenia, 16
Asia and Christianity *and
   see* individual country,
   30, 165–6, 176
Assemblies of God, 152
Athletes in Action, 255

B

Bagamoyo Mission
   Station, Tanzania, 81–2
Baker, Thomas, 42
Banda, Hastings, *98*, 102
Bannu, Pakistan, 202–4
Barnes, David, 244
Barnett, Henrietta, 218
Barnett, Samuel, 223
Barrett, David, 12, 23, 166
Basket, Fuegia, 134–5, *135*,
   139–40
Beagle, HMS, 134, 135
beer, 65, 91
Bible,
   correspondence
      course, 211
   distribution, 190
   and mission, 12, 15
   and the Quran, 209
   translations and
      editions, 20, 58, 69–
      71, *240*
   truth of, 216
Bisorio people, 57–60
*Bitter Cry of Outcast
   London, The*, 219–20
body-building, *240*, 261–2
Bokassa, Emperor, *98*, 98
Bold Mission Thrust, 27
Bolivia, 145–6
Bonnke, Pastor Reinhard,
   100, 100–3, *114–15*, 131
Booth, William, 215, 223–
   8, *224*, 230–2
Bosch, David J., 23

Bowen, Godfrey, 252
boxing, 105, 228, 230
Bradlaugh, Charles, 216
Brazil, 134, 148
Bridges, Lucas, 134, 142–3
Bridges, Thomas, *134*, 138–
   42
Bright, Dr Bill, 28
Britain *and see* England,
   Scotland, Wales,
      19th-century
      missionaries, 220–2
   church attendance, 26,
      125, 216–18, 244
British South Africa
   Company, 96–7
Browning Settlement,
   London, 223
Burgman, Father Hans,
   124, 125–6, 131
Burma, 176, 186
Burton, Dr Jill, 212–13
Burton, Graham, 188–9,
   211
Button, Jemmy, 134–5,
   135, 136, 138

C

Cacoban, King of Fiji, 42
Cadman, Elijah, 225, *226*,
   226
Cambridge University,
   222–3
Campolo, Tony, 242
Campus Crusade for
   Christ, 28–9, 255
cannibalism, *18*, 41, 41–2,
   48–9, *134*
Capuchin Franciscans, 65–
   9, *78*–9
Carey, Walter, 104
Carey, William, *18*, 18–19,
   23
cargo, 45, 52, 55, *55*, 64
Carnegie, Reverend David,
   97
Catholic Society of the
   Divine Word, 52

celibacy, 91, 162
Chalmers, James
   (Tamate), 20, 41, 43–9,
   44
charity, 218
Chiang Mai, Thailand,
   171–2, 186
Chick Publications, 60
Chile, 141–4, 152, 161, *162*,
   164
China, 166, 170, *174*, 176,
   179, 185–6
China Inland Mission *and
   see* Overseas Missionary
   Fellowship, 19, 178
Chishawasha mission,
   Zimbabwe, *93*, 96
Christ for all Nations
   Crusade, 100–1, 103
Christian Mission *and see*
   Salvation Army, 225
Christian Pakistan Radio
   Broadcasting Services,
   211
Christianity, 15–16
   in Africa, 101, 108–9
   in Asia, 165–6
   Celtic, 17
   in England, 17
   in India, 18–19, 30, 53,
      191, *233*, *237*
   and Islam, 202–6, 208–
      10, 212, 214
   in Japan, 178, 181, 184
   in Pakistan, 211–12,
      213
   in Thailand, 170, 186–
      7, *200*
Christians, numbers of *and
   see* church attendance,
   15, 29–30, 166, 190
   Asia, 30, 176
   India, 30
   Papua New Guinea,
      71
   Pakistan, 189
   Thailand, 187
Christians, Roman
   persecution, 16

Church Army, 228, 229, *231*
church attendance, *and see* Christians, numbers of, 125
    Brazil, 148
    Britain, 26, 125, 216–18, 244
    and charity, 218
    and class, 217–18
    England, 216–17
    Japan, 182–3
    North America, 25
Church of England, 217
Church Missionary Society, 20, 72, 89, 192, 201–2
Church of the Nazarene, 241
church planting, 178
churches, 108–9, 217–18, *243*, 244, *245*
cinema, 28
cities and religion, 216–17
City Missions, 218
Clarke, Ian, 127–9
class, and church attendance, 217–18
cleanliness, 21–2, 62–3
clothing, 47–8, 89–90, 139, 217
Coggan, Dr Ruth, 203
Cole, Alfred, 138
colonialism *and see* imperialism, *43*, 93–6, 98, 123, 206–7
commerce, 94–5
computers, 28
Congress for World Evangelisation, 165
Conolly, Captain, 203
conversion,
    benefits of, 21, 90–1, 230, 232
    disadvantages of, 91–2, 181, 209–11, 232
cooking, as means of evangelising, 181
Cox, Stella, 181
crucifixion, 67–8, 169
Crusades, 206–7
Crutwell, Father Norman, 63

D
da Silveira, Gonzalo, 85–6
Dahle, Lars, 166
dance, 62, 64, 98, *99, 106*, 106–7

Darwin, Charles, *134*, 135, 216
Davies, Dave, 206
Dawson Island, Chile, 142–3
de Bresillac, Monseigneur Marion, 83–4
de las Casas, Bartholomeo, 133
de Vera, Father Jose M., 184
Denison, Edward, 222–3
Despard, Reverend George, 138
disease *and see* medicine, mortality rates, name of disease, 84–5, 173
Divine Word Airways, *51*, 53
Dooley, Peter and Elizabeth, 144–5
Dove, Father John, 12, 107–8
drama, 58–9, *66–7*, 78–9, *257, 258, 259*
Driscoll, Father Dan, 149, 151, 164

E
East India Company, 175
Easter, celebrations in Papua New Guinea, 67–8
Ecuador, 161–3
education,
    in Africa, 98, 104–8, *120*
    in Chile, 164
    in Japan, 181, 184
    in Pakistan, 207–8
    in Tierra del Fuego, 144–5
Edwardes College, Peshawar, 205
Edwardes, Sir Herbert, 201
Eliott-Lockhart, Steven and Rhydwen, 76–7
Ellis, A. B., 90
encomienda, 133
Endo, Shusaku, 184
England *and see* Britain, London, 17, 215–32
Erskine, Commodore J. E., 46–7
Eshlemen, Paul, 28
Eskimos, 21
Ethiopia, 16
Europe, as target of

American evangelism, 241–2, 262
European Christian Sports Congress, 255
Evangelical Alliance Mission (TEAM), 180, 206
evangelism *and see* missionaries, missions, 54–5, 60, 162, 187, 246
    in Chile, 164
    in Europe, 241–2, 262
    in Latin America, 147–8
Evans, Robert, 246, 262
Executive Ministries, 255

F
faith missions, 28–9
Falkland Islands, 137–9
Far East Broadcasting Company, 163
Fearnehough, Bill and Sheila, 178–83, *179*
Ferrcira, Christavao, 169
Feuerbach, Ludwig, 216
Fiji, 41–2
finance, 123–4
    Campus Crusade for Christ, 28–9
    Church Missionary Society, 20
    Japanese church, 182
    New Tribes Mission, 57
    radio and TV stations, 162–3
    Seventh-day Adventists, 62
    Southern Baptist Convention, 26
    Summer Institute of Linguistics, 69
flower-sellers, 222
folk medicine, 56
Foote, Alison, 203–4
forgiveness, translation of, 71
Forman, Charles, 192
Forman Christian College, Lahore, 192, 208
France, 216, 241, 244–6
Freyburg, Reverend Paul, 53–6
Friends from Abroad, 190
Frontiers, 190
Frumentius, 16
Fuegians, *134*, 134–43, *135, 140*

Full Gospel Central Church of Seoul, 30
fundamentalism, 57

G
Gardiner, Captain Allen, *134*, 135–7
Garrida, Lura, 256
Gatu, John, 123–4
gift trails, 145
goitre, 174
Goodgame, Dr Rick, 12, 129–30
Got Kwer, Kenya, 112
Graham, Dr Billy, 165, 241, *248*, 248, 250–1
Great Salvation Fair, 227
Greater Europe Mission, 246
Greely, E. H., 89
Greenland, 18, 21
Gregory the Enlightener, 16
Gregory the Great, Pope, 17, 64, 182
Grimes, Father Damian, 103–8, *104, 106*
Groom, John, 222
Gundaphorus/Gondophares, Indian King, 191
Gusii people, 90–3

H
Hallelujah Doctor, *226*, 227
Hand, Bishop David, 60–1, 77
Hannington, Bishop Jim, *20*, 83
Hare, Macon G., 60
Hawaii, 32
HCJB broadcasting station, 162–3
healing, *100*, 100–1, 103, 109–10, *110*, 173
Helm, Charles, 97–8
Hewett, Captain Napier, 87
Hidden Peoples, 27
Hideyoshi, Japanese general, 168
Hill, Octavia, 220
Holy Ghost Fathers, 82
Hoover, Willis C., 161
Hour of Power, 262
Huddlestone, Trevor, 123
Hudson Taylor, James, 19, 178, *179*
human potential movement, 244
human rights, 146–7

Hunt, Bunker and
Caroline, 28
Hurley, Captain Frank, 50–
1
hut tax, 96
Huxley, T. H., 232

I
Iemitsu, Japanese shogun,
169
Ieyasu, Japanese shogun,
168–9
Impacto Chile, 152
imperialism *and see*
colonialism, 19, 22, 42,
49, 94, 201–2
*In Darkest England and the
Way Out*, 40, 215, 230
inculturation, 64–71
India, 18–19, 166, 175, 176,
191, *233*, *237*
numbers of
Christians, 30
numbers of
missionaries, 53,
192
Indian Mutiny, 192
Indo-China, 176
Indonesia, 53, 176
International Media
Mission, 262
International Missionary
Council, 123
Iqbal, Dr Muhammad, 188
Ireland, 17
Islam *and see* Muslims,
188, 190, 191–2
and Christianity, 202–
6, 208–10, 212, 214
Islamabad, Pakistan, 188,
189

J
Jacobs, John, 261–2
Jake Nation, 108
James, Dot, *70*, 70
Japan, 12, 54, 166–70, 176–
85
Jay, Reverend Osborne,
220–1, 228–30
Jesuits, 17–18, 86, 93, *95*,
96, 166–9, *195*
Jesus film/Jesus Project, 27,
28, 204
Johnston, Sir Harry, 95–6
Johnston, Steven, 258
Jones, Clarence, 162–3
Judson, Adoniram, 19, *38*

Jukes, Reverend
Worthington, 193, 201–
2
juogi spirit, 112

K
Kakure-Kirishitan, 176
Kalelombe, Patrick, 264–5
Kampala, Uganda, 129
Kane, Dr Herbert, 15, 19,
30
Kaunda, Kenneth, *98*, 98
Kawilorot, ruler of Chiang
Mai, 172
Kennaway, John, 72
Kennell, Bob, 12–13, 57–60
Kenya, 27, 53, 104, 112, 125
Kenyatta, Johnston
(Jomo), *98*, 98
Kimbanguist Eglise, 122
Kisumu, Kenya, 125
Kiwoko, Uganda, 127–8
Knight, Andrew, 214
Kuruman Mission,
southern Africa, 86

L
Lahore, Pakistan, 191, 192,
205, 207, 208, *234*, *236*
language, 19, 28, 162–3,
262
Afghanistan, 201
Africa, 105–6
Burma, 186
Ecuador, 161–2
Japan, 180
New Guinea, 44
Papua New Guinea,
69
Tierra del Fuego, 139
Latin, as medium of
worship, 65, 121, 161
Latin America *and see*
individual country, 134,
147–8
Lawes, Reverend R. G., *41*,
43, 45–6
Lawrence, John, 139
Lawson, Reuben, 163
Lehtinen, Kalevi, 247
leprosy, 12, 107
Let Europe Hear, 246, 262
liberation theology, 148–
52, 161
Lion, Eduard, 109
Lisu tribal people, 186
Livermore, Tom, 250
Livingstone, David, 72, 82,
85, *113*

on conversion, 103
on mission, 81, 88, 93–
4
Lloyd, A. B., 72, 81, 95
Lobengula, Mashona king,
97
Loewenthal, Isidore, 201–2
London, 219–21, 264
London City Mission, 218,
222
London Congregational
Union, 220
London Missionary
Society,
in Africa, 86–7, 97
in New Guinea, 43, 49
on Tahiti, 31–2, 41
Love Europe campaign,
214, 241
Luwere triangle, Uganda,
127

M
McClung, Floyd, 242, 256
McGilvray, Daniel, 170–3
McKenzie, Charles
Frederick, 85
malaria, 23–4
Malawi, 102, 125
Malik, Bishop, 212
Manarah Book Ministries,
190
Manferd, Manny and
Becky, 163–4
Mansfield House, London,
223
Marae people, 31–2
Marangonia, John, 123
Maria Legio, 108, 112, *114*,
121–2, *122*
marriage, in Japan, 185
martyrs, 23–5, 73
in Japan, 169
Latin America, 149,
149
numbers of, 23
Sierra Leone, 84
Marxism, 208, 246
Masai people, 27
Mashona people, 97
Mathews, Richard, 135
Matthew, Father, 68–9
Mearns, Reverend
Andrew, 220
measles, 141–2
medicine,
in Africa, 27, 109,
127–8

in Pakistan, 202–4,
207–8
in Thailand, 172–3
Mendi, Papua New
Guinea, 65–8
militarism, and mission,
227–8
Mill Hill Mission Society,
90–1
millenialism, 26–8, 30, 163,
165
Mission 89, 241, 248, 251–2
Mission Festival, 123
missionaries *and see*
evangelism,
missionaries,
numbers of,
missions,
in 19th-century
Britain, 220–2
and anthropologists,
146–7
image of, 19–20
inspiration of, 22–3
power of, 32, 86–7,
141
purpose of, 12–14
social status, *43*, *88*
standards of living, 26,
57, 59, 66, 69, 125–6
training of, 26, 241
women, 22, 23, 48,
203–4
missionaries, numbers of
and see missionaries,
12, 15
19th century, 87–8
Africa, 123–4, 127
Church Missionary
Society, 20
India, 53, 192
Indonesia, 53
Japan, 178
Kenya, 53
Latin America, 147
male:female ratio, 23
New Tribes Mission,
57
Papua New Guinea,
53
Missionaries of Charity,
264
Missionary Aviation
Fellowship, 27, *51*
*Missionary Heroes, Stories
of Heroism in the
Mission Field*, 21
Missionary Learning
Center, 26

*Missionary Travels and
Researches in South
Africa*, 72
missions *and see*
evangelism,
missionaries, and
individual country
or name, 19, 27–9,
19th century, 37
20th century, 25, 29,
265
and airlines, 53, 57
and colonialism, 93–6,
98, 123, 206–7
definition, 148–9
countries closed to,
25, 176
and imperialism, 19,
22, 42, 49, *94*, 201–2
and militarism, 227–8
and politics, 102, *150*,
151, 152, 164, 172,
250
and social
programmes, 131,
230–2
world's largest, 69
Moffat, John and Emily, 86
Moffat, Robert, *86*, 86, 92
Moghul Empire, 191–2
Mongkut, King of
Thailand, 170
Moody, Dwight, L., 249
Moravians, 17–18
Morocco, 190
Morris, Colin, 123
Morrison, Dr John Reid,
226, 227
Morse, Eugene, 185
Morse, J. Russell, 185–6
Morse, Robert, 185–6
mortality rates, 23–4, 75, 84
Mother Teresa, *12*, 12, 264
Mount Calvary, Kenya,
112
Mugabe, Robert Gabriel,
96, *98*
Mugabe, Sally, 102
Mulago Hospital,
Kampala, 129
Murray, Sir Hubert, 49
music, 260–1
Muslims *and see* Islam,
190, 202, 214, 234–5
Mutemwa Leprosy
Settlement, Zimbabwe,
107–8
Mutendi, Bishop Samuel,
109–10, *110*, *116*

Mwene Mutapa, African
King, 85
Mzilikazi, Ndebele king,
86–7

N
Namasagali Secondary
School, Uganda, 105–7,
106
Namayango boys' school,
Uganda, 105
naming, 89, 92
Ndebele people, 86–7
Nestorian Christians, 166
Neuendettelsau Lutherans,
52
New Guinea *and see* Papua
New Guinea, 42–52, *47*
New Tribes Mission, 57,
59, *75*, 145–7
Neyrand, Father, 12, 183–4
Nicaragua, *148*, 149, *150*,
151
Nigeria, 264
Ningram people, 63–4
Nkomo, Joshua, 98, *98*
No Longer Music, 260–1
nomadic groups, and
settlement, 27, 58
North America, 18, 19, 25–
6, 262–4

O
Old Umtali Mission,
Zimbabwe, 88–9
Ona Indians, 142–3
Ondeto, Baba Simeon, 112,
121–2, *122*
Ononge, New Guinea, *47*,
49–50
Operation Andrew, 251
Operation Mobilisation,
211, 214
Overseas Missionary
Fellowship *and see*
China Inland Mission,
178–80
Oxford University, 222–3

P
Pakistan *and see*
Islamabad, Lahore,
188–93, 201, 204–5,
211–12, *213*
education, 207–8
and Islam, 188, 191–2

medicine, 202–4, 207–
8, 212–13
Palau, Luis, *240*, 241, 242,
247, 252–5
Pandapieri, Kenya, 125–6
Papua New Guinea *and see*
New Guinea, 12–13, *21*,
35, 53–71, *74*, *75*
Paris, 257–9
Parks, Dr Keith, 25, 26, 30
Patagonian Missionary
Society, 136
Pathan people, 193, 201,
204–5
pay-back, 44–5, 71
penance, 17, 24–5
Pennell, Dr Theodore, *202*,
202
Pennell Memorial
Hospital, Bannu, 203–4
Pentecostal Assemblies of
God, 262
Peshawar, Pakistan, 192–3,
201, 213
Philippines, 165
pidgin English, 44, 55, 68
Pierce, David, *259*, 259–61
pigs, 62, 66
Pino, Nick, 152
Pinochet, General, 152, 161
Pioneer Column, 96
Pioneers, 63–4
Pleasant Sunday Afternoon
(PSA) Society, 227
politics, and mission, 102,
150, 151, 152, 164, 172,
250
polygamy,
Africa, 91–2, 112, 121
New Guinea, 44
Papua New Guinea,
56
Tierra del Fuego, 139
Pomare, Tahitian king, 31–
2
Pont, Ron, 205–6
Portugal, 17–18, 125, 133,
134
Potts, Denise, 70
Power Team, *240*, 261–2
prayer, power of, 31, 165
Presbyterians, 29, 170, 192,
201, 244
prostitutes, 255–7
Protestant churches, 14–15,
17–18, 25–6, 246
PSA (Pleasant Sunday
Afternoon) Society, 227
Punta Arenas, Chile, 144

Q
Quichua language, 161–2
Quiver, 21, 221–2
Quran, 209

R
radio, 28, 52, 162–3, 211
Reesink, Geere, 69–70
renunciation festivals, 55–6
'Rev 89', 241
revenge, 44–5, 71, 203
revolution, 216
Rhodes, Cecil, 96, 97
Ricci, Matthew, *167*
rice Christians, 45
Robertson, Pat, *249*
Roman Catholic Church,
14–15, 17–18, 27,
29, *150*
in Africa, 90–1, 123
in France, 245
in Japan, 184–5
in New Guinea, 44, 49
in Nicaragua, 149, 151
in South America,
132–3
as target of
evangelism, 60,
147–9, *162*, 246
and traditional
cultures, 64–9
Roman Empire, 16–17
Rouse, Ruth, study of
missionary vocation, 22–
3
Rudd, Charles, 97
Rushdie, Salman, 189, 212

S
Sacred Congregation for
the Propagation of the
Faith, 64
Sacred Heart Fathers, 49–
51
St Augustine, 17
St Boniface, 17, 61
St Brendan, *132*
St Columba, 17
St Patrick, 17
St Paul, 15–16, *33*
St Thomas, 166, 191
Sal Lo Fasso, 63–4
Salvation Army, 224–6,
226–8, 230–2
Santiago, Chile, 164
Satan, in New Tribes
Mission teaching, 60
Satanic Verses, 189

Schmidt, Bishop Firmin, 65–6
Schuller, Reverend Robert, 262, *263*
Schweitzer, Dr Albert, *13*
Scotland, 17, 125
sculpture, *84*, *116*
secret believers, 211
Seoul, South Korea, 30, *238–9*
settlement, and dependence, 27, 58, 59
Seventh-Day Adventists, 61–3, *77*, 90–1
Shaftesbury, Earl of, 222, 227
sheep-stealing, 63
Shields, Paula, 255–6
Shinjuku, Tokyo, 183–4
Shinto, 177–8, 181–2, *182*, *193*, *198*
Shona people, *96*
Siani people, 70–1
Sierra Leone, 84
Silesian Fathers, 142–3
Sims, George, 219
sing-sings, 62, 64, 66, *80*
Skinner, Harriet, study of liberation theology, 161–2
slavery, 81–2, 85, 94
Slim *see* AIDS
social reform, 131, 230–2
Society of African Missions, 83–4
Society of Jesus, 86, 96
Society for Promoting the Employment of Additional Curates in Populous Places, 217
South Africa, 18, 102
South America *and see*

individual country, 132–43
South American Missionary Society, 41, 136–8, 141, 142, 144
South Korea, 30, 176, *238–9*
Southern Baptist Convention, 25–7, 130, 147, 164, 178
Spain, 17–18, 133
sport, 255
Stan, Father, 91
Stanley, Chester, 62–3
Steger, Father Len, 213–14
Stevenson, Robert Louis, 31, 32, 43
Stewart, Andrew D., 31
Strauss, David, 216
Sulak Sivaraksa, 187
Summer Institute of Linguistics, 69–70, 146–7
Sundkler, Bengt, 123
Survival International, 147
Swaggart, Jimmy, 12, *14*, 152
sweepers, 212

T
Tahiti, 31–2, 41
Taim Bilong Masta, 56
Taiwan, 176
Tamate (James Chalmers), 20, 41, 43–9, *44*
Tank, Pakistan, 204
Tanoa, King of Fiji, 42
Tanzania, 81–2
targetting, 253–4
Taxila Eye Hospital, 208
TEAM (Evangelical

Alliance Mission), 180, 206
technology, as means of mission, 27–8, 59, *92*, 248–9
television, 28, 162–3, 251, 262
Tell Wales, 241, 252
tent-making, 214
Thailand, 170–4, 186–7, *200*
Thousand Years of Uncertainty, 17
'Thrust Paris', 241
Tierra del Fuego, 41, 134–45
tobacco, 45, 45–6, 96
Todd, Reverend Courthope, 222
Tokyo, Japan, 12, 183–4
Tonga, 41
torture, *168*, 169
Toynbee Hall, London, 223
Tozer, Bishop William, 85
Trans World Radio, 163
Tribal Air, 53, 57

U
Uganda, 12, 104–7, *106*, *128*, 127–31
Ukarumpa mission, Papua New Guinea, 69–70
Unevangelised Fields Mission, 245–6
United States Centre for World Mission, 27

V
Valignano, Alessandro, 168
Vatican Council (Second), 64–5, 148
Verjus, Father Henri, 24–5

Virgin Islands, 19
Voice of the Andes, 162

W
Wales, 241, 244, 252–4
Walker, George and Harriet, 57–8
Watercress and Flower Girls' Christian Mission, 222
Whitefield, George, 249
Williams, John, *73*
Wilson, Stephen, 257–9, *258*
witchcraft, 173
Women's University Settlement, 223
World Council of Churches, 122, 148–9

X
Xavier, Francis, 166–8

Y
Yaghan Indians, 134–9
yellow fever, 84
Youth With A Mission, 242, 256
Yuqui Indians, 145–6

Z
Zero Grazing, 129
Zimbabwe, 12, 86–9, *93*, 96, 107–8
Zinzendorf, Count Nicolas, 18, 19
Zion Apostolic Church, 110–12, *118–19*
Zion Christian Church, 109, *116*
Zionist movement, 109–12